“Everything is possible when you are armed with knowledge, passion, and determination.”

Marvin Alballi

Praise for *Restaurant Excellence*

"*Restaurant Excellence* is a must-have for those entering the industry for the first time, a great reminder for a seasoned restaurateur of what makes a successful concept and a how-to guide on ensuring it lasts!"

Alan Watts – President, Asia Pacific, Hilton

"I have known Marvin Alballi professionally for several years, and I am thrilled to see his excellent new book, *Restaurant Excellence*, see the light of day. It is truly a unique how-to guide for all aspects of the restaurant industry, clearly written and easy to understand. If I could suggest one book to current and future restaurant professionals, it would be *Restaurant Excellence*."

Michael Ellis, co-founder and CEO of Passionomy.tv, former chief culinary officer at Jumeirah Hotels and Resorts, and former global director of the world-renowned Michelin Guides

"I have known and worked with Marvin for close to ten years, and he is consistently excellent in his work. And this book is no exception. It is concise, thoughtful, and full of practical ideas you can use today. I highly recommend it."

Mike Ferretti, CEO, The Great Harvest Bread Company

"Knowing that Marvin is a passionate hospitality professional with integrity, experience, and a deep understanding of the industry, I couldn't wait to read his first book on hospitality management. And it didn't disappoint! It's a must-read for anyone who's serious about making a difference in restaurant hospitality. Written in a logical, thoughtful way, you won't want to put it down. It should be required reading for all foodservice professionals."

Warren Erhart, president at White Spot Restaurants

"*Restaurant Excellence* is useful, practical, and full of tactics and tools to succeed in the restaurant business. Chefs can learn a lot from *Restaurant Excellence*! A great resource."

Andres Marcelo Urresti Ferrel, executive chef, InterContinental Abu Dhabi, UAE

"The market is full of hospitality management books, but not many match the caliber of this comprehensive book. Culled from Marvin Alballi's personal experiences over time, it is a logical, practical guide to achieving success in restaurant management. He is a hospitality educator passionate and focused on instilling ought-to-know knowledge, and this book, rich with fail-safe tools, reliable tactics, and excellent tips, is a must-read for all contemplating entering the restaurant business or sustaining themselves successfully in this highly competitive space."

Sunjeh Raja, CEO and director, The International Centre for Culinary Arts (ICCA Dubai)

"Marvin is a food and beverage specialist, and having written the ***Restaurant Excellence*** book, he will help F&B professionals to build and manage better restaurants. It's important to get the fundamentals right for success, and Marvin's book is rich with tactics and strategies to win in F&B. Excellent content!"

Andreas Pfister, director of operations (Eighteen Hotels), Northern Gulf at InterContinental Hotels Group

"With a lifetime of experience in restaurants and bars, Alballi invites us to more deeply understand the foodservice industry and offers a framework and practical advice on how to elevate and improve food and beverage experiences, operations, and teams. This is a must-read for anyone in the business."

Eric Lent, former senior vice president Upscale Brands, Restaurants & Bars, IHG Hotels and Resorts Worldwide

"Marvin Alballi brings his broad experience to bear on the complex management of today's foodservice and hospitality endeavors. After several years of unprecedented challenges and overwhelming labor and supply issues, this book brings clarity and focus back to the dining experience. Clear, concise, and practical, this book is a necessary resource and an inspirational roadmap to rediscovering joy and success in your operation."

Mark T. Schuur, president and chief financial officer, Caffe Darte LLC

"*Restaurant Excellence: The Ultimate Guide to Success in the Food and Beverage Industry* is a very useful tool for marketers, finance leaders, designers, foodservice professionals, business owners, chain leaders, hospitality trainers, chefs, and many more. A real professional gem for the hospitality and service industry."

Panayiotis Hadjiloizou, business consultant and certified master trainer, former lecturer at the Higher Hotel Institute Cyprus

"*Restaurant Excellence* is an encyclopedia and resource that provides pragmatic, common sense, extremely valuable information, and practical advice on how to be successful in the restaurant and hospitality sectors. I recommend using it as your dictionary and a guide to achieve excellence in your operation. It is based on years of incredible food service experience by Marvin. Eat it up!!!!"

George Michel, Former COO of Global Markets at Brinker and former CEO of A&W Restaurants USA and former CEO of Johnny Rockets

"Mr. Alballi takes a macro look at the operations, marketing, and financial aspect of the foodservice industry. His many years of being a hands-on operator as well as an international operator makes his book, *Restaurant Excellence*, an excellent asset for a new restaurateur or someone who is looking to improve their bottom line. Wealth of knowledge. Highly recommend it."

Edgar Rahal, chairman of the board of the British Columbia Chefs' Association and past president

"After reading the book, I feel there are a lot of small details I need to learn or review. This book really helps me to step back and relook at how I manage my operation. It will remind you that our environment is always improving and our skills and focus also need to be updated.

Restaurant Excellence will support you in the right direction and will give you all the knowledge to perform well from the beginning—giving the best food and service is the key, but another key is to know your operation and targets."

Remi van Peteghem, culinary director, chez Resorts World Sentosa

"*Restaurant Excellence* covers everything you need to know about running a successful restaurant from someone inside of the industry. Whether you already own or are just starting off, this book will help you become a better manager and a better leader and give you a better understanding of your guests."

Lucy Todish, senior director of marketing & product innovation, MTY Food Group

"Running restaurants is easy, isn't it? In *Restaurant Excellence*, Marvin, with his many practical years of experience, delves into the key tactics and practical steps to operational success. In Marvin's easy-to-read-and-understand format, this is a must-read for those considering entering this exciting profession/lifestyle right through to those seasoned (excuse the pun) operators who need guidance, tips, and reassurance along the journey. Well done, Marvin."

Ivor Prestwood, former hotel general manager at InterContinental Hotel Abu Dhabi

"I had the opportunity to work with Marvin when I was the CEO of Caribou Coffee. His passion for his work was contagious, and I developed a formula for success in Customer Experience: P+E+S=Ef (Product + Environment + Service + The Experience Factor). This simple algebraic formula is like any formula—if you take away one part, you don't get the same answer. *Restaurant Excellence* teaches the lesson that you must do it all, all the time, to be successful. There are no shortcuts, and Marvin's book breaks it down writing about every detail to create a successful business by understanding success is in the small details."

Michael Coles, author of *Time To Get Tough: How Cookies, Coffee, and a Crash Led to Success in Business and Life*, former CEO of Caribou Coffee, co-founder of Great American Cookies

"*Restaurant Excellence* is extremely useful for both experienced and young chefs. It covers all the essential food and beverage business components and topics. It helps chefs become and act like true entrepreneurs and business owners. *Restaurant Excellence* is a must-have for every restaurant chef, manager, or owner."

Simon David Wipf, executive chef at Four Seasons Resort and Residences at the Pearl Qatar

"For as long as I have known Marvin, he has always displayed great passion for the hospitality industry. His experience and love for the industry shine through as a lifelong advocate for our profession. ***Restaurant Excellence*** is a must-read for both experienced professionals and those who are entering the industry. His book is rich with 'insider information' and anecdotes for a long and successful career in hospitality."

Marcus Routbard, cluster executive chef, The WB Abu Dhabi, Curio Collection by Hilton, and Doubletree by Hilton Abu Dhabi

"Marvin put his decades of experience into writing ***Restaurant Excellence*** to help anyone at every level of hospitality. There is a huge population of people who love the idea of owning a restaurant, running a restaurant, but sadly only see it for face value. It takes a vast amount of hard work to understand the financials, overhead needs, and how much money you will need to float yourself in order to be successful. Marvin will help with the menu that you present and understanding craveability to resonate with guests. I so appreciated the opportunity to read his book to get his unique point of view. This book should absolutely be in culinary education curriculum. The knowledge that his pyramid blocks in every section present for every aspect of restaurant operations is amazing. A great read for anyone in hospitality."

Howard Lee Ko, executive chef of Ce La Vi Restaurant Dubai

RESTAURANT EXCELLENCE

The Ultimate Guide to Success in the Food and Beverage Industry

MARVIN ALBALLI

Restaurant Excellence: The Ultimate Guide to Success in the Food and Beverage Industry

ISBN: 979-8-9867483-0-6 (Paperback)
ISBN: 979-8-9867483-1-3 (E-Book)

Cover illustration: Nimu Muallam

Cover design and interior design: Andy Meaden

Interior illustrations: Nimu Muallam

First printing edition 2022.

CONTENTS

ACKNOWLEDGMENTS

I would like to thank my wife, Vera, and son, Alex, for their incredible support during the past three years. Their patience and support allowed me to spend countless hours researching and writing this book. I love you so much!

My lifelong friend and mentor, Von Kennedy. Your support, care, mentorship, and advice have helped me throughout my career.

Ivor Prestwood, thank you for your valuable input, guidance, and advice.

I am also very fortunate to have known and received support and feedback on several chapters:

On Kitchen Management and Culinary Procedures: Chef Will Stanyer, Chef Nikolaos Tsimidakis, Chef Mathieu Balbino, Chef Yann Le Coz, Chef and director of F&B Jaehak Lee, Chef Christophe Louis Prud'homme

On Training: Panayiotis Hadjiloizou, Kris Ina Buenagua

On Design: Terry Chiu, Brian Tepen, Bina Pollack

On Finance: Kelvin Lum, Rony Habib, Mazen Salha

On Marketing: Lucy Todish, Kathryn Quick

On Service and Hospitality: Jerome Barbeau, Elena Gorba

I also would like to thank Chef James Kennedy, Sunjeh Raja, Chef Howard Ko, Culinary Director Remi van Peteghem, Matthew Broderick, Jeff Slutsky, Micheal Ellis, Priscilla Martel, Courtney Brandt, George Michel, Sonia Gawlick, Virginia Anne Newton, and Georges Farhat and his F&B team for their help with photography.

Editors: Sara DeGonia, your hard work, valuable insights, and passion helped me take this book to a new level.

Herb Schaffner, thank you for your patience, hard work, and creativity.

Graphic Design: Nurhida Muallam

Photography: Angelo Vassiliades

Lastly, I would like to thank all the foodservice professionals I have worked with throughout my career. You taught me everything that I know of the food and beverage industry.

INTRODUCTION

Fine dining with the wealthy. Gold-plated forks and knives. This is where I started in the restaurant industry in 1993 as a part-timer. The restaurant had a live band and classic ballroom dancing; the experience was like theater to me. Raised in a middle-class family, I loved and was astonished by the glamour, showmanship, restaurant design, and elegant food presentation. My job was to polish cutlery and stack clean dishes when they came out of the dishwasher. Still, I asked the management to train me in the kitchen, dining-room service, and management. I wanted to learn everything about the restaurant buisness.

Inspired by that experience, I knew I had found my calling and decided to pursue the food and beverage industry after high school. I studied the American Hotel and Hotel Association Educational Institute courses in food and beverage management. In my studies, I learned about fine dining and classic cuisine from chefs Marie-Antoine Carême, Auguste Escoffier, and Paul Bocuse. My dream was to become the food and beverage director of a luxury five-star hotel.

I am privileged to have experienced one of the world's most colorful restaurant industry careers. Typically, in the restaurant business, if one works in franchised restaurant chains, chances are they will continue in that domain; and if one works in fine dining and hotels, they will continue working there. I am very fortunate to have worked for all of the above in both entry-level and senior-leadership positions—which has given me extensive knowledge and unique insights; massive exposure to a variety of cuisines, service styles, and business models; and a different, non traditional perspective. Such colorful exposure inspired my creativity and armed me with enormous industry knowledge. I have worked in nearly every category, segment, and type of restaurant and eatery in the industry: catering, ferry boats, sports arenas, airports, fine dining, premium casual, casual dining, fast-casual, fast food, ice cream, coffee, Michelin star, Italian, Arabic, Belgian, Brazilian, Japanese, Chinese, Turkish, American, Thai, French, Indian, Spanish, Greek…and the list goes on. I took every opportunity to learn all that I could about these segments and concepts. At one point in my career, I led 776 restaurants across twenty-six countries in Europe, the Middle East, Asia, and Africa.

My passion for learning started at an early age—at my hotel school, I borrowed and watched all the American Hotel and Motel Educational Institute videos. *All* of them!

My house had hundreds of menus. I would go to restaurants, dine there, and take their menus home with me because I loved menu design, food descriptions, and culinary offerings. I always took time to speak to and connect with food servers, chefs, managers, and restaurant owners—I loved listening and learning from each one. Today, I can walk into any kitchen, any restaurant in the world, with the confidence to add value and improvements.

I am obsessed with quality, creativity, and operational excellence. For example, I am always searching for better information, such as the ideal way to cook a specific dish or ingredient. I am always asking questions such as: What is the best honey, olive oil, chocolate, bread, and pizza in the world? Why? Is there a better ingredient? A better way? Is there a chef out there who has a better recipe? If so, what is it?

I wanted to write this book for several reasons.

Firstly, the restaurant industry has one of the highest failure rates globally, and I want to help. It is sad to see people invest their life savings in opening a restaurant for it to fail after two to three years. My LinkedIn post opposite had 73,000 views and 1,422 likes from the foodservice industry professionals who agreed with my statement.

Unfortunately, many people think the restaurant business is simple and straightforward and requires no working experience. They think they know the industry because they are well-traveled, eat out a lot, or can cook good food for their friends and family. But the restaurant business is complex and requires expertise, systems, procedures, and outstanding leadership. As Anthony Bourdain so eloquently said, "If anything is good for pounding humility into you permanently, it's the restaurant business."

Secondly, I want to share my experience with fellow industry professionals. This book is a result of twenty-nine years of experience managing more than a thousand restaurants in over thirty countries. This book focuses on practicality and real industry examples based on working in management, kitchens, and dining rooms. I did not want to write only theory—or what many people call fluff. I wanted to help you improve your restaurant after reading each chapter and putting the ideas into practice. If I were to describe this book, I would say, "*This book is about what culinary or hotel schools may not teach you.*"

This book focuses on practicality and real industry examples based on working in management, kitchens, and dining rooms.

Thirdly, my goal was to write the most comprehensive, valuable food and beverage book in the world. In our industry, you rarely find a book covering every single aspect of the business.

This book took three years to complete and includes valuable feedback from top chefs, marketers, food and beverage directors, multi-unit leaders, hotel training leaders, restaurant designers, finance leaders, global marketers, CEOs, and business leaders. **At least three high-profile industry professionals reviewed and critiqued each chapter.** For example, Exceptional Food Quality and Kitchen Management (Chapter One) was reviewed by chefs who were trained by or worked for celebrity and Michelin-starred chefs Paul Bocuse, Gordon Ramsay, Jason Atherton, and Pierre Gagnaire.

I have spent more than 230 hours researching, reading, and ensuring I have valuable advice to impart. I spoke with and interviewed more than thirty-six food and beverage top professionals from North America, Europe, the Middle East, and Asia. All this to say, I believe I have done my level best to prepare a rich, all-encompassing guide for readers worldwide, and I look forward to hearing about all your success to come. Let's begin!

Building the Pyramid Together and Putting the Restaurant Success Formula to Work

This section will present how this book is structured to provide the building blocks of the perfect formula to achieve restaurant success.

This is the first layer of the pyramid.

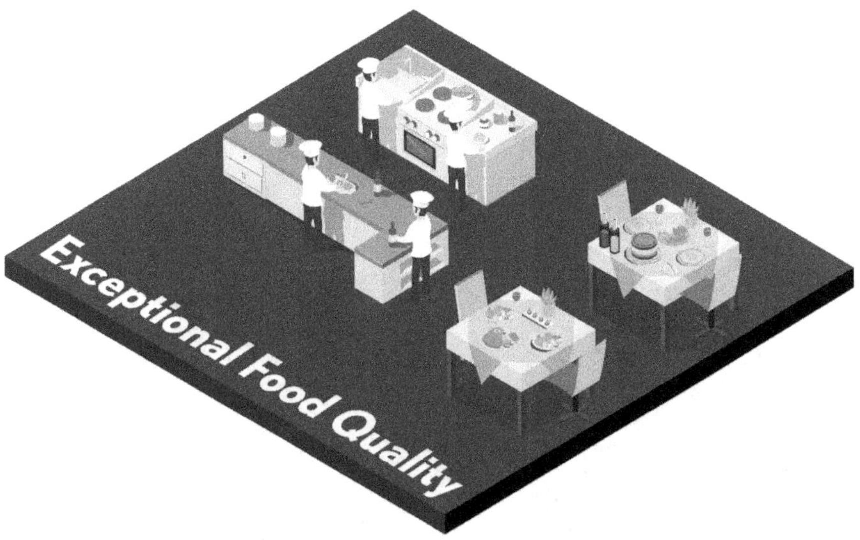

Imagine for a moment that you and your family are dining at your favorite restaurant. You expect and receive a great experience, beginning with delicious food and drinks. The food is beautifully presented and served at the right temperature. The food tastes amazing, it is fresh, flavorful, and colorful, and everyone loves their choices.

Now, let's add one more layer to the pyramid.

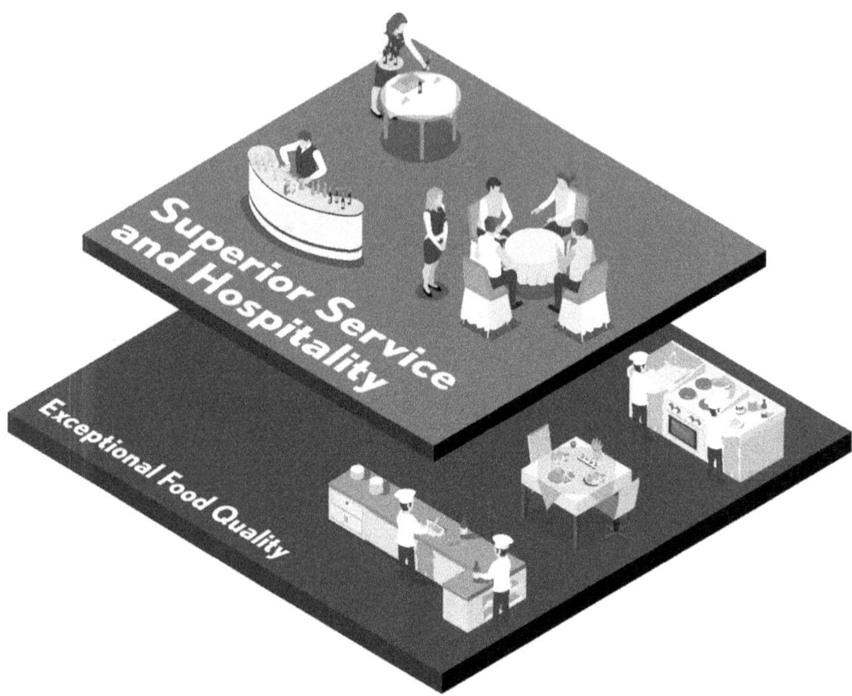

When arriving, your greeter pleasantly smiles and welcomes you with enthusiasm. The greeter walks you to your favorite table. Your food server welcomes you with a genuine smile and remembers your name and your favorite dish from a previous visit. They make excellent recommendations when you are not certain what to order. The service is paced appropriately, neither rushed nor slow, anticipating your needs without interrupting your conversation and experience.

Now, let's add one more layer to the pyramid.

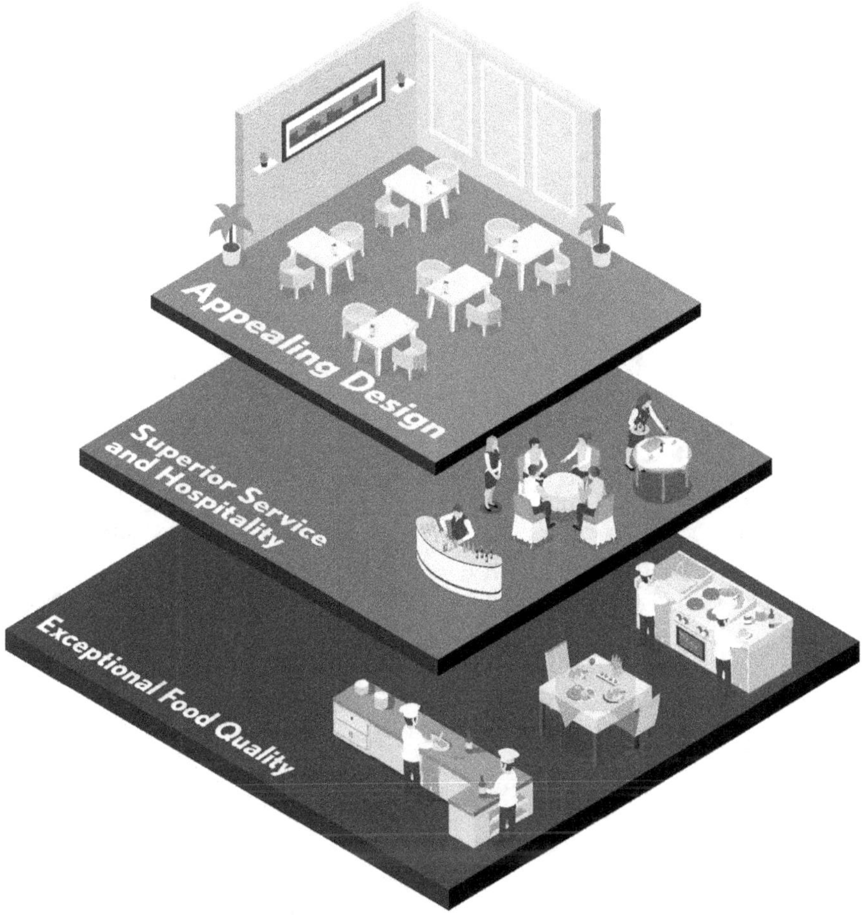

You love the music complementing the ambience; you love the design; you feel the restaurant's vibe and the energy. The restaurant is gleaming, squeaky clean, and well-maintained.

Now, let's add one more layer to the pyramid.

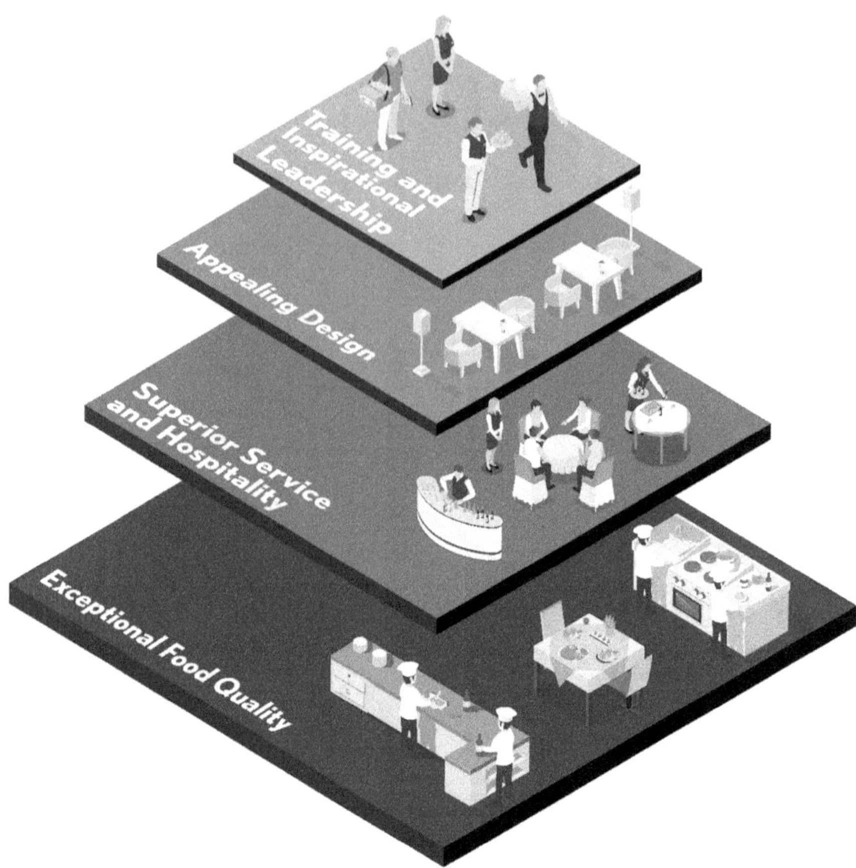

This restaurant's team is highly trained. They know the menu inside out and all the ingredients. They are confident, pleasant, and motivated. Their restaurant manager is friendly with great leadership skills and stops by to ask, "How was your meal?" to ensure guest satisfaction. The team is inspired and engaging with their guests.

Now, let's add one more layer to the pyramid.

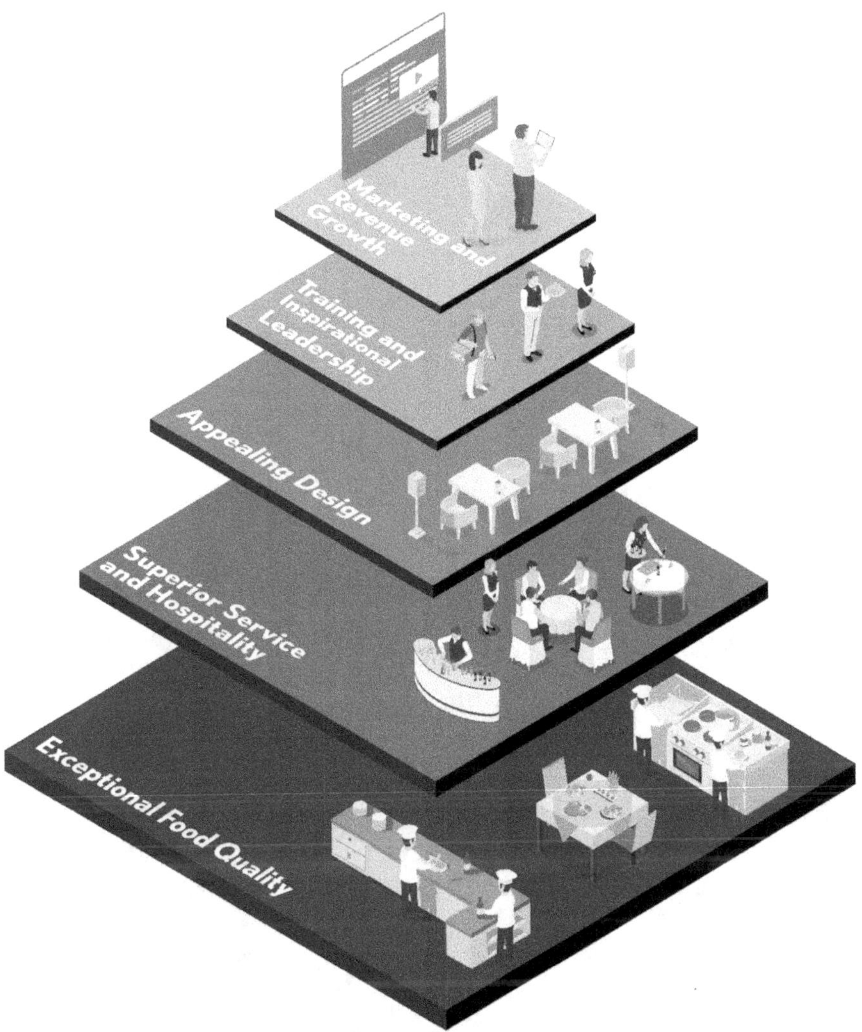

You may have initially decided to visit this restaurant because it was highly recommended by a friend or you saw favorable posts on social media, such as Instagram, Facebook, or Yelp. This restaurant markets well. Food photography was professional, presenting the food in an appealing way, exactly how it was presented on the plate.

Now, let's add one more layer to the pyramid.

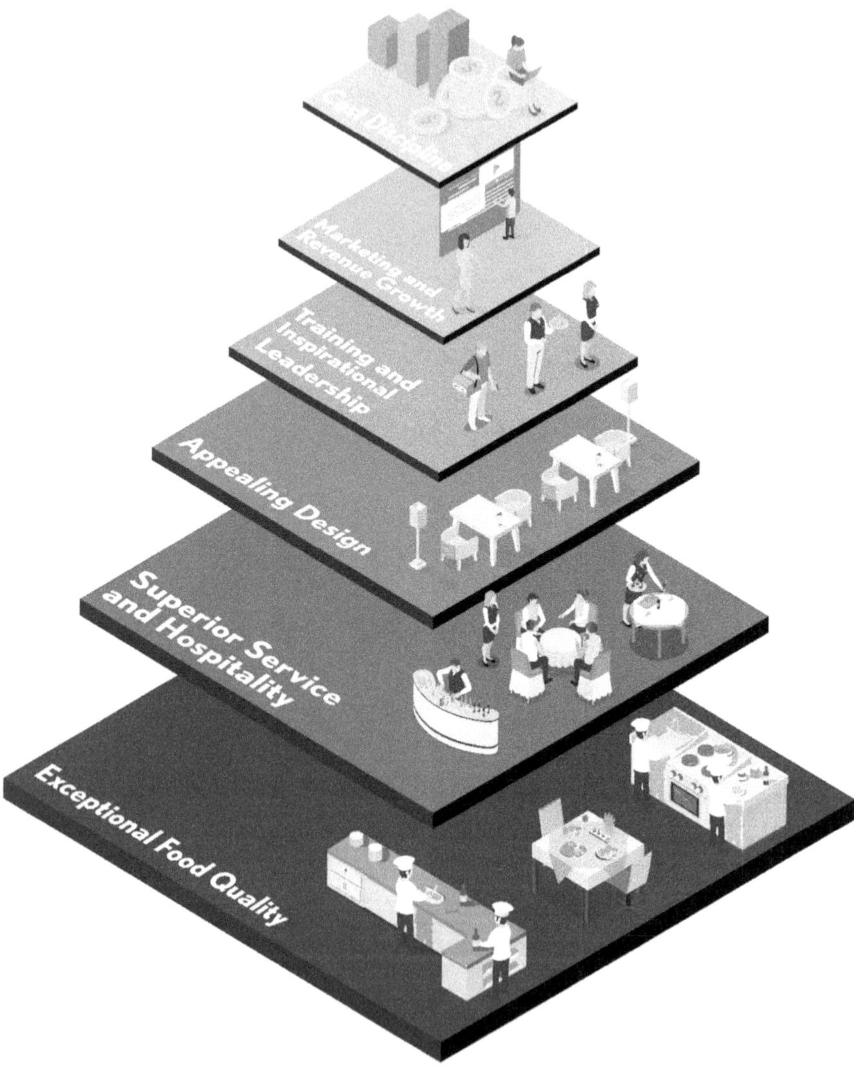

At this restaurant, the manager knows and manages costs without ever hurting or lowering quality. They are aware of every expense, and at the same time, they are laser-focused on driving revenue/sales.

Now, let's add the final layer to the pyramid.

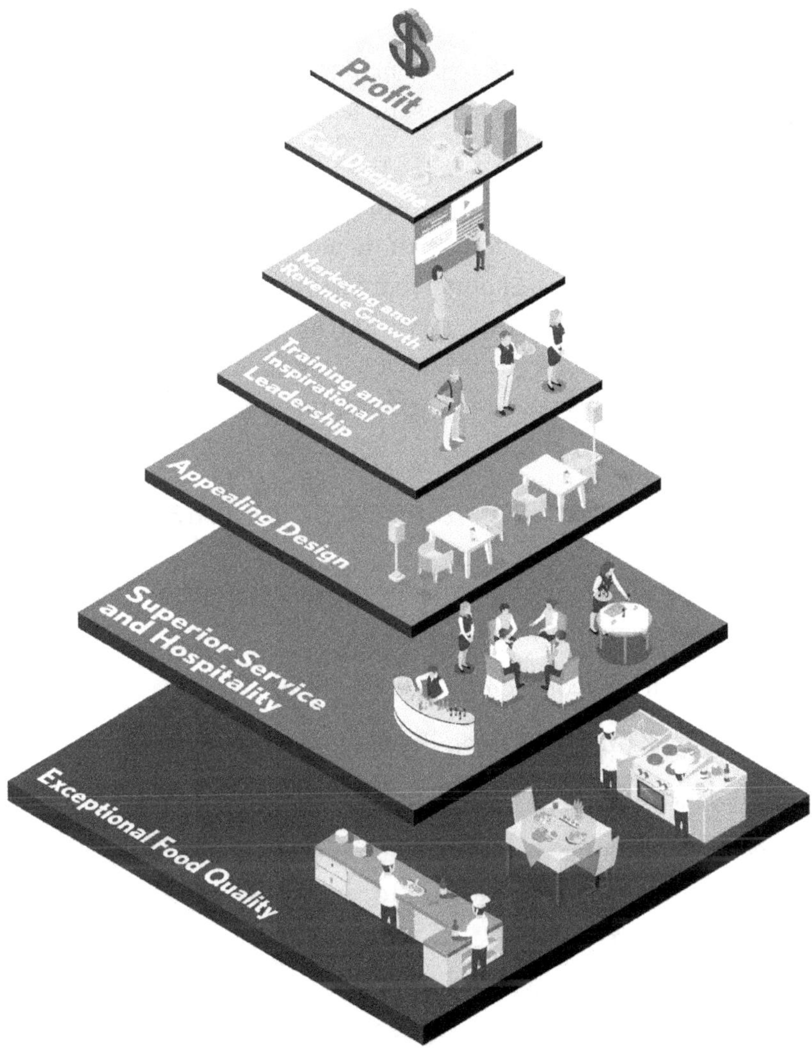

As shown in the illustration, I described a superior guest experience resulting from a successful, well-managed restaurant. This outcome doesn't happen because of hard work or good food alone. The manager in the example above is focused on serving great food in a pleasant atmosphere by a highly trained and motivated team. They are cost-conscious and careful with operations expenses, while at the same time being quality, guest-experience, and revenue-generation focused.

When you put to work the tactics that I share in this book—which results in great food, excellent service, an inviting atmosphere, a well-trained, motivated team, and stellar financial and leadership skills—**sales and profit are a natural outcome.**

I would like to highlight that most restaurants' trouble begins when managers and owners spend too much time on the top part of the pyramid and not enough time on the bottom four layers. When restaurant managers, owners, and F&B leaders focus more on cost, marketing, and how to generate sales, and less time on food quality, service, guest experience, team leadership, and training, the results can be rather damaging in the long run.

How to Get the Best out of This Book

As you read each chapter, test the ideas, try them. Don't race to finish the book. If you have questions, reach out to me on:

- LinkedIn (linkedin.com/in/marvinalballi);
- Facebook (Marvin FoodandBev);
- Instagram (@marvin_alballi_fnb).

If you need additional support, I also provide online and/or in-person learning sessions and business advisory to restaurants, hotels, business owners, and board members.

At the end of each chapter, you will find a table with several questions. Whatever you answer with a *No* represents a gap in your operating model. I also created a YouTube channel to support you: *The Restaurant Excellence Book_Marvin Alballi.*

Each layer of the pyramid represents a chapter in the book. I have also included a chapter on Operational Excellence (Chapter Eight), which recaps the first seven chapters and summarizes all the tools, systems, and procedures, as well as a chapter that shows how to take your food from good to excellent

(Chapter Nine). I conclude with Chapter Ten: learning and gaining valuable insights from top restaurant industry leaders and celebrity chefs.

Lastly, I would like to say that restaurant owners, managers, and staff work hard to serve the public. It is important not to take this for granted and instead express our appreciation for this fantastic, fun, and endlessly creative industry that touches all our lives.

Good luck with your food and beverage journey!

CHAPTER ONE
EXCEPTIONAL FOOD QUALITY AND KITCHEN MANAGEMENT

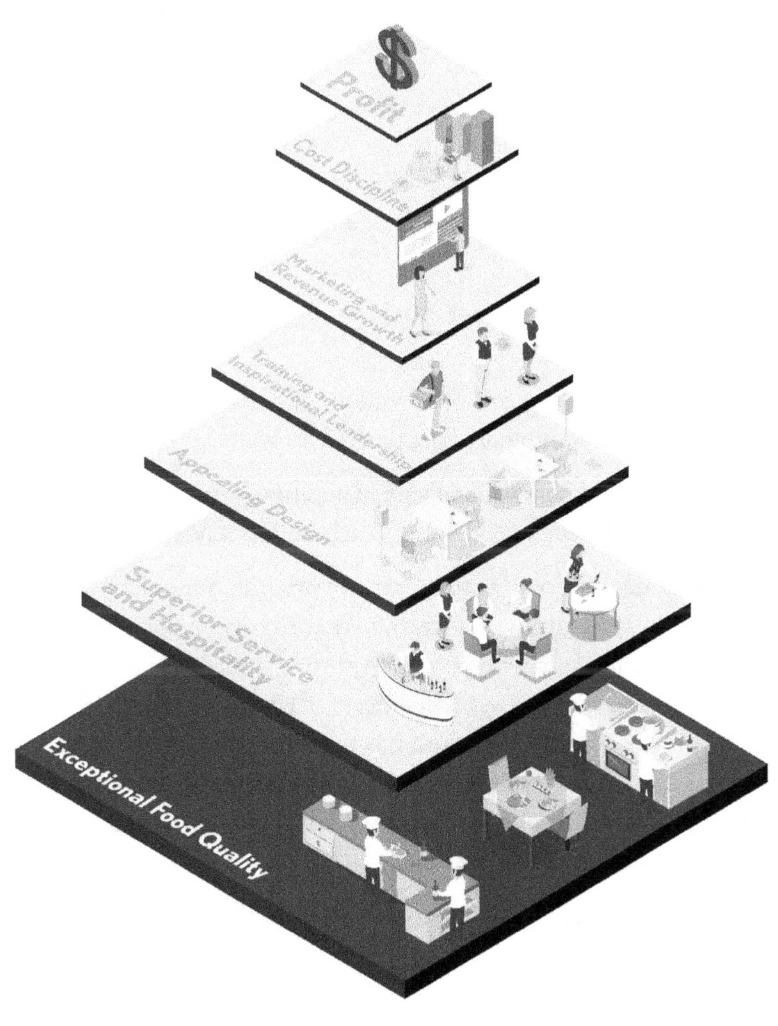

I have put food quality at the base of the pyramid, as it is the most critical part of our business.

I have traveled to more than forty countries where I observed mom-and-pop restaurants with a small or nonexistent dining room, no appealing design, and a location with very little or no parking. Still, many of these restaurants had long lines of people waiting to order and are successful despite everything they lack. Why? Because the food is fantastic. Swan Oyster Depot in San Francisco, and Kintaro Ramen in Vancouver, Canada, are two examples of this point.

The truth is that customers may forgive your restaurant for slow service, long wait time for a table, or a food server failing to remember the soup of the day, but they will never forgive bland, boring, or overcooked food.

Let me reveal how you can excel in this section of the pyramid, including the actions and systems you need to know to set your restaurant apart from competitors. Let's start with the most important part of a restaurant operation: food quality and effective kitchen management.

The Quality of Food and Beverage

The kitchen is the backbone of your restaurant. If its operation breaks down, the restaurant will undoubtedly fall apart.

Here I talk about kitchen management and how to succeed in serving great quality food, which depends on factors including but not limited to:

1. Consistency in quality, temperature, presentation, taste, and portion size. This can be difficult to achieve, but you can excel if you follow the ideas and tools that I will share with you. As Anthony Bourdain said in the Netflix show *Jeremiah Tower: The Last Magnificent*, **"The beast, the religion of any restaurant, is consistency. The food has to be the same every single time. It must be as good. That requires total vigilance, meaning the ability to stand in an incredibly busy kitchen with hundreds of meals going out all around you and you are aware of every plate."**

2. Great recipes, and adhering to them one hundred percent of the time, that will keep customers coming back for more. (I will explain this component in detail later.)

3. Ingredients. Buying the most expensive ingredients is unnecessary unless you operate a high-end, Michelin star–type restaurant. Good chefs make great food from good, quality ingredients and ensure suppliers are always consistent with the quality specifications that the chefs have developed. Purchasing the right ingredients at the right price will allow you to have wide options in your menu according to the customer's needs and concept/outlet positioning in the market and enable you to match your customers' spending power. *(Positioning, in short, is understanding and defining your target audience, competitors, price point, the image you want to portray to your guests, and the segment you play in, such as QSR, fine dining, or fast casual. Your team must also know and act in accordance with your positioning.)*

For example, some customers are willing to pay more for certain dishes, such as premium steaks and a wild catch of the day, while other brands can still be successful with lower-end cuts of meat due to their pricing and market positioning. It's important for chefs to avoid blaming lack of success on the inability to buy the most expensive ingredients in the market.

Build the right network of suppliers. Think of them as an extension of the chef's team because, in a way, they work for them. A good relationship between the chef and suppliers who can understand the philosophy of the chef makes a significant difference.

Source local, organic products as fresh as possible and as often as possible. It makes a huge difference in flavor profile and shows your support for your local community and the well-being of your customers.

4. Talent and leadership. This is about the skill level of the chefs and cooks you hire, but more importantly, the training and development you give them. In Training and Inspirational Leadership (Chapter Four), I share several training methods and procedures. It's important to mention the need for an ongoing and extensive level of activities in training. Chefs must also participate in industry events and competitions and attend supplier events to enrich their knowledge and understand business trends.

The talent of the chef needs to go hand in hand with the concept of the restaurant. Many restaurants fail because they do not invest in hiring a chef of a good caliber or profile. If a chef cannot adapt to the concept and is not qualified enough to adhere to the menu requirements as per the restaurant theme, it is a recipe for disaster.

Leadership and the working environment that head chefs create play major roles in the success or failure of the kitchen. The work environment should encourage creativity and discipline (but not fear) and be positive, fun, and inspiring.

5. Management skills: Most chefs got into the business to cook and are not keen on performing management tasks. Great kitchen managers/head chefs understand that their duties include supervision, food ordering, receiving, storing, inventory management, scheduling, business forecasting, hiring, and firing—for better or worse, the everyday, tedious tasks associated with being in charge. Unfortunately, senior chefs are rarely given management training—something that is far too often overlooked. It often takes years of trial and error for some before they learn managerial tasks and to be compassionate, nurturing, and understanding of others.

6. Constantly taking food from good to great. In this chapter, I cover the necessary philosophy to do just that. It's All About the Food (Chapter Nine) covers tips to take food to a new level and avoid common mistakes.

7. Supporting factors for achieving quality include equipment selection, proper layout, maintenance, and pace of service.

In the next section I will cover consistency, the craveability factor and its impact on repeat visits, the right approach to developing great recipes, and key culinary principles, such as flavor, aroma, procedure, and execution.

Consistency

Consistency can be the most challenging goal to achieve, but it is also the most critical aspect to ongoing success. The steaks should be as great on a slow Monday evening as they are on a busy Saturday night. Consistency determines consumers' trust—or the lack of it. McDonald's is probably the best example of demonstrating consistency on a global scale (regardless

Consistency determines consumers' trust—or the lack of it.

of what one might think of their food offering). You'll want to ensure that no matter how busy your restaurant may be, the staff can produce the same high-quality dishes. This attention to detail and taste will separate your restaurant from average establishments. When you plan your menu, avoid focusing solely on the content of the physical menu—such as categories or types of dishes. You should also consider how likely it is that the desired product will be deliverable to the required standard, day in and day out, regardless of any unexpected circumstances, like staff shortages or turnover.

Systems for achieving consistency include:

- Kitchen line checks. The line-check system is key to achieving consistency. I will explain it in detail toward the end of this chapter.
- Menu tasting—frequent tasting of entire dishes with your team (cooks, chefs, and food servers), not only by their individual components or specific ingredients, which is how line checks are typically conducted. This should include chefs producing the dishes for all the team to taste and learn, not solely for senior management tasting and decision-making on what goes on the menu.
- Team training. Involve other departments in this task. You won't have the time to do it alone, except when you conduct pre-shift briefings as a training method. See Training and Inspirational Leadership (Chapter Four) for a full discussion on training.
- Portioning tools. Use cups and tablespoons instead of grams and pounds during service and when finishing/building dishes. It's easier and faster to portion this way. No employee should start trying to measure 85 grams in the middle of service or try to weigh three ounces of mushrooms as per the example on the following page. One cup of sliced mushrooms is far more accurate and faster to utilize. The best approach is to create recipes with weight, measurements, and metric components as per the chart on the following page.

	Weight	Measurement	Metric
Sliced Mushrooms	3 ounces	1 cup	85 grams
Diced Onions	1 ½ ounces	¼ cup	42 grams

If a dish requires one cup of diced tomatoes, I make sure that the tomato pan on the kitchen line has one measuring cup in it, ready to use before the shift starts. (This is how the line-check program works.)

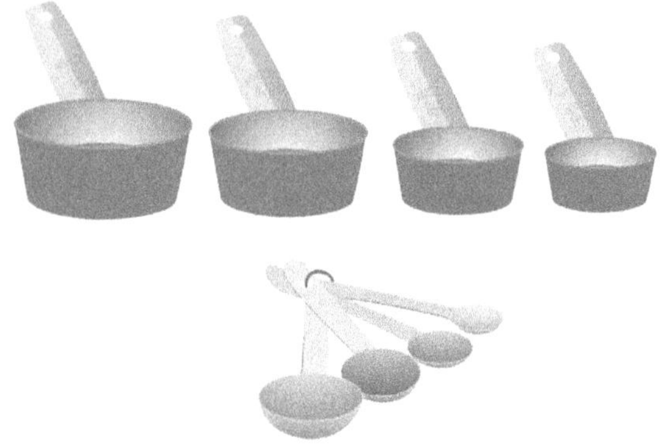

- Well-constructed recipes, which means clear procedures and clear portioning measurements, without hidden prep recipes that don't exist or were not provided to the team.
- Suppliers adhering to your well-written, clear specifications.

The Craveability Factor

Your restaurant success begins when people start craving your food. **Ask yourself: is my menu craveable?** Are people ready to drive out of their way to come to my restaurant because the food is worth it?

I often think back to an episode of *Seinfeld.* Watching the "Soup Nazi" scene, I realized that food was—*and will always be*—the most important aspect of any food and beverage business's success.

In the scene, guests line up in the freezing cold of a New York City winter because the soup is incredible. It's not too unusual to see that—I have worked and traveled to many countries where I have seen similar mom-and-pop restaurants with counter service and only one to five menu items, each cooked to perfection, with a long line of people outside.

In the TV show, the restaurant is poorly designed and has terrible service, and the Soup Nazi charges you for extra bread, but business is still going strong. Why is this? Maybe because it's dramatized for television, or maybe because the food is worth craving and people are addicted to it.

Ask yourself: How craveable is my food? Is **quality obsession** part of my restaurant's DNA? Are guests willing to drive to my restaurant, wait for a table, and perhaps pay slightly more to buy my food? Do you have signature dishes that no one can match in your city? Is your restaurant currently the talk of the town because of its unique dishes and incredible taste? Presentation is important, but beautiful dishes are only worth something if they taste amazing too. Spending time, effort, and resources and putting great effort into presentation without considering taste and craveability is a mistake countless chefs make.

Your restaurant's success begins when customers begin to crave your food.

You should constantly examine your menu development approach and philosophy and continually raise the bar. Restaurant design, service, marketing, pricing, and positioning are important, but none of these qualities exceed the importance of the taste, quality, and of course, **craveability** of your food.

Flavor, Aroma, and Cooking Procedure

The success of a recipe will depend on the art and science of menu development. The science aspects are the cooking techniques, while the art is mixing flavors to create something unique and design eye-catching presentations. It's relatively easy to teach science, but art is more of a natural talent. Art is when you create the right mix of flavors, textures, combinations, and presentation that evokes emotions!

The art of mixing flavors is about coherence and contrast: sweet-and-sour sauce or salty-and-sweet ingredient combinations (think of recipes with salt and sugar, such as chocolate-covered pretzels or salted-caramel ice cream).

What other factors contribute to a successful recipe? Fats, acids, spices, sauces, and methods of cooking (grilling, braising, pan baking, frying) make a difference in how flavors react. If your goal is to serve the best food in your city, conducting ongoing training and building a better understanding of your cooking methods, flavors, and aromas will add a lot of value to your cooks' knowledge and help them understand the critical nature of certain steps in the process. Continually training your team is a key factor and will be covered more in Training and Inspirational Leadership (Chapter Four) and It's All About the Food (Chapter Nine). For example, teach your cooks why it's important to skim your frying oil often (so fried food looks golden brown instead of deep dark with burned or black speckles—and when you remove food particles from fryers, you slow down the pace of oil breakdown). Or why we should stir hot food in the bain-marie every twenty minutes (so sauces and soups don't form a skin). Or why meat should be allowed to rest after cooking and before slicing (because the juices will be reabsorbed into the fibers of the meat. If you skip resting, you will lose more

The success of a recipe will depend on the art and science of menu development.

flavorful juices when you cut the meat. If too much heat escapes, the meat may grow cold before serving. Resting is arguably the most crucial stage of cooking meat [and often seafood too], and to maximize flavor, this process simply cannot be skipped. It literally finishes the "cooking process," and not adhering to it properly will yield undercooked and tough meat or fish). All these examples are great training topics for your team.

Chefs also need to develop different flavor profiles as per their restaurant's concept positioning. Sometimes it should be simple flavor direction, and other times it should be complex flavor approach. To achieve simplicity in procedures yet complexity in flavors, chefs need to work with their ingredients and seasoning to build a body of flavor. For example, this can be a well-developed cooking stock instead of stock powder, sea salt instead of iodized salt, or a well-combined pepper mix instead of only black pepper. However, don't get sucked into an excessive number of gimmicks—such as adding several Instagram-influenced dishes using smoking guns and the like (one or two dishes is okay)—or adding unnecessary complexity to dishes with many garnishes, microgreens, sauces, and toppings in order to try and stand out from your competitors.

Far too many chefs do this and lose touch of what is important: producing a great-*tasting* plate of food. **Complexity is the enemy of consistency.**

The point I want to make here is that each team will have cooks with varying degrees of skill and experience, which affects menu complexity. You will need to appoint a senior member of your kitchen team to take the time to go over the steps, methods, and techniques used for each recipe, as well as the reasons you cook items a certain way, especially for new hires. Don't take shortcuts—consistency is too important to not give it the attention it deserves.

Lastly, you need to create a unique flavor profile for your menu. It's your identity. **Don't create a dish with the same ingredients and taste that everyone else has in the market.** Understand your trading area and what your customers want.

You need to create a culture of learning, quality obsession, and distinctive menu offerings. How many times have you been served a Caesar salad or mushroom soup that tasted exactly like every other restaurant in town? Failure to separate your restaurant from the crowd is a nightmare from the standpoint of building a unique selling proposition.

Key Principles and Methods for Successful Kitchen Management

To build success in kitchen management, I will talk about applying the following ways of working: including food testing and obtaining feedback from guests and your team before you launch any new dish. I will also talk about the use of prep sheets and their impact on product freshness. Additionally, I will explain the correct frequency of introducing new menu items, removing non-moving dishes as per your product mix report, the importance of creating signature dishes, developing a quality-obsession mentality and culture, and the significance of the kitchen line-check system.

Food Testing

Test before you launch. Your dish needs to score 9 or 10 out of 10 on guests' surveys to make it onto the menu. If the dish is averaging scores of 8 or lower, it's not good enough. Take at least twenty surveys for each dish. This step will save you money and prevent potential losses in marketing, food cost, and waste. And, on a more basic level, you will not risk launching an unpopular menu item. A common mistake in this area occurs when restaurant owners and managers do the tasting internally and decide to launch a menu item because they like it, without getting customers' feedback first. They get excited and launch new menu items only to find out after a few weeks that the food didn't resonate with their customers. They change the menu again or, worse, fire the chef.

A common mistake in this area occurs when restaurant owners and managers do the tasting internally and decide to launch a menu item because they like it—without getting customers' feedback first.

Before you launch any new menu item, create the dish, and start selling it as an "off-menu," limited-time offer (LTO), or daily special in order to obtain customers' feedback on its price, taste, temperature, presentation, and portion size. I also ask for our chefs/cooks and food servers' feedback. Sometimes new dishes create bottlenecks in the kitchen or load one piece of equipment/kitchen station far more than the others.

Typically, I would plan for the next quarter's new dishes during the previous three months. Some restaurants prefer capturing the feedback in a more subtle fashion through table visits. That's a good approach, but not as comprehensive.

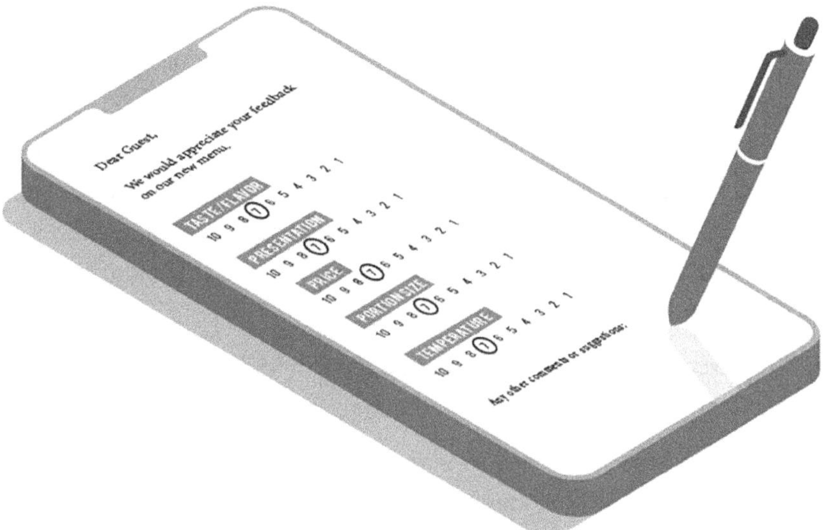

Proper Surveying:

1. Hand the above survey to your guests (at least twenty).
2. Gather at least twenty surveys for each new dish.
3. If the average score is only 8 out of 10, make adjustments, such as changing the recipe, or remove the dish and work on another. Your goal is a score of 9 or 10.

For soon-to-open restaurants, prior to opening, do the same exercise with focus groups.

In general, I never launch any dish (or any program, any new uniform, new menu design, new glasses, new software, and the list goes on) systemwide before I test in at least two to three restaurants.

Use of Prep Sheets

To run an efficient kitchen and serve fresh food, you must be prepared to prep the correct amount of food based on demand/service needs, which can fluctuate daily. **Your daily goal must be to serve all prepared products by the end of the shift and finish the day with minimal or no leftovers**, so you can start with fresh products the next day. Using prep sheets will help you achieve that.

Prep amounts impact shelf life, waste, and freshness, and therefore should be decided based on a historical product mix. As your kitchen manager or chef starts the morning shift, the first thing they need to look at is prep for the day based on historical averages, bookings, weather conditions, or any events nearby. Some chefs follow their intuition and rely on communication with front-of-house staff to predict daily demand, but I prefer a more structured way of forecasting prep amounts.

If you average twelve steaks on Sunday, and you find two leftover steaks from the night before, you should write a note to your cooks to prep only ten steaks.

If you don't have this tool in place, your cooks will either overprep or underprep steaks. One cook might decide to prep twenty while another might prep only five. In one real-life example, I was evaluating a restaurant that prepped forty-four steaks but only sold three per day! Imagine the impact on freshness and waste levels that smart prep can have.

Example Prep Sheet:

Items	Par	On Hand (from the previous night)	Need to Prep
Sirloin Steak	12	2	10
Hamburger Patties	20	5	15

PAR *indicates the minimum required quantity of a food item. You can create two PARs: one for slow days and one for busy days or weekends.* ***On Hand*** *refers to items found in the cooler today from the day before.*

Note for hotel chefs: One move hotel chefs make is to put leftover food on the buffet and say they don't have food waste. For example, you have leftover lobster and put it on the buffet for your hotel full-board customers instead of trashing it. This creates two problems. Firstly, your customers will expect lobster on the buffet on their next visit. Secondly, you deceive yourself and your Profit and Loss/Income Statement (P&L) by recording you had no waste.

Sometimes chefs might consider a certain food item unacceptable for one service but deem it okay for another, like a promotional or buffet offering. This approach is dead wrong. It means the chef is willing to sacrifice quality and hasn't thought about the potential downfall of this mentality. My rule of thumb is, "When in doubt, throw it out."

My rule of thumb is, "When in doubt, throw it out."

Introducing New Menu Items Every Quarter

Avoid changing the entire menu or launching new dishes too often, such as every week or every month, when a new executive chef joins your team, or whenever you see a drop in sales/revenue. A better method is to introduce four to six dishes once a quarter while removing non-moving dishes.

If you change the entire menu, you place tremendous pressure on your kitchen, and consistency will suffer. A new menu requires a massive amount of training. Another factor to consider with launching an entirely new menu is that guests who like items from the previous menu may stop returning to your restaurant since they can no longer find their favorite dishes and the restaurant's identity has somewhat changed.

If you want consistency and proficiency, avoid launching new dishes too often (every week or every two weeks, or every month). When you introduce a new dish, you will need to conduct pre-launch training for back-of-house and front-of-house employees. Everyone should score 100 percent on their new menu and recipe knowledge quiz. (One hundred percent because you do not want employees to know only 90 percent of the information. What if the 10 percent they don't know contains allergens? How would a cook execute a menu item if they only know 90 percent of the steps or ingredients.)

New menu items impact your kitchen equipment load, kitchen organization, and purchasing. For example, if you introduce more fried items to the menu, make sure your fry station isn't falling behind and causing bottlenecks. I would also like to mention the confusion that it can cause for the front-of-house team. If they are overwhelmed by too many changes, they will not be able to clearly describe or sell new menu items to guests. Have they received the training needed? Have they tasted the dishes themselves?

Most complaints and mistakes occur after introducing new dishes, as your team needs time to adapt and excel. The key thought here is to introduce dishes quarterly and to **excel at what you currently have on the menu.**

Additionally, changing your menu often is not the solution to declining revenues. This thought may surprise some chefs, marketers, and restaurateurs. Although it may sound smart on paper, in practice it's usually counterproductive, misleading with its short-term gains, disruptive to consistency of operations, and results in a negative guest experience. My advice is that **focusing on perfecting what you currently cook and serve is always the best approach**.

Don't change menu items because of a single customer complaint. Food and service are subjective. Our childhoods train our palates to become attached to the foods we grew up with. Do make changes based on receiving *repetitive* concerns, product mix performance, and *repetitive* food servers' feedback. Regrettably, I see restaurants remove menu items or change ingredients because one guest complained. Yes, only one.

My advice is that focusing on perfecting what you currently cook and serve is always the best approach.

Lastly, I think for a restaurant to really improve, every change should be for the better. A chef should take time to consider whether new dishes are improvements to the menu instead of merely changes. If the answer is no, perhaps there needs to be further consideration of the need for change. This requires experience and maturity as a chef.

Developing Signature Dishes

Having signature dishes is important from a market positioning standpoint. You will need to create dishes that make your restaurant famous or distinctive. **If a restaurant has no signature or specialty dishes, it will never have an identity or a following.** This could be a chocolate cake that can't be found anywhere else or a marinade for your chicken that no one can match in terms of taste and flavor. Success is about standing out, not fitting in.

A good restaurant should have at least two signature dishes in each menu category that stand out in a customer's mind and give it a competitive advantage over others (don't group all of them and place them on a single page on your menu). For example, your restaurant may be the only restaurant in town that serves a uniquely flavored smoked meat or gluten-free soufflé. **When it comes to creating signature dishes, flavor will always be more important than presentation.** If your menu offerings are too similar to other restaurants, guests may overlook your restaurant when deciding where to dine.

Signature Dish

Sometimes, dishes can become signature menu items without too much of a marketing push or without highlighting the dish on the menu as a signature dish. Chef Will Stanyer (the former head chef at a Michelin-starred chef Jason Atherton restaurant), whom I worked with, created a codfish dish that sold far more than he expected. In fact, it was so popular that he couldn't remove it from the menu even though he wanted to. He had interest in trying other codfish recipes, but he set his ego aside and had the maturity as a chef to realize that leaving the cod dish on the menu was the right choice for the restaurant. It was never removed from the menu and never dropped in popularity.

The more general and generic you act with menu planning or brand positioning, the less customer trust and respect you will receive.

Think of a pan-Asian restaurant versus a Japanese restaurant. Where would you choose to eat sushi? Most likely at the Japanese restaurant because you know it's their specialty, and you trust they will be good at it. Don't try to be everything to everyone. Don't fall into the "variety" trap. Customers trust specialized brands. If you want to order a steak, you will probably choose Texas Roadhouse simply because steaks are core items at Texas Roadhouse. Lastly, it's about creating your own culinary identity; it's not strictly about trends, Instagram, or what other chefs are doing or creating.

In this vein, watch out for how your restaurant is portrayed on online platforms like OpenTable, Google, Tripadvisor, or Yelp. Perhaps you identify as a British restaurant, but some websites are misrepresenting your restaurant as Mediterranean with incorrect descriptions of menu items and signature dishes. Monitor for this sort of hiccup, consider why it occurred, and be aware of how this can impact your business.

Developing a Mindset of Quality Obsession, Product Freshness, and Integrity

I've already explained the importance of high-quality signature dishes. But your approach and mindset should be about creating a culture of "quality obsession." Think about an easy-to-execute menu with high-quality ingredients. High quality doesn't necessarily mean only sourcing but also the way we cook. The more complex and elaborate your menu, the harder it will be for your team to be consistent; the less consistent you are, the more disappointed guests will be.

A culture of quality is about more than food. It's about everything in the restaurant, from the lighting and music, staff uniforms, and guest napkins to the plates and cutlery, and the list goes on. You must have a perfectionist mentality and high standards.

When it comes to food, your restaurant becomes unstoppable when "quality obsession" is ingrained in your culinary team's mindset. Quality obsession is different from just quality improvement, i.e., buying better quality ingredients. It's about reaching another level of passion for culinary success. This can manifest as a chef deciding to cook à la minute, prepping ingredients as close as possible to service time in order to maximize freshness and taste, or slow-smoking meat with a specific herb mix for more than eight hours.

Chef Jeremiah Tower said, "I think that the genius chef is the one who puts out the perfect ingredient, does as little as possible, but makes it go from a perfect ingredient to something spectacular. I wanted that kind of elegant simplicity."

Quality obsession requires a serious commitment and holding your team accountable to adhering to recipes that were created by the head chef. Problems occur when the kitchen team doesn't follow recipes or decides to get creative. In the franchise-chain world, adhering to recipes and franchisor standards is paramount to success. For example, if your franchise standard states that you can only hold burger patties for thirty minutes in the heat chute, but the franchisee/restaurant operator holds patties for one hour to save money, he/she ends up serving low-quality food. If your brewed coffee holding standard is forty-five minutes, but you hold it for one hour or more, you end up serving bitter/expired coffee. My most important advice to you is this: The closer you are to following standards, recipe steps, and operating manuals, the more successful you will be, and the opposite is true. It has to be an obsession!

The closer you are to following standards, recipe steps, and operating manuals, the more successful you will be, and the opposite is true.

Another element is product integrity. If a piece of beef is listed as USDA Prime on the menu, regardless of circumstances, the chef should never compromise on the quality. Many inexperienced chefs would make the decision to switch USDA choice for cheaper, lower-quality meat to cut costs based on the assumption that their customers won't notice the difference. A chef, or any other member of the restaurant staff, should never compromise on their integrity this way. I firmly believe that once you lose the trust and confidence of the consumer, there is little you can do to recover it. Sooner or later, you'll have to close your doors for good.

Product freshness is also key in building a quality-obsession mentality. In one of the restaurants I managed, we used to prep food twice a day. Yes, that meant higher labor cost. But it also meant more sales/revenue because guests loved our fresh food. Here is an example: sliced tomatoes prepped at 7 a.m. and served at 8 p.m. would taste fresher and far better if they were prepped at 6 p.m.

Cook Less, More Often is another key element of quality obsession and should be every chef's mantra for achieving great product freshness. Cooking lower quantities more often leads to better taste, less temperature deterioration, improved flavors, and better aroma. Consider french fries. When you fry them to order, you are frying fewer fries more often. The benefit is that you will have a hot and fresh product. The same is applicable to most menu items. Think of salads, mashed potatoes, baked goods, and sauces made from scratch for pasta.

If you want great taste and fresh food, you need to coach your team to follow this mentality. With one of the international brands I worked for, we had a bakery in each restaurant. We used to bake bread twice a day, which released the wonderful aroma of freshly baked bread into our dining rooms. Our guests absolutely loved it. Making lower quantities means higher product turnover, which means fresher dishes and better flavors. A good kitchen leader should be able to clearly train and inspire their team to come around to a new way of thinking and working to achieve a better product and deliver the best possible guest experience.

At the end of the day, the shortest route to sales and repeat visits is serving high-quality fresh products.

The Kitchen Line-Check System (A Technical Guide)

Line checks are one of the most important procedures you need to complete when preparing for a lunch or dinner service. I conducted line checks every day for forty-five minutes for four-and-a-half years in a restaurant that generated $200,000 per week with few or no food-related complaints. Line checks ensure food-cost control and, more importantly, that food quality meets specifications, food is portioned correctly to the proper weight, and ingredients are rotated appropriately (first in, first out). A good line check prevents unnecessary problems and headaches during service.

The goals of conducting line checks are:

1. Defining quality while establishing universal and clear quality identifiers for all your restaurant chefs/cooks and all prepped food items and ingredients.
2. To provide valuable information that enables chefs and restaurant managers to serve great products consistently.
3. To take the guesswork out of operations, relying on agreed-upon quality standards among cooks and chefs in the restaurant.
4. The food and ingredient description in the line-check form is a highly valuable training tool. Use it during the pre-shift briefing or while conducting your line check.

So, what is a line check and how does it work?

Kitchen line checks allow you to catch your restaurant's mistakes before your guests do, reducing food voids and comps. (Void is when you delete an item from the Point of Sales system. Comp is when you serve food as a complimentary, free-of-charge dish due to mistakes or service delays; a positive comp includes, for example, serving a dessert free of charge for a birthday celebrant.)

Line checks will enable you to check for kitchen- or buffet-line readiness. Line checks ensure proper portion controls are in place, backups are thawed, and the line is stocked and ready for the rush, providing consistent execution and raising guest satisfaction. Another reason to complete line checks is to ensure your food is prepared to the standards you developed. It is high quality, safe, and ready to serve to your guests.

> This may surprise you, but I encourage restaurant and hotel GMs to enter the kitchen, spot-check food, and confirm that prepped ingredients match the line-check description on the checklist.

Perform a line check before each service period. A thorough checklist should be in place for each station, including fry, grill, salad, expediter, and prep, and needs to be run through by a trusted, senior member of the team who is fully trained and well-versed in the requirements across all sections of the kitchen. This may surprise you, but I encourage restaurant and hotel GMs to enter the kitchen, spot-check food, and confirm that prepped ingredients match the line-check description on the checklist. The idea here is to create a culture of only accepting the exceptional and to ensure that all levels of management understand the importance of food quality.

The checklist should include a list of every item on the station with proper holding temperatures for each, a brief flavor-profile description that is written and developed by your head chef, and great quality-description points. This step is key, as it aligns everyone in the kitchen to the same page to have a shared understanding of what the prepped ingredients should look, taste, and feel like.

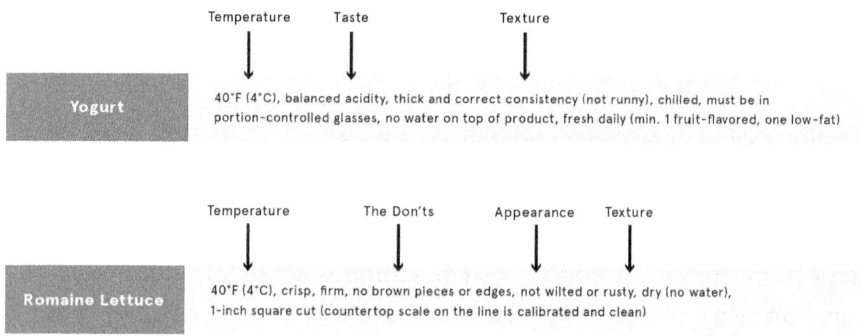

The proper size for portioning and measuring spoons, spoodles, ladles, scoops, or measuring cups should also be listed. Any other utensils or items needed for shift execution should also be listed, such as tongs, towels, pans, and sanitation buckets. Cooks can also use this checklist to set up their stations properly.

Of course, not all restaurants go to this level of detail. This type of intricate and well-structured program may be a foreign concept to some chefs. You hardly see this in Michelin-starred or independent restaurants, but what you will see is a different form of line check. I once asked Michelin-starred chef Pierre Gagnaire and Michelin-starred chef Jason Atherton about their line-check systems, and they both told me that chefs must check everything before the shift starts and must taste all sauces. Additionally, in one episode of *Eater* on YouTube dated January 2020, with twenty-one million views, executive chef Mark Lapico from Jean-Georges NYC said, "So, 5 p.m., the whole crew is at family meal, we usually take this time as the last moment of the day before service starts, where we can really break open every container, put a spoon into every sauce, and make sure that all the mise en place is tight. If something is not right, now is the time that we are going to remake it. The last thing in the world we want is a customer to point out what we have done incorrectly. Are the chives cut properly? Is the dill hydrated? Is the caviar cold enough?"

In Michelin-starred restaurants, the head chef is the expeditor. He or she tastes everything and visually checks every plate before it leaves the kitchen. They are the line-check leaders, but without the detailed checklist below.

When performing a proper line check, you must taste, touch, smell, and weigh all prepped products. Have these tools at hand:

- Laser or regular digital thermometer;
- Sanitizer wipes in case you use the thermocouple;
- Gloves;
- Line checklist on a clipboard;
- Teaspoons (thirty teaspoons or more, as you can't dip the same spoon in different items) and ramekins for tasting;
- Scale for pre-portioned items, as an example, spot-check and weigh pre-portioned veggies, sliced turkey, or pre-portioned penne pasta.

How Does It Work?

The chef or restaurant manager (if your brand trains GMs in-kitchen) checks every ingredient on the kitchen line at least half an hour before the restaurant opens for business. If the restaurant's opening hour is 4 p.m., then at 3:30 p.m., all prep/mise en place must be 100 percent completed. If not, you will miss out on checking several items, which defeats the purpose of the entire task.

A line check starts by signing and writing the date, the time, and the name of the person conducting the line check (important for record-keeping and accountability). The person then conducts the check by tasting, touching, visually inspecting, smelling, or weighing products to make sure they **match** the "quality-identifiers description section" written in the line-check form.

Identify the items that are wrong with the chef/cook on the section, responsible for its production or not. Enable them to either taste, touch, or smell the item to understand why it is wrong and therefore feel empowered to identify such issues themselves ahead of time, which should help ensure the smooth flow of operations.

If the item matches the required specifications, a checkmark is noted on the line check and the temperature is recorded. If the item does not match the specified quality (too salty, too dry), an **X** is marked, and the chef or kitchen manager will communicate immediately with the back-of-house team to rectify the issue.

As you can see in the image, the chef portions a small amount of soup in a ramekin and is tasting the product to make sure it matches the description on the checklist.

At the end of the line check, the manager and chef must briefly discuss the findings or write the feedback in the restaurant's communication log for a later discussion with staff, so issues do not repeat themselves. For example, if the lettuce is brown and dry every other day, the log will reveal potential issues.

In some countries, line checks are considered legal documents to support conformity to health-and-safety requirements. You must keep checklists on record.

How do I write the line-check quality identifiers? The restaurant manager or chef can write the quality identifiers for ingredients, keeping the following points in mind:

1. Temperature: the correct holding temperature for the item.
2. Taste: such as tangy, sweet, or sour.
3. Texture and touch: thick, runny, or soft.
4. Color and appearance: deep, dark red or bright green; for example: tomatoes.
5. Smell: Does the product have the right aroma, or does it have the right smell? For example, when ground meat is old it tends to smell foul or sour. If that's how meat smells, it needs to be discarded.
6. The don'ts: how to know when something has gone wrong. For example: turkey slices must not be salty, cheese must not have dry edges, and meat should never be slimy.

This example explains the above:

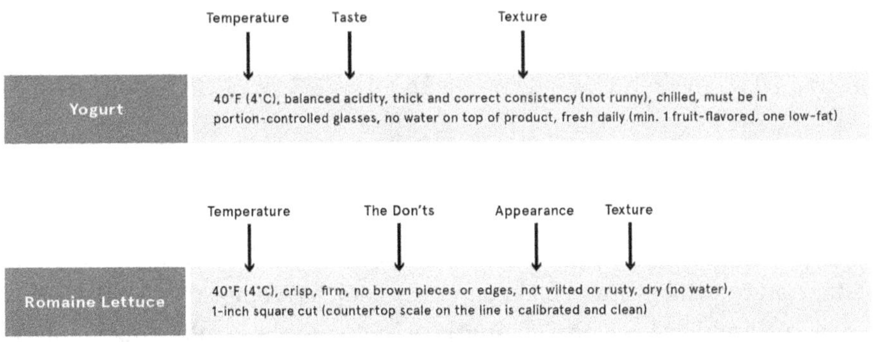

The top reason for lack of consistency in any restaurant is the absence of clarity and consensus among cooks around taste, look, texture, cut size, and aroma of finished prep ingredients. If you believe that romaine lettuce must be cut one-inch wide while another cook believes it should be one-third-inch wide, there will be no consistency. That's why you need to **spell out the quality identifiers as per the romaine lettuce example on the previous page**.

One additional part of the line check is making sure you have the right portioning tools and other smallware ready on the line before opening. These need to be stated on the line-checklist form. If you need a 5 oz. ladle for soup, it should be written in the soup section. The last thing you want is to only start looking for a 5 oz. ladle when the first order comes in. More examples: chopping boards, knives needed on the line, tablespoons, grill brush, squeeze bottles—in other words, every tool that you need must be ready on the line thirty minutes before the door opens for business.

I highly recommend using portioning spoons instead of grams or pounds when writing a recipe. Instead of writing that you need 8 fluid ounces of something, just place one cup into the pan on the kitchen line. Your cooks don't need to stop to measure 8 oz. of fluid every time; they can just use one cup. Likewise, instead of asking your cooks to portion 64 grams of corn kernel into a salad, just ask them to fill half a cup.

Lastly, please follow your local municipalities' rules and regulations for temperature standards, and make sure each cook has completed certification in food safety and hygiene. **Every month, ask your cooks to take a quiz on food**

safety and analyze the average score to assess what teachings are missing. A common problem in our industry is the notion that "all my cooks are certified in food safety and no additional training is required by the management team," but I often see a huge gap in food safety practices and knowledge even directly following certification.

Below you will find a short sample of a line check.

Breakfast Line Check

Date: 27-Oct-2022 **Time:** 5:30 a.m. **Conducted by:** Mike H

Item	Morning Shift	Quality Identifiers
Salmon, Smoked		40°F (4°C), glossy, not dried out, especially edges, not too salty. No off smell.
Cold Cuts		40°F (4°C), fresh, small portion, rotated, not dried out, especially the edges, minimum 4 types.
Romaine Lettuce		40°F (4°C), crisp, firm, no brown edges, not wilted or rusty, dry (no water), 1-inch square cut.
Display Chiller		40°F (4°C), hang-in thermometer checked, clean glass.
Yogurt		40°F (4°C), balanced acidity, thick and right consistency, chilled, must be in portion-controlled glasses, no water on top of product, fresh daily (min. 1 fruit-flavored, one low-fat).
Hash Browns		140°F (60°C), golden brown, not oily and not soggy, not more than 5 minutes holding time on buffet under heat lamp.
Sausage		140°F (60°C), moist and golden brown, natural case, not salty, not dry.
Bacon		140°F (60°C), freshly cooked, not overcooked, individual pieces, crisp and not chewy.
Sautéed Mushrooms		140°F (60°C), fresh white button mushrooms, sautéed with herbs and butter à la minute. Crisp, not soft.
Grilled Tomatoes		140°F (60°C), grill marks visible, ripe, and uniform size, no bruises, juicy, not oily or dry.

Zoning

Another key principle that falls under line check or general kitchen organization is **zoning**, which basically means placing items in the same place all the time. For example, if the diced tomatoes pan is placed on the right-hand side of the reach-in cooler, the team will not move it to another location or even to the spot next to it.

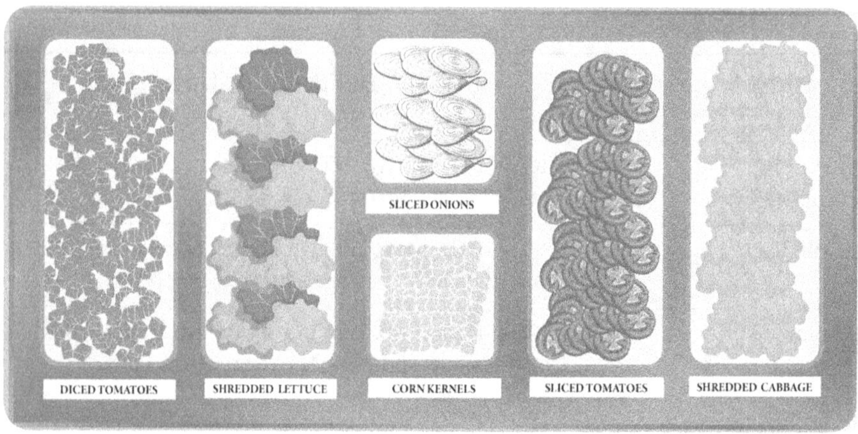

I would coach staff to always keep ingredients in the same spot. This way your team will end up working just like a blindfolded bartender who can spot a vodka bottle without even looking. Building a dish becomes very fast and second nature. If you change the location of ingredients by even one spot, you slow down the team. I use a mobile label printer, such as the one in the photo opposite (stand-up freezer), and attach labels on refrigerator doors, reach-in coolers, and dry store, so everything remains in the same area. It can also help new employees: it will be easier and faster to locate things; faster means a smoother kitchen and fewer labor hours.

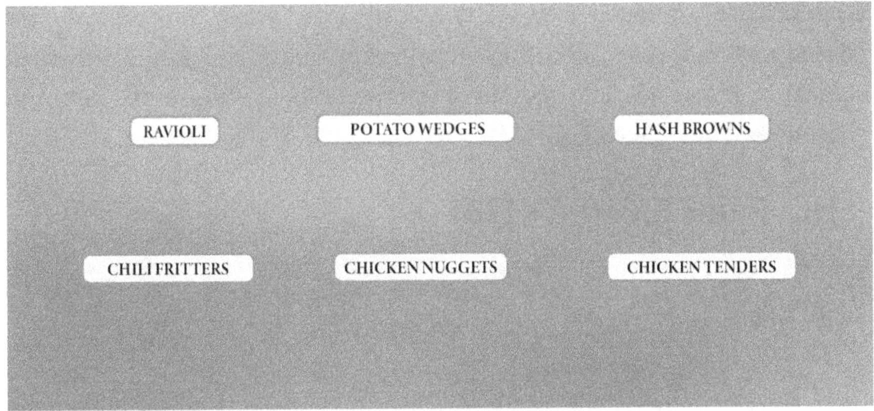

This is how a stand-up freezer door would look like in my restaurants. Cooks don't have to "search" for products. Every item has a zone with a clear label at the freezer door. It takes ongoing supervision and spot checks to create a discipline around zoning and kitchen organization.

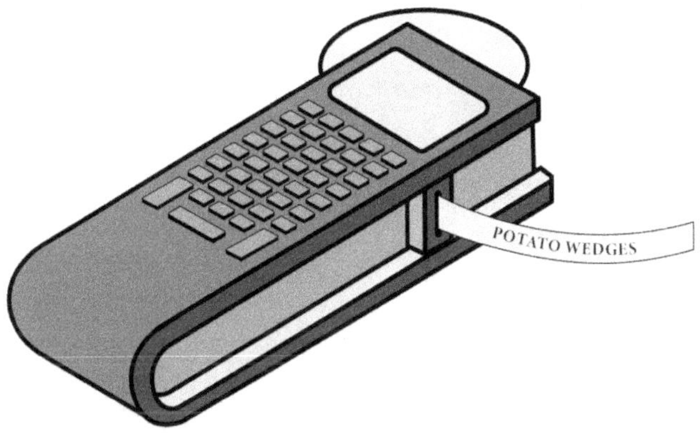

A label machine is one of my favorite tools to help my kitchen team stay organized and efficient. I use it in dry-storage areas, freezer, coolers, racks, kitchen line, prep area, food servers' station, and the list goes on.

Shelf-life

One more important system that you will need is a shelf-life checklist. This checklist will have all your ingredients' names and when they expire. For example: guacamole expires by end of shift; raw filet steak shelf life is forty-eight hours. At one of the restaurants that I worked for, we gave each cook a pocket-size laminated shelf-life checklist so that when they prepped and labeled an item we were all consistent with expiry dates and product freshness standards. It was not left to different interpretations. We also had one large sheet posted in the kitchen.

SHELF-LIFE CHECKLIST

ITEM	FROZEN LIFE	THAWED AND REFRIGERATOR LIFE	FRESH LIFE
Burger, 4 oz	N/A	3 days	N/A
Beef Chili	4 months	7 days	N/A
Philly Steak Meat	4 months	2 days	N/A
Steak, Ribeye	4 months	2 days	N/A
Tuna, 6 oz Yellow Fin	4 months	2 days	N/A
Chicken, Breast	4 months	48 hours	N/A
Cabbage, Red, Shredded	N/A	N/A	3 days
Cilantro, Fresh	N/A	N/A	2-3 days
Lettuce, Romaine	N/A	N/A	2-3 days

Lastly, line check documents the end process of a wider system that connects different processes and systems, such as proper receiving, proper holding, and proper product specifications. From the line check, you can also see if your ordering system, hygiene system, and preparation system are in working order. It's important to understand that your line-check document verifies that all the systems required to operate a kitchen from A to Z, i.e., ordering to serving, are working properly. Make it part of your kitchen DNA.

Developing Great Recipes

One of the first lessons hotel schools teach is how to standardize recipes. Unfortunately, when I visit restaurants, I find many recipes are poorly structured, leading to lots of mistakes. That is, they have missing ingredients, faulty seasonings, insufficient or poor instructions causing more work, or chefs haven't tested them. In many cases, restaurants don't even have recipes in place, especially hotel restaurants. This was shocking to me.

Let me share a principle called Standardization Always Meets Expectations, or SAME. Restaurants build consistency on constant recipe usage. If every cook uses an individual method to cook a dish, no two dishes will look, cost, or taste the same. One great practice is to have recipes laminated and placed in the kitchen, and to mandate that cooks use them while doing prep, no matter their level of experience. An amazingly effective way to make sure your recipes are read and used is to take one recipe in your hand during pre-shift meetings, refer/point to it often, read from it often, and discuss it with all chefs; afterward, post it on the kitchen notice board. This signals the importance of using recipes to your team. I always see cooks going to the notice board to read the recipe after the pre-shift briefing, which is exactly the goal. I also used to print copies and hand them out to all the cooks at the meeting. Daily discussions will encourage your cooks to understand and follow the exact steps.

If every cook uses an individual method to cook a dish, no two dishes will look, cost, or taste the same.

Additionally, the chef in charge must demonstrate actual preparation steps as part of a separate formal training program. I have also found social platforms such as WhatsApp very useful in this area—senior chefs can take responsibility to ensure that all new recipes are sent into a kitchen group chat. This also means that all chefs, regardless of their section or schedule, will have an electronic copy of every recipe that was introduced, which they can easily reference from their mobile phones, and more importantly, review before a pre-shift meeting. (The only possible drawback to this is confidentiality.)

Lastly, many people talk about the importance of quality, but few teach it. Chefs, restaurant managers, and food and beverage leaders must dedicate at least ten minutes a day to talk with their teams about one recipe and discuss how it can be correctly prepared and cooked to perfection. Making food quality part of your DNA is one of the most important factors for success in the food and beverage industry. Teaching others and learning from them is true leadership.

Raise the Bar and Aim High

When developing new menu items and recipes, ask yourself questions such as, "Are these recipes the *best* in my city? Are these recipes developed by top-class chefs like Jason Atherton, Alain Ducasse, or Gastón Acurio? What can we do better? Would these menu items achieve a 10 out of 10 score on customer satisfaction surveys?" (Refer back to the earlier section: Food Testing.)

I have stated before that you need good quality ingredients but not necessarily expensive ingredients; you cannot achieve greatness without affordable ingredients that fit your brand.

Everyone can make cheesecake or tiramisu, but not everyone has the best recipe. Challenge your chefs to always look for ways to improve their current recipe procedures (update and print new recipes when you improve them and have them handy for chefs to use always). That being said, if the dish is a high seller and very popular, then it's best not to make changes. As they say, don't mess with success.

Your goal should be to serve the best tiramisu in your city. Ask your chefs: "Is this tiramisu the best in our city?" Ask your guests: "Would you consider our tiramisu the best in the city?" If the answer is negative, find out what to do differently. These same questions apply to the rest of the menu. You must aim to serve the best food if you want to be the preeminent restaurant in your city. This is not just philosophical. You need to do the exercises, conduct the surveys, and ask the questions.

The Flow of Food

In this section I will talk about the process of food flow in your restaurant, from ordering all the way to serving. There are critical points and key actions, not only from a food safety standpoint but also from an operational excellence lens, that must be taken care of during each part of the cycle. I will begin with ordering.

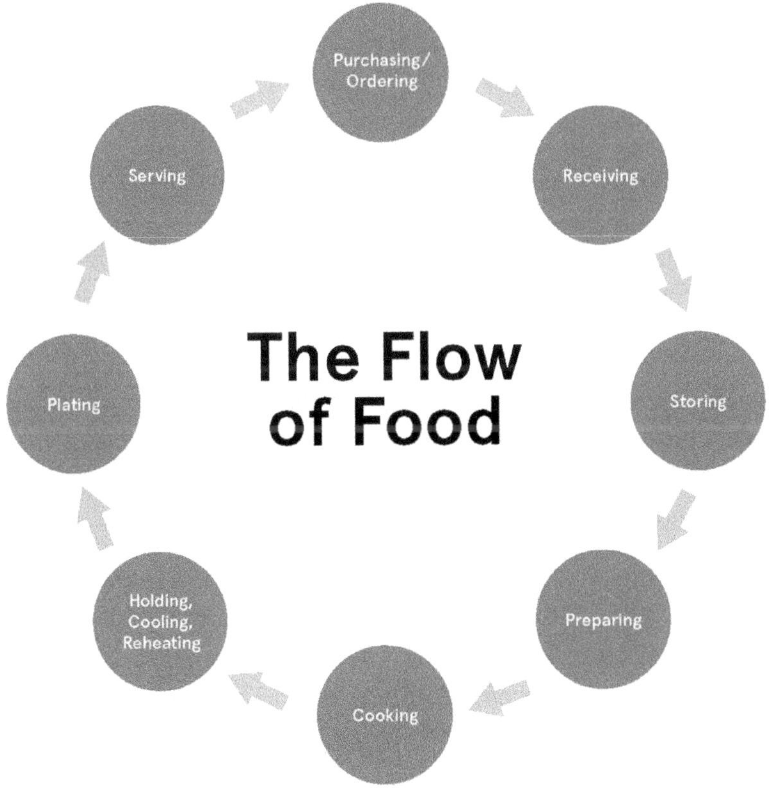

Ordering

Placing your food orders with your suppliers requires time and focus. As a chef or manager, you are trusted with money and how to spend it (the food order is a large amount of money to handle). Things go wrong when food orders are placed by managers who sit in their offices all day. Managers/chefs must go to the dry storage area, walk-in coolers, and freezers to physically check how much of each ingredient they have on hand. They must forecast their sales based on bookings, weather impact, events nearby, and product mix performance (historical sales). Establish a PAR level: *Periodic Automatic Replenishment or PAR levels are minimum and maximum quantity limits that you set for a certain item.* When the quantity approaches the minimum level, the item should be reordered. You must have a PAR level for busy days/weekends and another for regular days. You must have proper kitchen organization, proper lighting and access, proper labeling of products, and consistently follow FIFO (First In and First Out: the first product you receive goes to the back of the shelf, and product you had on the shelf before receiving the order goes to the front of the shelf. Use the slightly older item first and keep the inventory moving while maintaining freshness and avoiding expiration).

Some indicators of poor ordering include running out of products often, overstocked shelves, and conducting too many petty-cash purchases.

Receiving

Proper receiving is essential to accepting the correct products **as per the specifications that you have previously written and provided your vendor**—at the correct time, correct price, correct temperature, correct quantity, and correct quality.

Don't let the delivery vendor do everything for you. Inspect their work. Did you receive the correct quality at the correct price as per your order? Is the food safe? If you see ice crystals on ice cream tubs, that indicates the ice cream has been thawed and refrozen. Are the steaks frozen (if your restaurant orders frozen steaks), and if you order refrigerated, are they above the temperature danger zone? Are the tomatoes five-by-five inches, or are the avocados Hass avocados? Dairy and seafood are temperature-sensitive products—receive them at the right temperature without any compromise.

Don't delegate receiving to others. It's essential to the financial success of the restaurant, so it's best to guarantee it's done right by the restaurant manager or chef.

Product theft might occur during receiving; for example, a supplier brings ten cases of steaks, you count ten, you turn your back, and they keep one or two with them.

Discipline is key. You should have an agreed-upon delivery time with suppliers, so they don't show up during rush hours.

Don't delegate receiving to others. It's essential to the financial success of the restaurant, so it's best to guarantee it's done right by doing it yourself.

Michelin-starred restaurants place huge importance on relationships with suppliers. They compete to buy the highest and most expensive products. Their vendors and how they perform determine the success of their restaurants.

Storage

Now it's time to store the products. If you don't empty the original cardboard boxes and containers when you receive your food orders, be prepared for insect infestation.

Be sure to follow FIFO, as I covered in ordering. Place newly received products at the back of the shelves, and bring the old items to the front of the shelves.

Wash all vegetables and store in non-cardboard containers. When receiving, we use a process called "tagging," which is basically writing the date you received each product on the cans in order to maintain FIFO. Place vegetables, especially leafy ones, away from walk-in cooler fans to avoid drying them out.

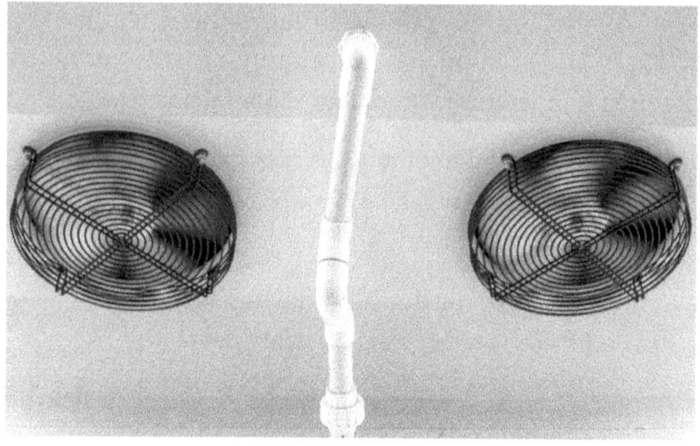

Placing leafy vegetables away from cold air from blowers will prevent drying them out.

Place meat in the coldest area of the cooler. If your walk-in cooler is connected to your walk-in freezer, place your thawed meat near the walk-in freezer area. It's typically the coldest area in the cooler, and the area near the walk-in cooler door is the warmest part of the cooler. Cover all products tightly to avoid cross-contamination or blood dripping from one container to other foods.

I find cleanliness to be one of the main issues of storage areas. You must wash all containers often so mold doesn't build up, clean shelves properly, and avoid rust buildup.

Enter your coolers at least once a day with your chef or kitchen manager to spot-check products. Ask questions such as: When was this product prepped? When does it expire? What's on the bottom shelf here? I see a large container of salsa; do we need this much for this shift? Most franchise restaurants have a shelf-life checklist for all products, which makes it easy to know when an item must be discarded. Develop your own checklist in line with your local health authorities and your own product freshness goals. (See the shelf-life checklist that I shared earlier.)

Be aware of slippery floors in walk-in coolers and freezers. Repair gaskets when needed, and don't rely on reading the temperature that's displayed outside the cooler. Go inside the coolers and read the more accurate hanging thermometers.

In the walk-in freezer, avoid ice buildup on the fans and tubes. Cover everything tightly to avoid freezer burn, and rotate products well. Place a nonslip mat in both coolers and freezers.

Don't store food on the floor anywhere in your kitchens. You must have racks that are at least six inches off the floor. Never store food, even in sealed containers, directly on the floor.

As you can see from this image, no product touches the floor. Everything is at least six inches above floor level.

Make sure prepped and ready-to-serve food (if held cold) is stored below 40 degrees Fahrenheit (4°C) and hot food is kept above 140 degrees Fahrenheit (60°C). In other words, all food must be out of the danger zone. In some countries, the temperature danger zone varies slightly. It could be 38°F to 145°F (3°C to 62°C). Check with your local health authorities.

I can't conclude this section without mentioning the food-storage chart, which is shown in the image below:

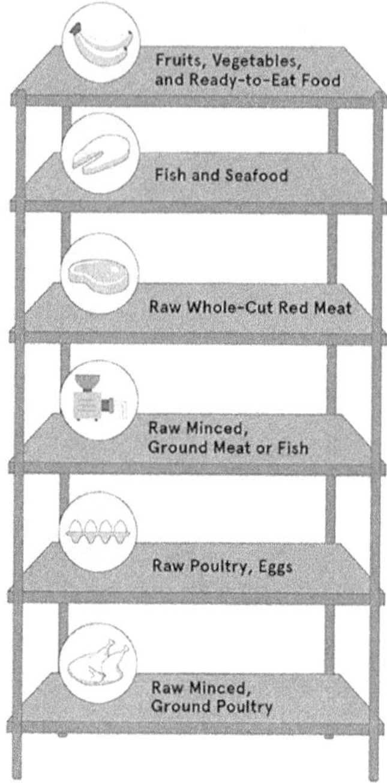

Prepping and Cooking

During this stage, training, supervision, talent, and adherence to recipes are paramount. How successful the finished product is going to be relies on how trained your team is; your shift supervision and holding the team accountable to high standards; the talent you hired and their skill level; what sort of learning attitude they have; and lastly, adherence to recipes and the techniques that you have stipulated in these recipes. The types of equipment and ingredients you use also play a major role.

My recommendation here is to keep a close eye on waste, the temperature of products during prep or final cooking, and the use of portioning tools. Many restaurants don't have strict portioning policies, causing taste, portion, and presentation to be different from day to day.

Holding

Holding has two parts.

Part One: when a dish is finished and under the heat lamp or in an ambient area of the expediter station (if the dish is cold). One common mistake I see in most restaurants is that either no one has turned on the heat lamps, parts of them are out of order, or the heat lamps are on but the dishes are not placed properly under them, causing them to be half-cold.

Part Two: when an ingredient is in a bain-marie or reach-in cooler, either stored or on kitchen-line setup. In both parts, the food must be out of the temperature danger zone.

It's important to talk about the concept of *zoning* one more time, which means each ingredient must have its own zone, and this zone must not change often. It's a good practice to label your racks in your coolers, and what's even better is to label the standup fridge doors with what is inside. This will help everyone locate products faster, which increases efficiency and saves labor hours. Line cooks must work like blindfolded bartenders, which means if pico de gallo is placed in a 1/3 pan on the kitchen line on the left-hand corner, **it should be there every day and must not move an inch!** No one should be looking for any items. All ingredients and tools should be in the same place, and everyone should know where to find them. Adherence to organization makes operations smoother, faster, and more efficient.

Menu planning starts before the restaurant is built.

Plating and Serving

Portion control and timing between appetizers and main courses is key. How many times have you been served your main course while you are still having your appetizers? Some chefs portion side items like mashed potatoes and grilled veggies way before finishing a steak, causing the side items to get cold. Presentation consistency and the old basic rule of serving hot food on hot plates and cold food on cold plates are also essential. I always make sure plate warmers are used for hot food and plates are chilled in the refrigerator for salads and cold items.

Menu Planning

Menu planning starts before the restaurant is built. It determines everything: selection of equipment, smoothness of operation, workflow, pricing, profitability, talent level, restaurant positioning, the look and feel of the restaurant, and guest satisfaction.

Some things to consider when conducting menu planning:

- Understand your location. Be mindful of your location and your impact on supplies. Don't try to be a seafood restaurant in the middle of the forest.
- Keep an eye on industry trends such as vegan dishes, plant-based, and gluten-free.
- Use seasonality to your advantage.
- Research your market. What is missing, or what can be better? If there are a few restaurants offering smoked meats in the area, but you know you have a superior recipe, and you can outperform them, consider adding smoked meat to the menu—as long as it fits your brand positioning, menu offering, focus, and strategy.
- Understand the demographics of your area, age, gender, ethnicity, and income level, and make sure your offerings match their preferences. Don't create a menu that targets teenagers in a senior-citizen community. Avoid the pitfall of creating a menu based on your personal preferences; conduct focus groups, interview guests, read industry magazines, and understand trends.

- Understand your equipment, cuisine, theme, future team talent level, supply chain, and pricing.
- Work on menu balance in terms of cooking procedures. For example, balance fried and grilled items, textures, and flavors. Don't create a one-dimensional menu. Keep in mind that menu balance also means equipment load balance. Lastly, think about additional revenue streams and whether the menu will be able to cope or fit. For example: delivery, takeout orders, and catering.
- Pay special attention to allergens, dairy products, and high-sodium products. Not only is there a legal aspect to declaring such ingredients but you also have a moral responsibility to adhere 100 percent to guests' requirements.
- Think of the story (positioning) that your food and restaurant wants to tell to the guest—otherwise it becomes a generic establishment without an identity.

A Note on Drinks:

To offer great drinks, follow similar advice to this chapter's guidelines, such as developing great cocktail recipes, receiving guest feedback before launching a new drink, conducting a line check before every shift, focusing on quality and creativity, creating signature drinks, purchasing proper supplies, and conducting frequent training and leadership exercises. Nearly every principle in this chapter is applicable to bar management.

General Kitchen Management Dos and Don'ts

The Don'ts

- Don't scream or yell. You won't be the next Gordon Ramsay because you scream, cuss, or yell at your team. Losing it during rush hours is the worst thing you can do to your team, as this causes panic and chaos. Treat your kitchen team well, even when mistakes happen. And if, at times, you do find yourself slipping up, I think it is important to acknowledge this and explain the reasons around it, either to an individual or to the team as a whole.

- Don't be flexible when it comes to using portioning tools. Lack of portioning tools results in inconsistent taste, portion size, and cost fluctuation.
- Don't overload one piece of equipment and underutilize others when planning your menu. For example, when you create a menu of appetizers, if most are fried, you will have a slow pace of service. Cooking and serving food will take a long time, fryers will be overloaded, and flavors will be mixed.
- Don't turn yourself into an admin/computer person instead of being a hands-on chef. Unfortunately, some chefs are distracted by social media and scroll through Instagram all day in their offices, and when they leave their offices, they just yell and scream at cooks. Some of the greatest chefs in the world—including Pierre Gagnaire and Jason Atherton—are still hands-on, cooking every day in the kitchen and treating their teams with the utmost respect.

The Dos

- Conduct kitchen staff surveys, and listen to their feedback. They are in the thick of it. The more you address their operational concerns, the smoother your kitchen will be. (Read more about this in Chapter Six: Cost Discipline, section: Team Engagement and Contribution.)
- Listen to guest complaints, especially the repetitive ones. Your customers' concerns will point out problem areas for you.
- Conduct monthly recipe-knowledge written quizzes. If you have ten cooks and the average kitchen-knowledge quiz score is 6 out of 10, it means you have not trained your team properly and given them the knowledge they need. (See Chapter Four: Training and Inspirational Leadership for more details on this topic.)

- Head chefs should be active in the community. PR events, industry events, and social media marketing can create a following. In many cases, customers follow the chef and are inspired by their creativity, style, and personality.
- Buy commercial-grade kitchen equipment. Commercial equipment must be made of noncorrosive elements like aluminum and stainless steel, proven to last longer. If you use a grill or microwave (the latter is not my favorite piece of equipment) that is designed for home use, you will have repair and maintenance problems, and speed of service will slow down, as home appliances won't keep up with the demand of a commercial kitchen.
- Define roles clearly. If the kitchen staff roles are clearly defined, and each employee knows their respective work, the restaurant works without any friction.
- Conduct a daily back-of-house shift briefing. It's the best way to cross-train your team and keep the standards high. (See detailed info in Chapter Four: Training and Inspirational Leadership.)
- Tour your kitchen several times during the shift.
- Introduce menu specials from suppliers once a quarter. It is a great way to offer diversity for the guest and provide an avenue of support for your suppliers, and it is typically advantageous for the company from a financial perspective.
- Create kitchen opening and closing checklists. Otherwise, someone will forget to turn off the fryer or the lights.
- Follow cleaning guidelines religiously—don't just tick them off. Follow due diligence records, as shown on the next page. Check in with your staff, following timely intervals.

Now, let's put the learning to action. If you answer with a *No* to any of the questions on the following page, it means you might have a gap or an opportunity in that area.

Evaluate your Kitchen Management

Question	Comments
Is our food consistent?	
Do we have great recipes?	
Is our food the best in town?	
Do we have a line-check program in place?	
Are my food vendors adhering to our specifications?	
Do we test and receive customer feedback before launching new dishes?	
Does each ingredient have a zone in the kitchen?	
Do we have a shelf-life checklist in place?	
Do we prepare food using prep sheets/ product mix?	
Do we introduce four to five new dishes every three months while removing non-moving dishes?	
Do we properly forecast prep quantities to ensure freshness and minimal waste?	
Do we have signature dishes? Are they different from our competitors?	
Do we train our kitchen team every day during pre-shift briefings? Do we explain one recipe every day?	
Do we create a culture of empowerment, encouragement, creativity, and motivation in our kitchen?	

CHAPTER TWO
SUPERIOR SERVICE AND HOSPITALITY

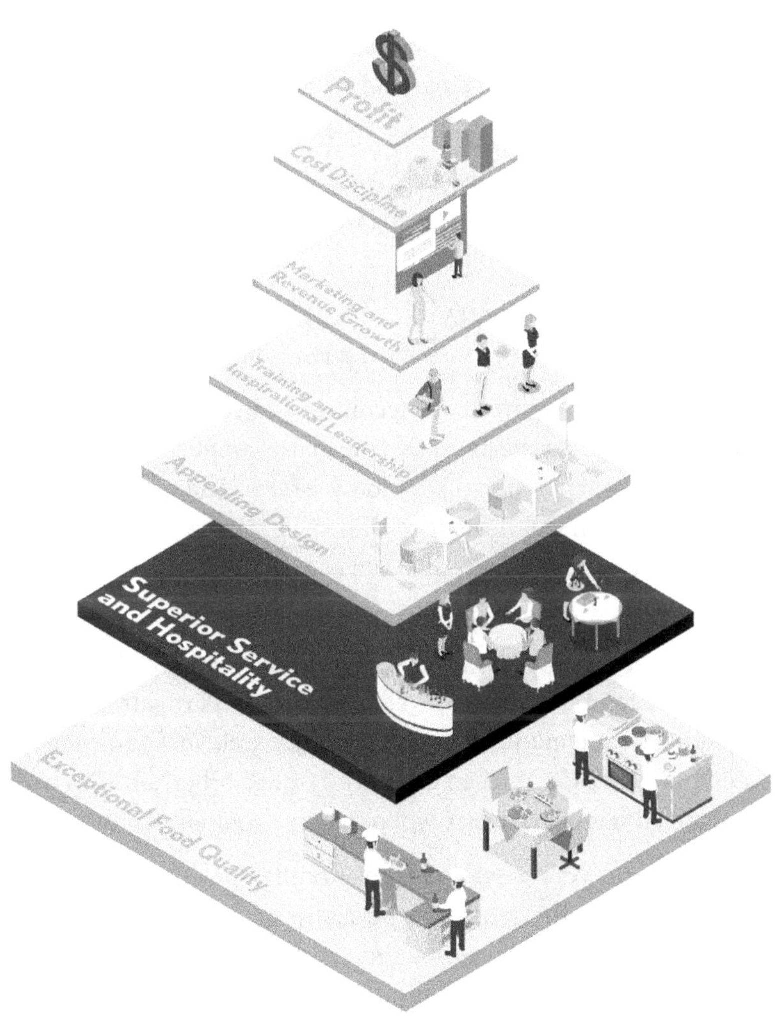

The restaurant industry is labor intensive. It relies on the human aspect—the human touch in serving people and, more importantly, connecting with them. Service and Hospitality impact how we feel about a restaurant's food and affect our experience and overall perception.

Service is a mixture of art and science. The art is knowing how to read your guests and anticipate their needs, so they don't have to wave to get served. It should be a seamless process—you anticipate and take care of your guests' needs before they ask. But it's also about taking command of your table. Some think service is about having a servant mentality by treating the guest as superior to you. In truth, it is about **leading your guests** to a phenomenal experience and making suggestions and recommendations while remaining humble and kind.

While it might seem obvious, the science aspect of service is about knowing your menu inside and out, remembering who ordered what, and recalling your guests' names and favorite tables.

Lastly, and most importantly, it's about going the extra mile and having a "whatever it takes" attitude to ensure the guest is happy.

Excellent service requires both technical and social skills to recognize, anticipate, and meet guests' needs. Some guests would argue that the best food in the world will not make up for lousy service. Additionally, the shortest way to generate significant sales is to cultivate happy guests who come back often. In this chapter, I will share different and essential aspects of service and hospitality.

Service and hospitality are two completely different things. Service is when you pick up the food from the expeditor window and bring it to your guest's table. Hospitality is about how you make people feel, how you connect with them, and how you care. You can get service from a robot, an ATM machine, or an automated service, but they will never give you hospitality.

Understanding your restaurant positioning (positioning, in short, is understanding and defining your target audience, competitors, price point, the image you want to portray to your guests, and in which segment you play, for example: QSR, fine dining, or fast casual) and the feeling you want it to portray is essential. It's mission critical that your entire team understands and believes in your positioning. One of the common issues I see—especially with fresh graduates from hotel and catering schools—in misunderstanding service style is, for example, when food servers try to serve your food in classic French formal style but in a casual-dining restaurant.

Before I begin discussing hiring, training, steps of service, suggestive selling, and other key pillars of successful service operations, I would like to highlight that service starts *before* guests enter your restaurant. It begins with their arrival to the building. Consider how valets welcome cars and how hosts and hostesses interact with guests. This must be part of the experience. It must be seamless and smooth. You will need to ask yourself: Are the valets friendly and well groomed? Is my host or hostess friendly, outgoing, and humble? The same applies to the departure experience.

A natural, genuine, and warm smile with open body language sets the tone for the entire dining experience. You don't have a second chance to create a first impression. Impress your guests with your enthusiasm and be cheerful. It sets the tone for the entire experience.

One fundamental principle to remember is that a guest has only two things to do: arrive and pay the bill. Anything in-between is the job of the staff. This means your service steps, procedures, and culture must be built around this mantra: **we own the entire process from welcoming the guests to taking orders, serving food with a smile, refilling drinks, and fulfilling special requests, all the way to payment and departure.**

Everything begins from the reservation step, whether it is booked by phone, email, or online. Is the reservation process smooth and easy? Could the guest easily communicate any special requests? First impressions are built from this stage. From looking at your website, your interior, food images on table-booking platforms, and other guests' reviews, guests start building an idea in their heads and begin to anticipate or visualize what their dining experience might be like.

Service is about empathy, and the right people should be empathetic and kind.

Let's start decoding what it takes to deliver outstanding services. The most important element by far is hiring the right people. Outgoing food servers who are friendly and genuine create a welcoming atmosphere that keeps people coming back. Service is about people, their personalities, and their attitudes. Employees are the face of a restaurant.

When recruiting dining-room staff, look for the right personalities, which is more important than their skill level. During job interviews, look for smiling faces and happy personalities.

Service is about empathy, and the right people should be empathetic and kind. Skills can always be acquired through training. As Anthony Bourdain said, "Skills can be taught. Character, you either have or you don't have."

I often hear operators complain about the inability to hire the "right people" due to pay scale. I disagree, and I have hired many brilliant food servers at a reasonable pay scale or even minimum wage. I hired them above all for their pleasant, outgoing personalities, and then trained them on service skills.

I believe you have to train, refresh, and refocus your team every single day. One of the best opportunities to train your team is during pre-shift meetings. It allows you to train your team for ten minutes daily (see Chapter Four: Training and Inspirational Leadership for more details).

Ensure that your service staff's product knowledge is flawless and that how they describe your food entices customers. Training builds confidence and confident food servers sell more, serve better, and deliver outstanding service.

This leads us to suggestive selling. When I started in the restaurant business, I attended many pre-shift briefings. Our dining room manager would ask all food servers to sell, sell, and sell, because we needed to hit the budget. I always thought, "What about our guests? Could they possibly be on a budget?"

Upselling, sometimes called suggestive selling, must focus on creating outstanding guest experiences rather than exclusively making your customers pay more money. Successful upselling may add more to the bill but not necessarily with intrusive techniques or by pushing dishes people don't want. Emphasis should be placed on long-term gains, not short-term wins. By this I mean achieving higher rates of repeat visits, improving your reputation, and generating more revenue. These goals are achieved by suggesting dishes and add-ons that make the meal more enjoyable. That's the cornerstone of suggestive selling—its primary goal should be improving your guests' experience with the added benefit of increasing your revenue.

Upselling, sometimes called suggestive selling, must focus on creating outstanding guest experiences rather than exclusively making your customers pay more money.

That being said, don't be afraid to suggest items that would otherwise be going to waste soon, or items of which you have plenty of stock. The key is emphasizing to your staff that it's not purely about profit but rather managing resources as a team.

On the revenue aspect, upselling is more effective when it is conducted in a seamless, smooth, and relevant manner. You can center your upselling initiatives on your guests' experience using the following suggestions.

1. Food and drink combinations, like red wine with a New York steak.
2. Add-ons include cheese on a burger, guacamole on a Southwest salad, or sautéed mushrooms on a steak.

3. Upgrades, for example, suggest a slice of tiramisu instead of taking an order for a scoop of ice cream, or recommend shrimp pasta instead of a shrimp sandwich.
4. Recommending popular menu items will keep your customers coming back for more.

The goal is to entice your guests to return more often. You make more money that way. You can increase their check average by suggesting add-ons that make their experience more enjoyable. Sometimes management chooses to place emphasis on items that generate more profit per dish rather than higher-priced dishes with lower yields.

Two types of guests come to your restaurant. The first type is guests who know what they want to order beforehand. They come into your restaurant having already decided what to order. But, you still need to upsell menu items to them reasonably.

The second type is guests who come to your restaurant without making up their mind about what they want, or who may not be familiar with your menu. They appreciate recommendations and comments to feel self-assured to order your food. Servers should be skilled at observing guest preferences before proceeding to upsell them.

The check-average metric is a crucial indicator of a business's health. It reflects your team's efforts and skills, menu merchandising, and in-restaurant marketing efforts, such as POPs, posters, and table tents/talkers. It's sad for me to visit a restaurant where the owners have made a substantial investment in their business, yet when I ask what their most popular dish is, they suggest their most expensive item. For some guests, this sounds like a rip-off. There is a fine line between being too pushy and being effective at suggestive selling. Food servers must be sales-oriented, acting with integrity and care toward their guests. They are experience makers, not just passive order takers.

Food servers must have integrity because, as I mentioned before, good service is not about making our guests pay the most. It's about making them enjoy your most popular meals and about suggesting great combinations and add-ons to make the meal better so they come back. Don't let them break the bank on one meal. Rather, entice them to return more often for greater long-term gains.

Another critical element is to ensure that you frequently provide opportunities for your staff to taste the food. The team needs to know how the food tastes before they sell it. They should know their favorite dishes on the menu—this knowledge becomes an essential tool in suggestive selling. It's impressive when food servers talk about their favorite dishes. It reflects pride and menu knowledge, which guests appreciate.

The team needs to know how the food tastes before they sell it.

Food servers must take an active role in helping guests make their selections. It's a fundamental aspect of their job. Food servers must not start suggestive selling solely when there is a contest or a reward by the manager. It must be an expected part of their job.

Sales phrases should entice the guests with suggestions or present guests with a choice between one alternative or another. Some restaurateurs believe that the golden rule concerning sales phrases is: don't ask any question that can be answered with a yes or no. Avoid asking questions like, "Would you like a starter?" or "Do you want coffee?" Instead, you can say, "Our desserts are incredible—would you like the chocolate brownie or the tiramisu?" This tactic may not always be successful, depending on the guest.

A great approach for add-ons is the following technique: "My favorite dish is apple pie, but I always get a scoop of ice cream to go with it." They are showcasing excellent salesmanship while remaining genuine.

Additional examples:

- "As a starter, may I recommend our beef carpaccio? It's thinly sliced raw meat drizzled with lemon juice and olive oil. It's delicious."
- "Can I start you out with an order of shrimp cocktail, or would you prefer to have our chef's signature salad for your appetizer?"
- "Can I bring your drink first? I recommend our mojito or famous hand-shaken margaritas."

- "For your dessert, would you like our famous chocolate cake or homemade strawberry cheesecake? Both are fantastic."

Additional sales phrase examples you can implement:

- "May I recommend...
- "We're featuring our kale salad with truffle oil as a starter today. Would you like to try one with a glass of wine?"
- "I would like to remind you that we have homemade desserts you will surely love."
- "My personal favorite is our sirloin steak ... *(I find this form of suggestive selling to be genuine and very effective.)*
- "Which one would you prefer?"
- "Let me tempt you with one of our specialty soups ..."
- "If you like the main course, wait until you taste our desserts ..."
- "How about bringing you two spoons to share a dessert?"
- "My favorite dessert is the apple pie, but I always get a scoop of ice cream to go with it." (As mentioned before, this example shows suggestive selling combined with an add-on.)

Train your team to use descriptive words. Examples include:

Bite-sized	Tangy
Spicy	Hearty portion
Amazing combination	Tasty blend
Rolled into one	Smothered
Fresh	Crispy
Authentic	Heaping mound
Toasted	Golden brown
Homemade	Home-baked
Golden crisp	Crunchy

Freshly ground	Thick and juicy
Mouthwatering	Tender
Piled high	Flavorful
Generously	Savoring
Seasoned	Drizzled
Garden fresh	On a bed of
Freshly grated	Medley of
Aged	Melted cheese
Warmed	Rich
Creamy	Moist chocolate
Relish	Freshly squeezed
Quenching	Perfect blend
Unique	Signature flavor

Upsell desserts after asking how a guest is enjoying their main course. For example, "Keep some room for our amazing chocolate cake."

At one restaurant I managed, we posted a simple chart of how many add-ons each food server sold per shift each week.

Example:

Food server	Sun.	Mon.	Tues.	Wed.	Total
John K.	13	16	22	16	67
Mike C.	10	9	11	15	45
George W.	6	9	9	11	35
Ken H.	4	7	6	10	27

John achieved the highest add-on sales, and Ken is the lowest at twenty-seven. This exercise helps create positive competition among food servers, increasing overall add-on sales. If one server (or whoever works the shift in his absence) sells five extra scoops of guacamole at one dollar each shift, five dollars a day times 365 days a year comes out to $1,825 in additional sales from only one add-on and one food server in one shift.

Pace of Service

In these next sections, I will cover several other fundamentals, beginning with pace of service. A common guest complaint is that food is served too slow or too fast. It is essential to monitor ticket times (ticket time is the duration from when food is ordered and entered into the Point of Sale machine [POS] to when it is served to guests). One effective way to measure it is by placing a digital clock near your pass-out window. Team members should keep track of the times and communicate with the chefs by name to ensure optimal ticket time.

For example, let's say an order goes into the POS at 11:00 a.m. for an appetizer. The chef prepares and places the item on the pickup window at 11:12 a.m. The food server writes on the ticket: order duration 12 minutes (11:00 to 11:12). If any dish exceeds the 12 minutes, the expeditor would inform the kitchen expeditor. This way, you keep the kitchen team aware of whether the food is coming out late. Oftentimes, chefs don't know that they are late in preparing dishes because they are focused and busy. It's helpful to keep them informed and alert. At shift's end, you will know which orders are taking longer than usual so that you can analyze and devise actions for improvement. (Please note: this is not fast-food thinking; this is about proper pace of service.)

> A common guest complaint is that food is served too slow or too fast.

You should also set standards for your kitchen staff. Some suggestions:

- Appetizers within eight to twelve minutes (dine-in restaurants);
- Main course within eighteen to twenty-two minutes (dine-in restaurants);
- Desserts within five minutes;
- Drinks within three minutes.

Without monitoring ticket-time duration or cooking-time duration, your team will unintentionally slow down, lowering your table turnover rate and, more importantly, impacting guest satisfaction, as the pace is slow and the food is late.

One more thing to keep in mind is that you don't want to serve guests their entrees while they are still eating their appetizers. That could lead to the main course getting cold, thus ruining the meal. This might seem simple, but it can be frustrating to guests.

Also, be sure to conduct biweekly silverware and chinaware inventories. A major cause of potential service delays is insufficient silverware or plateware due to loss or breakage. If you don't monitor inventory weekly, you will unexpectedly run out of something simple, like coffee cups. This could lead you to think you need to hire more people as you reach a false conclusion that the service is not efficient, or your dishwasher is slow, when in fact, the problem is in the lack of tools (in this case, cups), not number of employees per shift. When you are short of tools, you make it harder for your team, especially if you run a lean organization. They will need more time to locate tools and more time to serve guests.

Here is a sample inventory sheet:

Item	On Hand	Par	Required/Lost
Forks	66	120	54
Knives	80	120	40
Red Wine Glass	50	100	50
Side Dish	110	120	10

Let your team know the quantities lost and the cost to replenish items every week. This exercise will make them more responsible and self-aware. Similarly, frequently spot-check your trash bags. You most likely will see ramekins, knives, and forks in them.

To reaffirm, if silverware and chinaware are not monitored, losses will indeed happen, and you will suddenly need to place a large and rather costly silverware, glassware, or chinaware purchase order, which can sometimes get delayed by the purchasing department due to obtaining several quotes, signatures, and approvals from business owners.

Create Wow-Your-Guest Procedures

Your team's goal in every single shift (without exaggeration) is to wow your guests. Why? Because of this simple formula:

Average Experience = Average Sales

Good Experience = Good Sales

Wow Experience = Wow Sales

Your food servers should walk to their tables thinking: "I want to wow those guests. I want to impress them, not just serve them. I don't want to just meet their expectations, I want to *exceed* them and make their experience memorable."

Your food servers should walk to their tables thinking: "I want to wow those guests."

How do you wow your guests? How does your team go the extra mile to impress your guests? Does your team know specific steps, and do you provide them with the tools, knowledge, and training to empower them to wow your guests?

A wow example might be allowing food servers to serve three complimentary desserts to three tables per shift, surprising guests who didn't order desserts with a pleasant treat, exceeding their expectations. Restaurants begin to fail when they start to nickel-and-dime customers. Generosity is a hallmark of the foodservice industry. Brainstorm four or five ways to wow your guests, and share them with your food servers and cooks.

I believe the restaurant business is an entertainment business; it's a show business. It's like theatre—as soon as we open our doors, we are onstage. The show begins and we must entertain, dazzle, and impress our guests, and let them leave wowed. This notion has been translated to literally hundreds of new restaurants that combine dining with live entertainment, theatrical dancing shows, and singing. There is huge growth in this category of our industry, but regardless of whether you offer live entertainment or not, we have to build the notion in our team's minds that we are onstage. The restaurant manager is the director, the team is the cast, and we must amaze our guests to the point that they are eager to tell ten other people about their memorable experiences or write a wonderful online review telling everyone how they enjoyed our restaurant.

Wowing your guests creates memories. Meeting guest expectations is not enough to create customer loyalty. Service and hospitality are about creating memorable experiences that make people come back more often. The key word here is "memorable": the food taste, food presentation, personalized, genuine service, and the **surprise and delight element**—the wow element—is what turns one-time customers into loyal fans!

Sampling (Pass Around)

One of the best ways to create an interactive and more energetic dining-room feel is through sampling. Sampling is also a great way to increase sales. Let guests experience your food while providing you an opportunity for nonintrusive table visits. Some restaurant managers use sampling as an opportunity to ask guests about their experience—which is perfect because the last thing you want is an intrusive, sudden table visit.

When you offer food samples, your guests will learn what new dishes are coming, or they will discover other existing dishes, desserts, cocktails they have not previously tried, educating them about your menu variety. Sampling increases check average. I have had experiences where guests ordered desserts/cocktails/wine immediately after sampling. We won!

Menu Knowledge

Develop frequent menu-knowledge tests for your team. (I used to conduct weekly tests but made it fun and not intimidating; our servers often looked forward to the quiz, as I always gave out rewards for top scorers or most improved food servers.) Knowledge builds confidence, and confident servers are more focused and offer better levels of service to customers. Consider the following sample questions for tests:

- What ingredients are in our chicken salad?
- How many chicken wings are in the large order size?
- What dressing/sauce do we serve with the fried fish?
- Where does our chicken, beef, and lamb come from?
- Does our beef, lamb, and fish come fresh or frozen?
- Are our vegetables homegrown or imported?
- How is Alfredo sauce made; what are the ingredients?
- Fill in the blanks. For example: Pasta Alfredo is made with ______ pasta and ______sauce, topped with__________and ________.

Create steps of service, but keep it simple. After your host seats guests, they should mention the name of the food server and whether any menu items are unavailable during that day to avoid any disappointment (generally this shouldn't become a habit; all items must be available at all times).

Note: Steps of service vary from one restaurant to another based on service style, cuisine, or industry category. For example, the following steps are not applicable to casual-dining restaurants.

1. At the host station, greet your guests by name (if known from a reservation).
2. Food server: acknowledge your guest within thirty seconds of being seated.
3. Greet the guest by saying, "Good evening, my name is ___. I will be your server for this evening. Thank you for choosing ______(name of restaurant)."

   It's important to note here that to avoid sounding insincere or robotic, servers can personalize their greetings and not follow the script 100 percent.
4. Take the drink order, and repeat it back to the guests. Depending on the style of the restaurant, inquire if the guests are celebrating any special occasion.
5. Serve the drink order within three minutes of ordering.
6. When the guest is ready, offer to take the food order, explain daily specials, and suggest a specific starter by name or recommend the main course. If you serve a family, ask your guests if you can take the kids' orders first and if they would like the kids' orders delivered before the adults' meals. Ask if any guest has any allergies.
7. After writing the order, repeat it back to the guest.
8. Deliver starters, mentioning the name of the items clearly while serving them. Serve ladies and elderly guests first, followed by male guests.
9. After two minutes, or a few bites, make a quick quality check. *Ensure you are not interrupting guests' conversations with your check for satisfaction.*
10. Refill drinks if needed.
11. Before serving the main course, make sure silverware is set, plates are clear, and napkins are replenished.

12. Deliver main course items, remembering who ordered what, naming the items as you serve them.
13. After two minutes or a few bites, make a table visit. *Ensure you are not interrupting guests' conversations with your check for satisfaction. A great practice here is to inform your manager that the main course has been served at this table and give him/her the opportunity to conduct a table visit instead of having too many table visits by both you and the manager.*
14. Glance periodically over to the guests' table for cues and to note how far along a guest is in completing their meal. As guests finish their meals, clear dishes.
15. Offer and deliver specific desserts and hot beverages.
16. Always wait until guests ask for the bill; ensure the table is thoroughly cleaned before you deliver the bill. (Note: In the United States, customers are used to being presented with the bill even though they didn't ask for it. They usually don't find it offensive, especially if a restaurant is busy and needs to turn over tables. In other parts of the world, it's considered rude if food servers present the bill without guests' requests.)
17. Deliver the bill and finish the payment procedure *promptly.*
18. Thank the guest by his or her name and invite them back to your restaurant. The server may personalize this with a statement such as, "It has been my great pleasure to serve you tonight." After the server delivers the bill, continue service until the guest leaves. (Guests are often ignored after they have paid.) Servers must pay attention to whether the table needs any other assistance, such as refilling water.

> Guests are often ignored after they have paid.

Note: Different guests dine at your restaurant for different reasons; it is not a one-size-fits-all experience. Because of this, preset standards might not fit every occasion or every restaurant.

Passive vs. Active Service

Passive service occurs when servers simply deliver food without building any connections with the guest, without any type of hospitality or personal bond. The problem with such service is that it doesn't build loyalty or inspire repeat visits. Active service, on the other hand, involves genuinely caring about your guests, serving every table with the goal in mind of satisfying each patron and building a connection to the restaurant. The examples below demonstrate the difference.

Passive	Active
"What would you like to drink?"	"Can I start you off with our signature beverage, a lemon mojito?"
"Welcome to our restaurant."	"Welcome back, Mr. Johnson. Would you like to sit at your favorite table?"
Looks after adults only.	Entertains and interacts with kids as well.
"Here is our menu" (order taker mentality).	"Here is our menu. I would like to let you know that our ribeye steak is very popular, and our Monterey chicken is our number-one-selling dish."
Manager performs a flyby table visit.	Manager visits tables, introduces him- or herself by name, and asks specific questions, such as, "How's your steak?" or "How's your experience?"
"Thanks for coming. Bye, sir."	Hostess: "Thank you for coming. How was your dinner? We hope to see you next Friday for our seafood night."

Great food servers view their job as diverting. They enjoy themselves. They are having fun when they are at work. I once had a Webex call with about three hundred professionals during which I asked what they thought of as the most important aspect of service. Many attendees replied, "Food servers must have fun without getting too casual with guests." They must be cheerful and lively, not overly formal or grumpy.

Acculturation

Let's say you operate a French restaurant but your team members are not French, they are from different nationalities. What I call "acculturation" involves the importance of teaching them key and fundamental aspects of French culture: eating habits, table manners, and etiquette. For example, in Middle Eastern restaurants, Arabs use bread more than forks and knives. So, if your Arabic guests order hummus, they expect bread to be at the table right away. If you have employees of a different nationality, let's say the Philippines or India, they may not automatically know this, which can cause guest complaints. Or, when American customers ask for coke with ice, they prefer a lot of ice (full glass of ice cubes)—other cultures may provide only a small amount of ice, like one-third of the glass.

Russians start their meals with soup or cold cuts, while other cultures begin their meals with bread and butter. In South Korea, everyone waits until the oldest person has started eating. Only then can the rest of the diners at the table begin.

The way Arabs order the check/bill is different from the English or Americans. The hand gestures are entirely different. In India, a server standing at the table throughout the experience may be appreciated; in the US, guests want space and more privacy. And the list goes on. Such subtle differences make a huge difference in the experience for guests in different cultures.

Proactive Table Visits, Not Flybys

The number one difference maker in guest satisfaction ratings is performing table visits for every table, no matter how busy the restaurant manager is. Table visits must be viewed as a *top priority* and should not be pushed to the back burner or delegated to a server when the restaurant is busy.

When conducting table visits, remember to keep it short, simple, and specific.

Example:

"Good evening, my name is John, and I am the manager on duty. How is your steak?" (specific). *Some restaurants like to ask, "How's your experience?" as it covers everything: service, food, and atmosphere.*

Guest: "It's great, thank you."

You: "Great. If you need anything, please ask for me." (short and simple)

You should not sit with guests. It sounds obvious, but I've seen it happen. You should not talk about yourself or your life. Guests are here to talk about themselves, so make them the center of attention, not you. Lean forward and make eye contact without staring. Compliment them on their order choice in a genuine way ("The New York strip you ordered is my favorite").

I would like to stress here the importance of making sure the food doesn't get cold because of a long table visit. Even if the guest is chatty, make sure you excuse yourself and come back after they have finished their main course. I see this issue often, and it results in a poor culinary experience.

I would like to stress here the importance of making sure the food doesn't get cold because of a long table visit.

Please remember that we don't know what is going on with our guests' lives. Some are visiting because they are celebrating an occasion; some are ordering food for their sick spouse; some might have just returned from military duty or learned that they have a terminal disease; some may have just landed a dream job. We just don't know. So, by performing a friendly table visit and showing care throughout our service, we bring joy to their lives regardless of their situation. We make their day better! It's that powerful.

Avoid direct and abrupt table visits—it's too intrusive. Go to the table and remove a dirty dish, refill water, offer food samples, bring more napkins, and let the guests see and feel your presence *before* you introduce yourself and ask about their experience.

Touch the edge of the table, as this shows warmth. In fact, it's the reason some restaurants call table visits "touching tables."

Flyby table visits are bad for business. Let me explain it, it goes like this, "Hi folks, how is everything?" and then off to the next table. It's not genuine, too quick, and it shows the manager is not comfortable with table visits. Instead, slow down and show genuine interest in your guests.

Be friendly, but do not be overfamiliar. Overfamiliarity may appear unprofessional and make your guests uncomfortable.

Guest Feedback

In addition to table visits, you must have a system for collecting guest feedback. Use QR codes, surveys, or guest comment cards. The harder you work to listen intently to what your guests are saying, the more successful your restaurant will be. At the end of the day, it's all about the guests. After all, they pay our salaries.

Train your staff to deal with negative and constructive feedback immediately and with sensitivity. If a guest expresses concerns, the guest needs and expects a response. There is no point to a guest survey if it sits on the manager's desk under a pile of bills. I've seen managers throwing negative guest surveys into the waste bin.

Misleading Feedback (I Love It, but I Really Don't)

One of the major issues with our industry is that we occasionally receive misleading guest feedback. This happens when managers conduct table visits but the guest doesn't want to express their disappointments. Some guests are shy in nature, with friends and family and don't want to voice a complaint, in a rush, or just don't like to complain.

It also happens when restaurant owners/managers invite friends/social media influencers/industry professionals/members of the management team for a menu tasting or complimentary meal to get their opinion—or when suppliers or third-party marketers who want to do business with you provide feedback about your food. They often say the food is good or even amazing even though it might not be. Be careful with misleading positive feedback—avoid making decisions based on it.

Nine out of ten unhappy customers leave the premises without saying a word. Continue to offer online surveys and table visits. Monitor your guest-satisfaction scores, Tripadvisor and Google reviews, and all the available review platforms.

Your measurements of success are guests ratings, repeat visits, and revenue growth.

Work to Understand Your Guests' Needs

Guests dine at your restaurant for different reasons or occasions; adjust your service model for different diners. That's common sense, but it's not always obvious when you're in the thick of the rush. That's why preset standards or steps of service (as mentioned before) might not fit every occasion.

Here are different examples of when you need to adjust your service method accordingly:

A. Business lunches need quick service. If there is more than one guest, they may be engaged in business discussions, so don't interrupt their conversation.

B. Dinner date. Don't interfere in the conversation of the customers on a date.

C. Young adults having fun.

D. A guest who is alone and understanding whether they want to socialize or not.

E. Tourists on vacation who want to talk to you (as a food server from the local area).

F. Older adults who want good lighting and less noise.

G. For some guests, seating and table preference are critical to their experience.

H. First-timers: a guest at your restaurant for the first time. Do you have a method or procedure to help you identify first-timers? You could flag their table with red napkins (whereas you use white napkins for other guests) so all servers know that they're first-timers and will work to turn them into regulars.

I am often asked, "Should my chef do table visits?" If you have a well-known or celebrity chef, the answer is a clear yes, as long as such table visits don't disrupt kitchen operations. (It is more important that your guests receive their food on time, at the right temperature, taste, and presentation than that they speak to your chef.) If your chef is not a celebrity, then a chef's table visit is possibly something nice to have but not critical for the business.

Keep guests informed of what is happening using phrases such as, "I will be right with you," or, "Let me check on your order. I just checked with the chef; your food will be here in two minutes." These small touches tell the guests that we are not ignoring them and that everything is under control. This is particularly important if the kitchen is running behind. Don't wait for twenty minutes when the food is late. Attend to the guests and tell them what you will do about it.

Be Flexible with Guest Requests; Use Your Judgment

Examples:

- A guacamole, no onion request should not be a problem to fulfill.
- A guest wanting a table away from a noisy group of people shouldn't be an issue.

Remember Guests' Names and Favorite Dishes

A guest hearing their name is like music to their ears. It doesn't matter if you are in a full table-service restaurant, fast food, or coffee shop. You and your team should attempt to learn every guest's name.

Do not use numbers but instead say names when communicating with guests. Starbucks asks for a guest's name, and they write it on the cup because customers are human beings, not numbers. Many fast-food restaurants call guests by numbers—an embarrassing transaction.

Remembering a guest's favorite order shows you care. Customers love it when you say, "John, would you like to order the vegetarian omelet without onion, like yesterday?" Don't underestimate the power of remembering guests' names and favorite foods. It makes a massive difference in loyalty and repeat business.

Be Generous and Use Service Shock Tactics

Do not be penny-wise and pound-foolish. A complimentary slice of cake will not put you out of business. I often use service shock tactics for customers who frequent my restaurant five days a week. I would give my customer the entire sixth meal free without prior notice. When the check is asked for, I would say, "Thank you for being a loyal guest. Today your food is on me. Yes, on me! See you again soon."

Separately, your loyalty program must be generous enough to generate repeat visits. I will cover loyalty programs in Marketing and Revenue (Sales) Growth (Chapter Five).

Do Not Eavesdrop

The worst thing a food server can do is jump in on a private conversation, having overheard guests talking about football, politics, relationships, discounts, or something else. I mean anything. You simply must not do that. It is considered creepy.

Always Remember Who Ordered What

No matter what kind of restaurant, full table service or not, the worst thing you can do is scream the names of dishes as if you are at an auction. You shouldn't be asking, "Who ordered the steak?"

Too Much Service Is Not Good Service

Food servers should fade into the background. They shouldn't dominate the dining experience, and they shouldn't ask too many questions or try to interrupt every five minutes. That is not VIP service—that's terrible service.

Some food servers believe that the best way to impress a guest is by asking lots of questions and being at their table 100 percent of the time—or worse, staring at them expectantly. This idea is counterproductive. If a food server interrupts every three minutes, guests won't enjoy their meal.

Sometimes employees need to walk around, or act busy, rather than stand in one area watching the guests, which is annoying to many guests. They should anticipate needs without asking (like refilling water glasses). If you are refilling wine, pause slightly above the glass and then pour slowly. This gives guests an opportunity to signal to you if they do not want their glass to be filled or if they would like to have a half glass.

As a restaurant manager, always ensure that only one waiter is serving/communicating with a table (except the food runner, if any). Different servers coming to the guests' table asking the same questions makes guests uncomfortable, which does not reflect professionally organized service.

Follow the Guest's Path

As a manager, you should have a meal at a *different table every day* and come in from the front door just like a guest does. Do you see what your guests see? Observe. Do you see smiling food servers? Do you sense friendliness? Do you see cleanliness? Do you hear music? Is the air conditioning set at the right temperature? And the list goes on. See the interaction from the hostess station all the way through payment. Again, evaluate your experience just like a guest.

Hostess: Inquire About the Occasion

Hosts and hostesses play a major role in the guest experience. When taking bookings or seating a customer, they must ask about any specific occasion. This will help your team prepare better, especially for anniversaries or birthdays. Hostesses should walk with the guest when leading them to the table, not ahead of them. They should ask about their day, and let them know who their food server will be.

Hostesses should be warm and friendly. Arrogant and unfriendly hostesses can turn off your guests despite the delicious food and excellent service. It's a common issue in the industry.

Food servers must adjust their service style according to the occasion. A couple celebrating their anniversary probably wants minimal interruption. The same goes for people on business meetings during lunch, whereas a guest having breakfast and constantly looking at their watch likely wants faster service.

Food servers must adjust their service style according to the occasion.

Compliment Guests on Their Choices

Guest: Can I get the tuna ceviche?

Food Server: Excellent choice. It's one of my personal favorites. *(Only if it's truly your favorite dish! Being genuine is key.)*

Do Not Justify, Always Rectify

When there are guest complaints, the worst thing a food server can do is argue with guests or justify the situation. The following exchanges exemplify incorrect interactions.

Guest: My steak is cold.

Food server: Our heat lamp is out of order.

Guest: My food is late.

Food server: I rang in the order right away.

Don't justify or make excuses; just fix the issue right away. If a guest says their fries are cold, apologize and bring fresh and hot fries right away. Don't say, "We just fried them!"

Nod and Smile (Smiling Is Contagious)

Smiling gives your customers the feeling that all of your restaurant's team members are friendly and welcoming. Here's how it works: Let's say one of your food servers is serving tables 20, 21, 22, and 23, but table 26 or table 45 (far from his station) is served by someone else. What needs to happen is that when food servers pass by any guest at any part of the restaurant (even if they are not their own guests), they need to nod their heads in acknowledgment and smile. A smile is contagious. When you smile, people smile back at you, and it spreads throughout your restaurant, making the atmosphere more welcoming and pleasant.

Sit in your dining room and watch your food servers. Do they smile? Do they look friendly?

Every guest is my guest.

I would like to highlight here the importance of creating a service culture where every food server believes in the following principle: **every guest is my guest** regardless if the guest is seated in my section ore not. If a guest needs something, or if a server has a table that needs pre-bussing, for example, he/she would help and assist the guest. One of the worst service mistakes is ignoring guests because they are not seated in your service section/station. The mantra should say: every guest is my guest and every guest leaves happy because of me!

Duckwalk and Full Hands in, Full Hands Out

Food servers should walk in their stations by looking left and right at each table (similar to ducks). It sounds cheeky, but it is an effective way to cover eight tables in one go. If your food servers walk straight and look only at one area, they miss out on some table clues and cues such as empty plates, tables that need napkins, and water glasses that need to be refilled. Duckwalk is an excellent method for better productivity and guest service.

All food servers and managers must also follow "full hands in" and "full hands out" steps. When servers leave the dining room and enter the kitchen or dish area, they must come in with dirty dishes in their hands. Likewise, when they leave the kitchen, they must bring clean dishes, cutlery, or ready-to-serve food (but they must wash their hands before touching clean dishes or cutlery. It's advisable to have a handwashing station right next to the clean dishes areas). Full hands in/full hands out might be an obvious thing, but it can impact your team's productivity negatively if not done consistently.

A Hostess's Golden Question: How Was Your Meal?

Nine out of ten unhappy customers leave a restaurant without saying a word. A scary stat. We try hard to know how customers rate us. We do table visits and reward guests for completing online satisfaction surveys and guest comments cards, but your last opportunity to catch an unhappy guest is when they are leaving.

The golden question that your hostess must ask is, "How was your meal?" I have seen many customers vent right at the end of the experience (when they are about to leave the building). If a guest says, "It wasn't great," you can still win them back by giving them a complimentary coupon or having them speak with your manager.

When guests depart, they must leave with a positive last impression. It's your last opportunity to catch a problem. Guests often don't complain to food servers or managers, but they'll vent on their way out the door when your hostess asks the following golden question: how was your dinner? If they were happy with the experience, invite them for a specific occasion, if applicable. Say, "I hope to see you next week for our Italian night." If they were unhappy, ask a manager to talk to them and offer complimentary meal coupons as a last attempt to win them back.

"My Pleasure"

Saying "my pleasure" is a nice way to tell someone that you were pleased to serve them. Chick-Fil-A has made the words "my pleasure" part of their operating standards, instead of saying, "You are welcome."

I totally agree with Chick-Fil-A, but I also love it when employees use their own creative ways to appreciate guests, such as, "It was great serving you" or "Delighted to serve you."

Managers Need to Dine at a Different Table Every Day

You will notice that some tables may be crooked, not stable on the floor, and that certain areas need deep cleaning. You will experience what your guests will experience. When I was a restaurant manager, I often found areas that needed deep cleaning, or a booth that needed new upholstery, or tables that had loud music because they were too close to the speakers.

Dealing With Guests' Complaints: Use BLAST

When handling guest complaints, use the BLAST approach:

1. **B**elieve your guests. Don't question their *integrity (even the one percent of guests who are not reasonable with their complaint or not truthful).*
2. **L**isten when a guest complains. Listening gives your guest a chance to vent. Lean forward, don't interrupt, and lower your voice (when you lower your voice, they lower theirs too).
3. **A**pologize. Guests appreciate an apology, even if they are wrong. You can always say, "I am sorry you feel this way about our service."
4. **S**olve the issue. Let your guest know how you will solve the issue. Did you know that when guests face problems at your restaurant and you successfully solve their problems, they turn into loyal guests?
5. **T**hank your guest. A guest who complains is doing you a great service. Why? Now you know which areas you need to improve upon. Thank them for their patience and/or for bringing the issue to your attention rather than losing them silently.

Another approach would be to use a brief and well-conceived customer comment-card system. Send an email or, even better, a personalized card thanking the customer for completing the comment card and showing that you care by addressing any specific complaint.

One interesting fact is that most complaints happen when the restaurant is slow, not when it's busy. This is probably due to a lack of urgency and slacking.

As you have seen from all the tips and tactics I shared on the previous page, multiple actions are required to achieve great service. You will need to divide these actions among your team. Other aspects must be part of your training program. You will not be able to do everything alone.

Counter Service

Counter service allows only one opportunity in seconds to upsell because your guests are not likely to go back to the line/counter to order other items. A counter cashier or order taker can make or break an entire upselling program. Ensure that you do the following:

1. Hire the right person.
2. Train the right person.
3. Track upselling.

I would like to talk more about upselling tracking. As you know, what gets measured gets done. I would give counter employees an upsell target per shift and reward them at the end of the week—sometimes the day—for meeting their goals.

For example, today we need to upsell twenty-five add-ons of bacon on hamburgers. Keep a notepad next to your point of sale system (POS) so you can update as you take orders, similar to the image opposite. (Some may find the opposite outdated. If your POS can give you instant data, use that technology instead.)

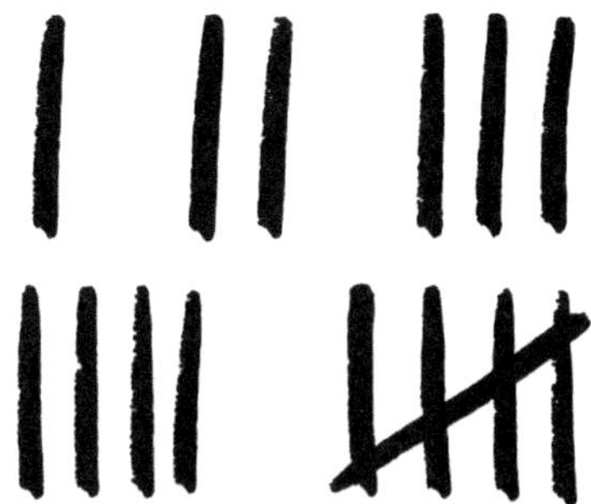

This kind of tracking puts the responsibility on the order taker/cashier to track upselling. They become more aware.

To see how effective this exercise is, try it one day without giving your employees a target and again by giving them a goal. If adding a slice of bacon on a burger is only $1, times two shifts per day, a target of twenty-five per shift times 365 days a year equals $18,250 per year. All that is needed is a focused manager to follow the above example.

With counter service, you have *only one shot* to make the sale—unlike full table service where you have several interactions and upselling opportunities.

Another example for increasing sales is something that I have done and tested at a Quick Service Restaurant (QSR) brand. Take a slice of brownie, cut it into *bite-size pieces*, go to the dining room, and offer it to your customers. You will notice that at least four or five customers will order it right away.

Simplify the ordering procedures and make sure your team is 100 percent proficient with using your POS system. Why? Long queues will negatively impact table turnover, guest satisfaction, and overall sales. If your menu allows the customers to request too many customizations, you end up complicating the ordering and plate-preparation process. I am all about customization, but there is a fine line between giving customers too many options and/or smoothness of ordering and food preparation and overall experience.

Simplify the ordering procedures and make sure your team is 100 percent proficient with using your POS system.

Use names not numbers: As mentioned before, Starbucks does this really well. When your drink is ready, they call your name, not just a number!

Personalize: Even though you operate a QSR or fast-casual brand, it doesn't mean you are all about mass production and devoid of personal touch. Simply by writing on the sandwich box a phrase like, "Proudly made by Ashley" (Ashley is one of your cooks) or "Enjoy your day, Mike," you take customer service to a new level.

One last note on counter service: there are three magical words that must be part of each transaction—*please* and *thank you*!

Common Service/Service-Management Pitfalls

In this section, I would like to share a list of *what not to do* so as not to ruin a meal. These small things can make a huge difference in guest experience. We learn best from our mistakes.

- Servers with bad breath, long fingernails, poor grooming. Likewise, servers wearing too much perfume, cologne, or aftershave.
- Food servers who do not know the daily special or soup of the day.
- Food servers don't know your restaurant's most popular menu items and can't advise guests. They have never tasted the food.
- Food servers who are unable to recommend meals.
- Food servers who rush customers into ordering.
- Food servers getting too casual with guests or touching them.
- Food servers jumping in on a private guest conversation or hovering near the table.
- Food servers talking about themselves during table visits.
- If/when a customer doesn't finish their meal and leaves their plate half-full, a food server fails to ask if there is anything wrong with the food. I always say to restaurant owners, if you want to know what your guests don't like, check your garbage. If you see many half-full salmon dishes coming from the dining room to the dish area,

it means your guests don't love your salmon. This honest feedback from the guest is as good as a table visit or a Tripadvisor review.

- Only interacting with the guests upon payment in order to get tips.
- Poor farewell. No food server or hostess saying anything to guests on the way out.
- Starting the meal with super-cold butter that guests cannot spread and cold, dry bread.
- Customers keep coming to the same restaurant for months, but the food server doesn't care to remember their names.

> If you want to know what your guests don't like, check your garbage.

- Paying more attention to certain guests than others.
- Removing guests' glasses from the table while refilling their glasses. If you are refilling a soft drink, bring a full glass to the table and remove the empty one. This makes drink refills seamless.
- The restaurant manager spends all shift near the hostess station.
- The restaurant manager comes to a pre-shift briefing unprepared, and the team is not prepared for the shift.
- Fake smile, fake welcome.
- Slow service during business lunch and fast service during a romantic or family dinner.
- Failing to adjust lighting for time of day when possible.
- Overpriced drinks or side dishes.
- Large restaurants that look empty and boring all the time. (Restaurant owners/managers must work with the designer to break up the dining room so it doesn't look super large and empty even when busy.)
- Taking too long to provide the check or process payment.
- Food servers asking too many questions or interrupting meals often.
- Failing to thank the guests for their visit and wish them farewell.

- Hostess station area is untidy.
- Doors are not opened by staff.
- Not greeting customers within thirty seconds.
- Not answering the phone within three rings.
- Not answering the phone with a "smile."
- Hostesses are not neat: poor grooming or uniform standards.
- Hostess staff is not facing the door or is displaying arrogant behavior.
- Unclean, torn, or dog-eared menus.
- Wait-list not used, and wrong times quoted. Restaurants must have a waiting list in place: write the names of guests, the number of people, and the time they were placed on the waiting list, and provide a reasonably accurate waiting time. Guests are extremely disappointed when a hostess says their waiting time is ten minutes but they end up waiting for thirty-five minutes.
- Servers asking guests how their food is while they are still chewing their first bite.
- Food servers touching silverware and glassware from the top or plates with fingers inside the plates.
- Some restaurants train their staff to pre-bus as soon as one guest finishes their meal, but if a couple is eating together, by removing the empty dish of one guest, you indirectly put pressure on the second guest to eat fast and finish their meal.
- Guests having to wave for waiters even when the restaurant is not busy.
- Two food servers arguing in guest view.
- Food servers or cooks smoking at the back or front of the restaurant while wearing your restaurant's uniform. For some guests this is a hygiene and cleanliness issue. Staff who smoke must wash their hands well, refresh their breath, and mustn't smoke in guest view.

- Food servers on their cell phones.
- Food servers with rude body language. See image below.

Guest-facing employees must use the appropriate body language; using the gestures in the image above is rude. Instead, use positive body language and an open palm.

- Super loud music or improper climate (too cold or too hot).
- Hostess not walking with the guest but instead walking way ahead of them.
- Food servers asking, "Would you like me to bring back the change?"
- Guests pointed toward a table instead of the host at least partially escorting the party.
- Clearing plates while guests are still chewing their last piece of food.

- Forgetting a special request that was made before arrival.
- Price difference between menu and final bill.

Tip: Use one tactic or tip from this chapter as a topic in your daily shift briefing.

Evaluate Your Guest Service and Hospitality

Question	Comments
1. Do we hire people with outgoing and friendly personalities?	
2. Do we train our team members during the pre-shift meeting every day?	
3. Does our suggestive-selling program help our guests enjoy their meals?	
4. Are my food servers well-trained at using descriptive words?	
5. Do we track upselling?	
6. Do we have procedures in place for proper pace of service?	
7. Do all our employees know our wow guest procedures and options? How about service shock tactics?	
8. Do we provide sampling/pass around every shift?	
9. Do we perform team quizzes for menu knowledge?	

10. Do we have clear steps of service in place?	
11. Do managers visit every table during every shift?	
12. Do we remember guests' names and favorite dishes?	
13. Do our food servers nod and smile whenever they see guests (not just guests seated at their tables/station)?	
14. Do we use BLAST to handle guest complaints?	
15. Do food servers perform duckwalks every time they manage a station?	
16. How are we doing with getting guest feedback? How do we measure the score?	
17. What's our loyalty program for repeat guests?	

CHAPTER THREE

APPEALING DESIGN AND AMBIENCE

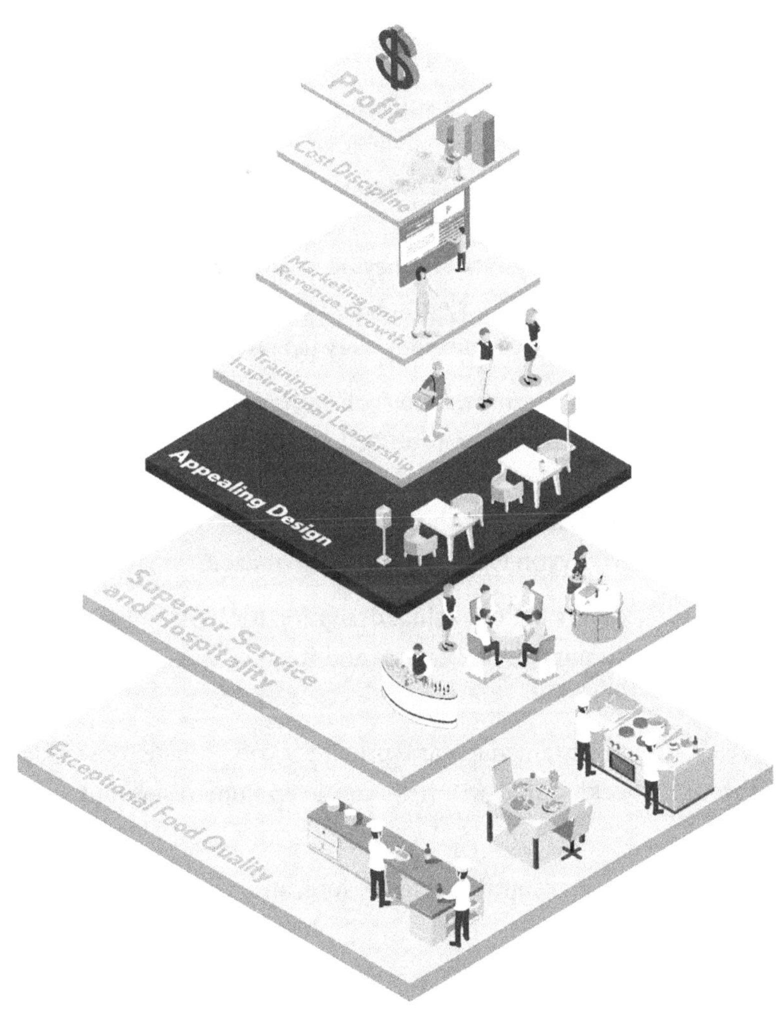

I have worked with designers, architects, and contractors while opening more than forty restaurants across the globe, from the conceptual through the construction phases and proceeding all the way to ribbon cutting at opening.

This section will cover the essential information to create a visually appealing and efficient restaurant with the right ambience and positive guest experience.

A restaurant's success is based on great food, excellent service, a well-trained team, and creating the best possible guest experience. But many times people choose restaurants because they love the décor and ambience.

People remember where they experience milestone events, especially spectacular meals. Design is the soul and spirit of any restaurant concept. Marketing, positioning, tableware and table setting, uniforms, and service style are all components of the design. Design is the image you want to portray to the world and the experience the guest has during their stay. Frequently, guests expect to pay a certain amount of money because of what they perceive of the design. At a classy, high-end restaurant, guests are willing to pay three times the price for the same mushroom soup they get elsewhere.

Conversely, if a restaurant's design is casual, guests expect more reasonable prices. Design can be used as a tool for both branding and entertainment or influencing a guest's perception. Think of restaurants built near/in huge floor-to-ceiling aquariums, or with a massive statue of Buddha, or with a large amount of greenery so you feel you are in the Amazon.

This chapter covers the following: designing for look and feel, efficiency and function, restaurant vibe and energy, and frequent design (costly) mistakes to be avoided.

I review design sustainability and provide a comprehensive weekly/daily walk-through checklist that will help you keep your restaurant in tip-top condition.

First, what elements contribute to the look and feel of your restaurant?

Design: The Look and Feel

Consider building an open kitchen that can be viewed from the dining room. It creates energy, activity, and theater. It suggests quality, cleanliness, and freshness. It says, *Look, we have nothing to hide*. But if you do, make sure that smells, smoke, and noise don't impact the dining-room experience. I like an open kitchen built with floor-to-ceiling glass or a large window showcasing the area. That way you can see the theater without the noise or smell.

In addition, I recommend keeping your restaurant on the smaller side. When restaurants are too large, they look empty and boring on slow or moderately busy days. Small restaurants often must operate with a wait list due to the limited availability of tables. Wait lists give guests the impression of popularity and exclusivity. It creates consumer curiosity.

When restaurants are too large, they look empty and boring on slow or moderately busy days.

Additionally, smaller restaurants have lower operating and fixed costs (utility, labor, maintenance, and upkeep). Please note that I am not recommending building tiny restaurants. I favor "smaller" efficient restaurants but not "small" restaurants. The restaurant must meet your realistic sales projections and your market, as well as operational needs.

The guest's experience typically starts on the street, but for our purpose, I will start with the restaurant's main entry. The restaurant's main doors should always be followed by the foyer (vestibule) and a second set of doors. This design element helps manage the interior temperature when the weather is too hot or too cold. By having double doors offset from the foyer area by four to five meters, you create a buffer—a "sense of arrival" that allows your guests to decompress and orient themselves before entering the restaurant proper. But if you have only one set of doors, all the cold or hot air will hit nearby tables when the front door opens. Also, your HVAC (heating, ventilation, and air conditioning) and exhaust systems will function far better with double doors.

Consider natural and organic elements to incorporate in the design, such as wood, stone, brick, and greenery (the choice of wood, stone, or brick will depend on your concept).

I am against using artificial, plastic plants. I encourage restaurant owners, as per the image above, to integrate more greenery and flowers, as they add a beautiful color, look, and feel to the restaurant.

Focus on sustainable materials that show your commitment to the environment and the reduction of pollution. I am a big fan of live plants that are easy to maintain, not plastic.

Different colors evoke different emotions. Some make us feel calmer, such as earth tones, blues, and greens. Warm colors—like reds, yellows, and oranges—are associated with active feelings. You see more of these colors in fast-food/quick-service restaurants (QSR). Most of their interior colors are flashy, and the chairs are not very comfy—they don't want customers to linger. QSR brands want quick table turnover. Apply color and lighting psychology in your restaurant

Different colors evoke different emotions.

design, allowing you to customize each space to be on-brand and adhere to the atmosphere and feelings you want to invoke or areas you want to highlight.

When it comes to lighting, high-end, classic, fine-dining restaurants typically use dim ambient lighting to create a relaxing mood and formal ambience.

Fast-food restaurants, on the other hand, build well-lit restaurants, splashing light everywhere. Many restaurant consultants believe that bright lighting can overstimulate guests and help achieve faster table turnover. Some design professionals believe that bright light conveys "cleanliness"—nothing to hide.

To create a visual connection from the exterior, build floor-to-ceiling windows: a significant element that showcases your dining room and creates energy. Visually, natural sunlight brightens up the space and saves energy. Pay attention to lighting, both natural and artificial, as well as direct and indirect throughout the day.

It's a critical design element that helps set the tone for a room and thus a guest's experience. Adjust the lighting to create the atmosphere that you want to cultivate. A dimming system with preset/preprogrammed scenes is a good investment.

In general, there are four types of lighting: ambient lighting, task lighting, decorative, and accent lighting.

Ambient lighting is also called general lighting. It's the natural light from your glass doors and windows, and in artificial form, the lighting that substitutes for natural light as it allows a general functional light level throughout the space. Ambient lighting sets the mood for the entire dining room.

Task lighting is used for performing tasks. These lights enable cooks to work and guests to read the menu and place their orders. **One common mistake designers make is excessive task lighting in dining rooms, making them look and feel like an office space.** Make sure you use a balanced approach between task and ambient light. The third type of lighting, decorative, is often used as task lighting at the table. Restaurant designers will introduce color and atmosphere with decorative light fixtures as a focal point when introducing a chandelier or sculpture fixture in the middle of a ceiling or with a pendant over a table for better menu visibility.

Use accent lighting or spotlights to highlight pictures, décor items, or anything you want to focus attention on. For example, if you invested in a beautiful brick wall with artwork on it, you can use accent lights to highlight the artwork and brick to create focus and ambience.

Choosing the right type of seating is essential. My rule of thumb is to **choose comfort over design**. Many restaurant owners opt for beautifully designed but uncomfortable seating. This choice hurts your business in the long run. Repeat visits will be affected, as the experience is associated with discomfort, not the otherwise enjoyable dining experience (for example, the tables are too low, too far; the chair is too hard or too small), all ingraining an uncomfortable experience in the guest's mind.

Use your awnings/canopies to educate potential customers about your offerings. Awnings are primarily used for fast-food, fast-casual, and casual dining. Awnings with large, printed words on them, such as pasta, pizza, or steaks, quickly tell customers what food you offer.

Canopies provide 365 days of marketing and customer education about your brand.

It's essential to understand your customer and brand when designing awnings. Some fine-dining establishments use awnings without any copy other than the name or logo of the restaurant. Awnings must be illuminated to attract attention, and the name and logo should be easily readable.

Apply artwork in the design. The type of art should match your restaurant's overall theme and contribute to the atmosphere you're creating. Consider murals, portraits, photography, wall finishes, sculptures, and graffiti. As mentioned above, use the appropriate accent lights to highlight each piece. Ensure your designer is considering your restaurant's cuisine when making design choices. Otherwise, your restaurant may end up with a confused personality and identity.

I also recommend your design include space for your guests to wait to be seated. Wait areas are part of forming a guest's first impression, and you should assign that aspect of the design its appropriate importance. Another key is to create inclusive seating options that build a variety of choices and create energy. Make sure you have both flex tables and booths—create combinations. Flexibility is important. Flex tables (tables that can be moved and connected) help with seating large parties. Pay attention to the number of tables for twos and fours required for your type of restaurant. Pay attention to the personal space for every customer seated: ten square feet per person in QSR restaurants and twenty square feet per person in high-end establishments. Some designers consider forty square feet per person more fitting for very high-end exclusive dining.

> Wait areas are part of forming a guest's first impression.

Consider having one private dining room, if you have space. It can be used for business meetings/lunches, VIP guests, and birthday parties. It gives your restaurant a competitive advantage and can be used for overflow dining at peak times.

Your restaurant design must also address how server and customer foot traffic circulates throughout the rooms. **Create a space for your staff to take comfort breaks. Give your team the space and thus the opportunity to recharge and reenergize.** Don't underestimate this point, as it affects staff motivation and appreciation of your organization.

Your design must factor in the method of payment and point-of-sale (POS) systems and how staff will access them.

The location and number of POS stations have a huge impact on pace of service.

Your designer should show you options for the distance between POS and tables. The number of tables and POS stations is balanced against the distance from the kitchen as it will impact the speed of placing orders, speed of service, and table turnover. I see this as a recurring issue in many restaurants.

Consider outdoor seating where possible. Outdoor seating is a competitive advantage for many restaurants as it creates a "destination."

Design Efficiency

I find most operators or owners spend a tremendous amount of money on front-of-house decor but often cut costs when it comes to the back-of-house working space and equipment selection. We must remember, **the kitchen is the heart of the restaurant, its engine**. What comes out of it (and how quickly) makes or breaks the dining experience for guests.

Here are some common mistakes I often see that you should share and discuss with your designer and contractor if you remodel or open a new restaurant:

- Include a pass-thru window with heat lamps over the hot plates. Too often dishes end up half-cold due to limited window space. Follow the fundamental rule of our industry: serve hot food hot and cold food cold. Watch out for air vents and diffusers blowing cold air above hot food areas or pass-thru windows. We faced this issue at restaurants I managed. All the food was getting cold fast because the pass-thru window had an air diffuser above it.

Other details to keep in mind designing your eatery:

- Does the dishwasher capacity and type support heavy operations?
- Poor exhaust ventilation or mechanical design including heating, ventilation (exhaust and makeup air), and air conditioning design resulting in high humidity during the summer (condensation on the walls, appliances, and tables) and a cold interior during the winter due to poor climate control. Ensure that the kitchen makeup air system incorporates air conditioning and heating, as you must provide an appropriate environment for staff.
- Is excessive noise a concern? Sound bounces off hard materials. Be sensitive in choosing finishes. This issue happens a lot in dining rooms where you have a hard flooring surface and an open (to roof structure) ceiling.
- In general, poor cleaning management processes and procedures form the main causes of cleanliness issues. Watch for potential cleaning issues related to wall-, flooring-, and ceiling-texture choices. Equipment must be easily moved and disconnected, such as placing shelving and equipment on castors. Keep ease of cleaning in mind when considering kitchen equipment layout and placement.
- Another major issue I often see is limited capacity for freezers and coolers. I prefer to have walk-in coolers and freezers instead of standup reach-in coolers and freezers. Walk-ins maintain better temperature and offer better space and organizational opportunities. Make sure your cooling storage facilities support your business volume. Also, think about dry goods, dishes, utensils, and catering equipment storage, as well as frequency of deliveries.

- Booth partitions: be careful of separating booths with high, dark-wood partitions that can leave customers feeling isolated, or tables too low or too far from the seats. Avoid installing booths with non-commercial grade, hard, unyielding, or cheap upholstery.
- Also ensure you have the appropriate number of outlets/connection locations for plumbing, gas, and electrical services. Ensure that these electrical outlets and service connections are where they should be in back-of-the-house areas and at guests' tables.
- Walls and pillars should not prevent or hinder guest and employee movement through tight spaces. Check that there is enough space for trash bins. Double-check all the details! Install good lighting in walk-in coolers and freezers. While working with the Saladworks restaurant chain, I was impressed with how one operator in Philadelphia built a walk-in cooler with large glass windows. It helps with supervision, and yes, it prevents theft, such as your staff eating in the cooler.
- Install the adequate number and appropriately sized kitchen cooking equipment, including griddles, fryers, and a broiler, to support demand. Restaurant owners make this mistake all the time, slowing down the entire kitchen: I often see a menu with several fried items and only one frying vat, which means slow service, not to mention that cooking fries with other items like chicken and fish can negatively affect the taste and creates a cross-contamination issue. The same happens when a chef's menu calls to finish many dishes in the oven, but the oven is too small. Take menu planning and seating capacities into consideration before making your purchasing decisions. For example, choosing a twenty-four- or forty-eight-inch flat grill will depend on your menu and seating capacity.

I often see a menu with several fried items and only one frying vat, which means slow service.

- Poor layout often results in a long distance between the dining room and kitchen, which negatively affects the speed of service and food temperature. This is also a common mistake.

- Install easy-access handwashing sinks in the dish area so that after servers leave dirty dishes at the dishwashing station, they may quickly wash their hands and pick up clean dishes to bring to the dining room. When this sink is not available, they skip handwashing and immediately pick up clean dishes with dirty hands. Hand sinks should be appropriately located and installed throughout the kitchen as well as the prep area.
- The location of the Point of Sale (POS) in your restaurant can dramatically affect your business's efficiency. As I mentioned before, if the POS and server stations in the dining room are too few or too far, this will result in slow ordering procedures and impact your labor cost. You will end up hiring more people to be more efficient. I see this happening often: three food servers form a queue to place an order, which slows down speed of service, table turnover, and makes you mistakenly believe that you need to hire more people.
- Ensure that your sound systems and sound distribution aren't distracting or annoying. Work with a sound or acoustic engineer to make sure your speaker distribution and sound level are appropriate for guests to have a conversation without speaking loudly. Avoid music that is either too loud or too low. Restaurant managers need to adjust the sound volume level according to how full or empty the dining area may be.

Other common mistakes include badly located BOH workstations from a workflow standpoint, inadequate lighting, several restaurants served by one kitchen, slippery kitchen floors, small grills, ill-fitting wall ovens, colliding doors and drawers, lack of worktable space, appliance cabinets, under- or overpowered exhaust systems, poor ventilation, lack of live cooking areas in restaurants, and noise pollution.

Additional Key Notes for Kitchen Design

Place your receiving area near the refrigeration areas and avoid placing cleaning chemicals near food. Store chemicals separately. For third-party delivery and takeout, think about delivery drivers' access or consider creating an off-premises dedicated section. Think about creating easy access without hindering customer parking and traffic. Then there are large catering events. If you want to build this aspect of your business, you have key questions to answer:

How can you transport catering equipment? Do you have large doors that equipment can fit through? Do you have a sufficient storage facility? And plating areas?

While designing your kitchen, prepare a detailed list or menu of all foods you plan to prepare in the kitchen. Visualize how each menu item will be prepared and served. Does your design allow for this to be done efficiently? If not, adjust.

Develop an equipment list for each kitchen station based on menu requirements and conduct time-motion studies to follow these steps. For example, study how your cooks will prepare a salad. Where would the containers be? What about smallware, mixing bowls, large spoons, and dressings? A time and motion study for each menu item can highlight inefficiencies.

Determine your service process for delivering complete dishes to the customer. Then, organize the equipment layout for each station and arrange the stations that share menu components next to each other.

Design your kitchen for maximum labor efficiency, safety, and functionality. Ensure sufficient room to move about freely when carrying smallware, pots, and bulky supplies. Cooks should not have to waste time and extra movement completing a task. This will increase efficiency, lower fatigue, and reduce workplace injuries. An ergonomically designed kitchen is key: employees should stand in one spot and do all of their work with minimal bending, reaching, walking, or turning.

Pay special attention to the proximity of the food-prep area and the food-storage area, including refrigeration equipment, for easy access. Place food-preparation stations near a refrigerator so that your back-of-house team can quickly and safely store raw food and ingredients until they're ready to be used.

Set up your expediter station and place it at the center of all cooking stations.

Handwashing sinks should be installed with backsplashes or side-splashes as needed to prevent contamination of nearby areas, and each must have soap dispensers and paper towel holders.

To achieve an optimal sales per square foot result, I believe that the dining area (especially in casual-dining restaurants) should take up seventy percent of the total area of a restaurant; the kitchen and prep areas should take up thirty percent. The kitchen space may increase depending on having walk-in coolers and prep and storage areas.

The staff room is also an important consideration and should not be overlooked. This is where you'll post your weekly schedule and staff announcements, train new staff members, and hold staff meetings.

Ensure you have allocated areas for recharging smartphones and laptops, especially in coffee shops (if people use your establishment to work or if you are in a business area where business lunch/meetings are prevalent). I have seen restaurants that were built with private dining rooms and had meeting facilities such as digital screens, speakers, flip charts, and other tools for group presentations, and they generated a great amount of revenue from business meetings/lunches. Having said that, the point here really depends on your business objectives, as guests may linger and table turnover may suffer.

Make sure you build distinct and specific kitchen working zones. Ensure your fry area, cold-prep area, flat-grill area, and/or broiler area have adequate space.

Also, make certain that you have under-the-counter refrigeration and sufficient storage for the shift without struggling with cross-contamination.

Think about a three-compartment sink that can be converted into work tables with stainless steel covers or even chopping boards—and plan for a small manager's office. The one I like is just a cabinet or closet that holds a PC, safe, and files and can be pulled in and out to save a lot of space. (The more prominent your manager's office is, the more time your managers end up spending in it. The last thing you want is for your manager to spend a long time in the office. You want them in the trenches with your guests and employees.) Lastly, don't forget to build separate staff restrooms that are also separate from food handling areas (you do not want cross-contamination).

Think about a three-compartment sink that can be converted into work tables with stainless steel covers or even chopping boards

It is the law in most countries throughout the world that your facility provides physical access for the disabled. You must address accessibility and/or accommodations; it cannot be ignored.

Once the kitchen is built, conduct mock training and do a stress test, which involves placing a large food order and building a scenario where your restaurant is full, with a long wait list. Then you can see how you would handle a super busy restaurant, where the bottlenecks are, and what needs to be worked on before the soft opening. In one stress test I conducted, we had lots of smoke coming out of the kitchen as the exhaust hoods could not keep up when every piece of equipment was on and entirely loaded. Also, our point-of-sale system (POS) repeatedly tripped and shut down. We learned a lot from that experience.

Create an Inviting Atmosphere: Energy and Vibe

Live entertainment, when done properly, can (as long as it fits with the concept/meal period) make a huge difference in the dining experience (assuming it generates the desired incremental revenue to cover its cost). Great live entertainment can make your restaurant a destination. Live entertainment helps restaurants with challenging locations.

For fine-dining restaurants, think of live piano and other instrumental music. For casual and fast-casual restaurants, bands might play popular and trending music. One common mistake is allowing music with profanity. Make sure you play the clean version of any song. I worked for a chain restaurant that sent/mailed its twelve hundred restaurants CDs with specific music. No manager could play any other music or even change the tracks. When corporate office directors completed the restaurant evaluation, franchisees would lose points if they played different music. I appreciated that the parent company wanted to play country music, as the restaurant had a country theme—the music reinforced and protected the brand's image and integrity.

Live entertainment helps restaurants with challenging locations.

Repair and maintenance: a great preventative maintenance program will keep your restaurant looking fresh, and even better, reduce your long-term costs. At the end of this chapter, I have shared a monthly/daily walk-through checklist that will help you keep your restaurant maintained and looking fresh.

Only managers (not food servers or hosts) should be allowed to adjust the thermostat (air conditioning and heating), lighting, and music selection and volume. Alternatively, opt for using preset, preprogrammed, or sensor-based systems.

Create a unique experience to strengthen branding. Embed design elements, including natural light, plants, paint color, wood elements, pictures, and decorative items.

Hire a professional lighting consultant. Lighting plays a massive role in the look and feel of your restaurant and changes throughout the day.

A Note on Sustainability, Environmental Consciousness, and Design

Customers appreciate when establishments use sustainable materials. Additionally, sustainable materials make a huge difference in the location's atmosphere. For example, I love vertical gardens because they present a unique way of displaying plants. I like installing them to dress up a dull wall and turn a negative design element into a positive.

A few items for consideration related to sustainability:

- Use environmentally friendly refrigerants for all refrigeration equipment and air-conditioning units.
- Ensure refrigeration equipment drawer and door seals are installed and in good condition.

- Utilize reclaimed materials when and where appropriate.
- Use operable windows and doors such as an overhead door, which is like a garage door that opens upward along a track on both sides of the door. However, there are many different kinds of openable doors that can be used in the restaurant environment. A French door or folding door, etc. can also be used, depending on the design. These doors reduce the use of the mechanical system and provide fresh air to the restaurant.
- Verify all openings throughout the restaurant are sealed properly.
- Use LED light fixtures throughout the restaurant.
- Install motion sensors wherever possible.
- Install programmable thermostats.
- Install automatic sunshades/blinds/lighting.
- Install plastic curtains at the walk-in cooler and freezer doors. They reduce your energy bill, prevent insects from entering, and maintain product temperature and shelf life.
- Install on-demand water heaters.
- Install waterless urinals.
- Ensure all plumbing pipes are properly insulated.
- Install low-flow pre-rinse nozzles for dishwashing pre-rinse sinks.

Facilities Upkeep Checklist

At least twice a week (some restaurants do it daily), restaurant managers must check the following physical aspects of the restaurant to make sure the restaurant stays in tip-top condition:

- Signage: all lights working; free of cracks and chips; clean and dusted.
- Parking lot: no debris or micro trash; no cracks or holes; well painted.

- Marketing banners: secured, clean, taut, and not flapping; not faded or torn.
- Sidewalks: no debris or micro trash; no major cracks or safety concerns; no sand buildup.
- Landscaping: no litter or micro trash; looks attractive; no dead shrubs or plants; no insect infestation.
- Awnings: clean, free of dirt buildup; no birds' nests; not faded, tattered, ripped, or stained; music speakers under awnings are working and clean.
- Exterior lighting: all lights working (landscape, awning, building, parking); appropriate wattage; adequate for safety; timers working correctly.
- Back dock area: doors closed and always secured; surrounding area clean, free of dirt and grease.
- Roof: rooftop equipment is clean and working (hood and HVAC); no trash or grease buildup.
- Windows: clean; no streaks or cracks; windowsills free of dust and dirt; no faded, cracked, or peeling paint.
- Front entry: clean; free of litter; hours of operations posted; no spills or standing water (wet-floor sign used if the floor has been mopped); door handles polished; wood on the door not faded, cracked, or rotten.

Interior:

- Foyer area: floor clean; no spills; clean floor mats; inside doors and windows clean; window ledges clean.
- Walls throughout interior clean.
- Blinds and light fixtures dusted; ledges clean.
- Indoor plants: watered; look attractive.

- Interior lights at proper setting/no burned bulb. Light fixture directed properly.
- Proper music volume level.
- HVAC units working properly; all HVAC ducts and vents clean.
- Décor items are clean and free of dust.
- Interior paint in good condition.
- Indoor plants maintained/clean/healthy.
- High chairs and baby booster seats clean/not broken.
- Bar area: back bar area free of odor; back bar neat and organized.
- Restrooms: clean; free of spills, odors, trash; dry; mirrors clean, no streaks, no smudges; toilets clean and flushed, in good repair; walls clean with no graffiti; trash container clean, not overflowing; all lights working; hand towels and soap stocked; HVAC components (ducts and vents) clean. Ensure the exhaust fan is working properly.

Final Thoughts

More and more restaurants are upping their game when it comes to design. In the age of social media, people like to snap photos and post about where they eat. People create memories in restaurants: they celebrate anniversaries, birthdays, graduations, even weddings, so how the restaurant looks and feels becomes part of people's lives and is vital to their choices.

Lastly, no matter how you design your restaurant, don't overdo it. Stay true to your brand. If your brand projects simplicity, stay true to that. Don't complicate it. Don't change who you are.

Many people enter the restaurant business because of their love of food or mistakenly think it's an easy business and requires no formal education or experience. But to create an economically viable business, the design, workflow, operational elements, and specifications of a restaurant space are essential and must work in concert together. Unfortunately, this is not well understood by many. If your budget permits, hire consultants for lighting, sound, HVAC, restaurant interior design, kitchen layout, and landscaping. Do not leave it in the hands of one person, like an overall restaurant designer.

Stay on top of repair and maintenance items. Refresh the look and feel; repaint walls; change mirrors; buy new plants; and the list goes on. Keep your restaurant fresh and clean. Create a vibe, play appropriate music, and create a welcoming, comfortable ambience and an experience that people love, enjoy, and return to again and again!

Note: This chapter doesn't have questions at the end like other chapters. I highly recommend that you use the facilities-upkeep checklist that I provided and refer to this chapter when you plan to open a new restaurant or remodel your existing one.

CHAPTER FOUR

TRAINING AND INSPIRATIONAL LEADERSHIP

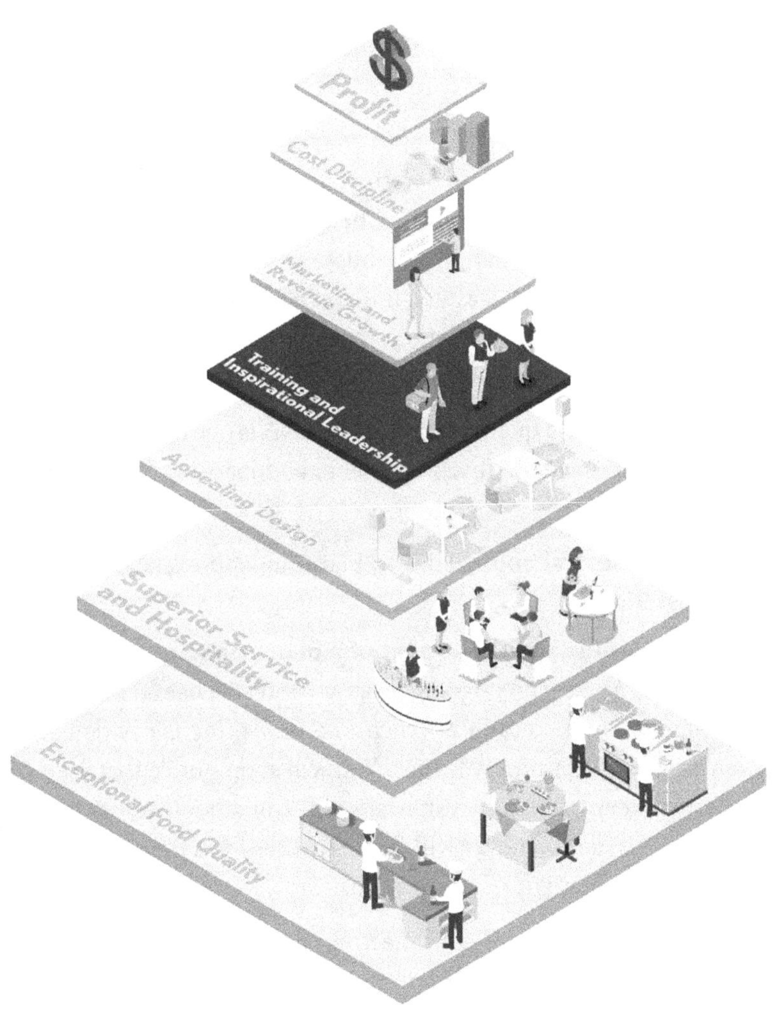

One of the key areas for achieving business success is building a highly skilled team. A skilled team makes everyone's job easier. Having a well-trained staff means lower labor cost, fewer mistakes, and a great guest experience.

Well-trained employees are profitable. If they know how to sell, they make you bucks. If they know how to portion, they save you bucks. You achieve your highest ROI when you invest in your people.

By putting time, effort, and focus into your restaurant's training program, you immediately emphasize your company culture for every new hire and existing employee.

Training should be part of your restaurant's identity and not an add-on that is initiated only when standards are not met. It should be planned, reviewed, and a part of everyday operations.

Many people talk about the importance of training and quality, but very few practice what they preach. Chefs, restaurant managers, and food and beverage leaders (no matter how busy they are, running large or small operations) must dedicate at least ten minutes a day to training their team. This could be as simple as talking with their teams about one recipe and discussing how it can be correctly prepared and cooked to perfection.

Making training and quality part of your DNA is one of the most important factors for success in F&B. Teaching others and learning from them is true leadership.

Let's discuss several approaches to planning and executing an effective training program.

First off, training should be part of a plan—an annual calendar—not randomly done. Make it an ongoing program and part of every shift. Use your pre-shift meeting as a conduit to teach one new thing every day. In ninety days, you'll have taught ninety things. You will soon notice that your team is getting better every day. Your restaurant will run smoother, fewer mistakes will be made, and staff turnover will decline, as they feel they are learning and growing their career at your organization.

If you cannot conduct pre-shift meetings because your team arrives at the restaurant at different hours, use another method: "Coach 'em in and coach 'em out." Simply take three minutes with each employee before their shift starts and talk about that day's goal and star dish of the day, and share a training tip. Here are some examples of training tips you can use in pre-shift meetings:

- Cooking training tips: A fried item is done when it floats. A grilled or baked fish is done when it flakes.
- Did you know that a dry towel is safer than a wet towel when holding hot pots and pans?
- When grilling a steak, never press it. Pressing steaks or putting weight on them to cook faster will result in bad quality, as it dries them out of their natural juices.
- How can we increase the check average of a burger? Suggest bacon or cheese as an additional topping. Suggest cheese or chili with fries.

These tips are also good examples of cross-training. If you are discussing the correct procedures for grilling a steak while your baker, expediter, fry cook, and prep cook are attending the briefing, they will learn from these tips about other stations. In this example, you are effectively cross-training them in how to handle the grill station. Once you put them in a formal training program in other stations, they will transition *faster*, as they have already gained a significant amount of knowledge about other stations from attending the daily pre-shift briefing.

The key to conducting an impactful pre-shift meeting is preparation. You need to come to the meeting with valuable training tips. This means you need to **pre-read** and decide what that tip is going to be. Don't just try to wing it—your team will quickly notice that you are talking about things that they already know, or you are adding no value.

> The key to conducting an impactful pre-shift meeting is preparation.

Key Notes for a Useful Pre-Shift Briefing:

- The pre-shift briefing is a great opportunity to excite and motivate your team before the service begins. Focus on the positives. Don't focus on what went wrong the previous day. You can and should bring up yesterday's mistakes, but do so in an indirect manner. Don't put any team members on the spot. For example, don't say, "John, your guests at table 40 complained about late payment." Make the pre-shift briefing fun and motivational, and make sure to praise your team.

- Ask specific questions. Asking, "Any questions?" is not helpful. Frame your questions around the goals for the shift, e.g., "Any suggestions on how we can sell twenty-two steaks tonight?"
- I use an acronym called MTTY for FOH and RTTY for BOH. M for menu item (R is for recipes for BOH), T for target, T for training and/or thank you, and Y for yesterday's challenges and successes. So, you discuss, describe, and taste one **M**enu item with the team, give them a **T**arget (sell X steaks per shift), and provide a **T**raining tip (for example, cook less more often to achieve freshness). **T**hank the team and keep them motivated, ask about yesterday's challenges, and provide tools or solutions to help them adjust. This way you are constantly improving the business and demonstrating great leadership.

Shift Briefing - FOH

Date ______________ Day ______________

MENU ITEM/STAR DISH OF THE DAY: Tenderloin Filet

This is the most tender cut of beef we have. It's a juicy, flavorful, and lean 8 oz. filet marinated for twenty-four hours with herbs and spices. It comes with sautéed wild mushrooms, grilled cherry tomatoes, mashed potatoes, and au jus beef sauce.

ADD-ONS:
Option 1: Add grilled shrimp on the side.
Option 2: Grilled asparagus
Drink: A glass of cabernet sauvignon

TARGET: Sell 5 tenderloin filets per food server
TRAINING TIP: When you receive a guest concern, don't justify, always rectify
YESTERDAY'S SUCCESSES AND CHALLENGES: (to be discussed)

____

OTHER INFO:
Number of bookings ______________
86 Items ______________
Waste ______________
Roster ______________

Lastly, and most importantly, celebrate yesterday's successes and wins—small or big. Inspire your team and fire them up!

- Avoid this common mistake: I often hear restaurant managers telling their team that they need to achieve the budget without offering any tips or tools to do so, which ends up being just words. A better approach would be to say, "We need to sell five sirloin steaks per food server during this shift." This way, you have a measurable and achievable target that will help you generate greater revenue on that day. **But remember to gently follow up with your team and what you set as a target one hour after the shift briefing.** Otherwise, targets won't be respected or, for that matter, anything that you decide in pre-shift. As the saying goes, people respect what you inspect.

Pre-shift briefing is one of the most important acts of leadership during the restaurant manager's/chef's workday. It sets the tone for the entire shift, and it's a training tool and motivation and performance driver! Always come to the briefing highly prepared and ready to teach and inspire your team.

Schedule training sessions once a month.

Build training classrooms based on your restaurant's needs or your guests' feedback. For example: late food or inaccurate orders are common customer complaints. Conduct training specifically on these two topics, not based on a generic topic. Schedule the session and decide on the venue and time. Send your team pre-reads. Such sessions have minimum interruptions or distractions, and they allow for in-depth analysis and a higher level of focus than pre-shift meetings. These sessions are often highly appreciated by team members, as it helps their career and shows your commitment to helping them grow and develop. Make them highly interactive, not a lecture. Randomly pick attendees to elaborate on topics and perform role-play. Divide them into groups and let them put their ideas on flip charts and share with others. Reward and excite them during the session.

These sessions are often highly appreciated by team members, as it helps their career and shows your commitment to helping them grow and develop.

One of the common mistakes I see in restaurant training classrooms is the absence of conducting training assessments. What usually happens is that team members end up attending training sessions on issues that are not problematic, making the session a waste of time. For example, say you hold a session on friendliness and the importance of smiling to your guests when, in fact, you have no problems in this area, and you always receive positive comments on your team's friendliness. Instead, if you always receive complaints about cold food, then the best use of your time is to conduct training on food temperature.

Training assessments are usually built from reviewing guest comments, team comments, and your own observations. Look for ways to identify what topics your staff is the most in need of training on. Use data, customer feedback, observations, and product feedback.

A critical point here is to ask for anonymous feedback from all attendees after the training session. Create a one-page survey and ask questions such as: What needs to improve? Was the session relevant? Did you gain new knowledge? Also, make sure to leave a section for them to write their feedback openly.

Build an in-house training team.

A restaurant manager with spare time never happens! Put someone in charge of training and build a training team with trainers from each station, such as one food-server trainer, one or two cook trainers, and one hostess trainer. These trainers will help you train new hires. The trainers will also be your future restaurant managers, which means your succession-planning program is in place and alive. Remember that trainers need to be trained too. They need to be trained, mentored, and given resources on how to train others. Trainers need to be trained on the art and science of training others. Don't just throw them in the deep end without showing them how to teach others. Training others requires knowledge, skill, and passion. See below for several tips on training your trainers.

Trainers' Training Tip:

One of the best methods for on-the-job training: **"Tell, Show, Do, Review/ Follow Through."**

1. **TELL:** Prepare the trainees and tell them what you will train them on. For example, how to cut chicken.
2. **SHOW:** Show them how to cut chicken.
3. **DO:** Let them do the task; ask them to cut chicken.
4. **REVIEW/FOLLOW THROUGH:** Let them do the task once again and review it together.

Remember to have your trainer sit or stand parallel (next to their trainees), *not* opposite to them. This will help trainees see the task or step from the same angle, which results in faster learning and, more importantly, less confusion. One more tip: avoid abbreviations and jargon. Keep your language simple and clear.

More tips for trainers:

- Patience, patience, patience.
- Don't comment on everything! Give the trainee room to make mistakes. Making too many comments makes the trainee less confident.
- Prepare. Trainees will always notice if you show up to the training unprepared.

- Motivate and encourage even if they make little progress.
- Keep in mind that different people learn at different paces.
- Explain the goal of the training for the day before you start the training.
- There will be times when no progress will be observed. That's totally okay.
- Some trainees are faster learners than others. Don't be frustrated with slow learners.

Consider the following topics for team training:

- How to upsell (roll-play).
- Adhering to recipes: While holding a recipe in your hand, ask kitchen employees about proper steps, amounts, and dos and don'ts. Having the recipe in your hand while conducting pre-shift briefings shows the employees the importance of using and adhering to the steps of that recipe. One major issue in the industry is that cooks don't stick to recipes. There are many benefits to using a recipe, such as portion control and consistency in taste and presentation, which leads to guest satisfaction.
- How to handle a guest's credit card that is declined.
- If you have non-English-language speakers, consider teaching one English phrase every day, such as, "Don't say to the guest, 'I am sorry,' every time you try to ask about their meal or serve a dish." In international markets, English proficiency is a major issue. I used to share a phrase every day with the team and correct mistakes. They loved it, and our team sounded professional and developed great communication skills. Imagine the impact on the image and reputation of the restaurant.
- One cooking method or observation for your kitchen staff. For example, skim your frying oil often to prevent the oil from breaking down fast.

- Learning which menu items are highest selling, vegetarian, low-salt, and least or most expensive.
- Finding the right balance between too much and too little interaction with guests at their table.
- Learning about multitasking and consolidating skills.
- Successfully selling guests appetizers or desserts.

Develop FOH Star Dish of the Day/Daily Feature manual and preset calendars.

The Star Dish of the Day manual, which every restaurant should create, is a great tool to use with the front-of-house (FOH) team during pre-shift briefings because it helps those staff members learn all about your menu and encourages them to use sales and mouthwatering descriptions, which are particularly important to highlight the value and uniqueness of your food to your customers.

It shows your food servers *how* and what to upsell. The tool highlights key quality and service notes to deliver great-quality food. (See quality and service notes on the following page.) The finished dish photo will help your team, especially your expediter, deliver consistency in food presentation. It will guide your team to identify whether the dish is up to standard when they pick it up from the kitchen pass window.

Star Dish of the Day Manual

Dish Name:

Tenderloin Filet

Sales Description:

This is the most tender cut of beef we have. It's a juicy, flavorful, and lean 8 oz. filet marinated for twenty-four hours with herbs and spices. It comes with sautéed wild mushrooms, grilled cherry tomatoes, mashed potatoes, and au jus beef sauce.

Add-ons:

Option 1: Add grilled shrimp on the side.

Option 2: Grilled asparagus

Drink: A glass of cabernet sauvignon

Quality and Service Notes:

- Preset the table with a steak knife.
- Rim of the plate should be clean. Plate must be warm.
- Serve immediately, as steaks left under heat lamps continue to cook.
- Ask the guest for preferred doneness. After serving, ask the guest if the steak is cooked to their preferred doneness: rare, medium rare, medium, medium well, or well done.

Preset Shift Briefing Calendar

In conjunction with the Star Dish of the Day manual, create a calendar to make sure you cover and rotate through all menu items in pre-shift briefings. I recommend using a calendar like the one below. If you have thirty dishes, you will need thirty days to cover the entire menu. After that, continue repeating the same calendar.

Repetition is one of the best ways to learn, and staff turnover is high in the foodservice industry. One of the key benefits of having a calendar in place is that it helps your team to prepare themselves for the day before the briefing. In fact, in all my management roles I mandated that the team came prepared to discuss, sell, and describe the Star Dish of the Day.

One more advantage of having a calendar in place is the fact that, since each shift has a different manager, you want all managers to discuss the same dishes. Otherwise, you end up with different focuses and miss discussing other dishes.

Once again, ask your team to come to the briefings prepared by reading about the Star Dish of the Day from the manual before the briefing starts, or even a day in advance. Create a learning habit.

Daily Briefing Calendar (topics)

Sat Feb-01	Sun Feb-02	Mon Feb-03	Tue Feb-04	Wed Feb-05	Thu Feb-06	Fri Feb-07
Beef Brisket	Cobb Salad	BBQ Ribs	Mushroom Burger	Lasagna	Spaghetti Bolognese	Paradise Pie
Don't justify, always rectify	Body language dos and don'ts	"My Pleasure" vs. "You are welcome"	Nod and Smile (Smiling Is Contagious)	Remember who ordered what	Share five mouth-watering words	Share three upselling ideas

You can see from the above table that not only do we know what the Star Dish of the Day is but we also know what training tips we will discuss. This helps your team to come prepared to the briefing. I always ask my team to read the table above and prepare for the next day. This way the briefing is far more effective.

Conduct biweekly menu knowledge tests and quizzes.

Menu knowledge for front-of-house employees and recipe knowledge for back-of-house employees is key. The better your team knows the ingredients, procedures, allergens, and sales phrases, the more confident they will be to prepare and/or sell the items.

Your goal is to have every single employee at 100 percent menu knowledge. Don't settle for anything less. Why? If one employee knows only 99 percent of the ingredients and forgets to tell a customer about an allergen, and the customer gets sick, that's because they forgot the 1 percent of one dish. Very recently, one tourist in Mexico passed away as he was allergic to sesame; he asked the service team, but they mistakenly gave the wrong answer and served his food with sesame. One hundred percent menu knowledge is that serious.

Take a look at this example kitchen quiz for the back-of-house team, showing three questions. This quiz is not applicable to the front-of-house team.

Name of Employee: John White   Date: Aug. 10, 2020
Position: Prep Cook

Answer the following twenty questions:

1. Choose the correct answer. What is the correct cut size of romaine lettuce for salads?
   a. 2" wide
   b. 1" square
   c. .5" square
2. At the fry station, the enemies of oil are: salt, soap, food particles, high temperature, and water.
   True   False
3. When working at the flat grill, you must scrape the grill's surface every time before placing fresh patties on it.
   True   False

If you have ten cooks and the average test score is 60 out of 100, it means there is a kitchen knowledge gap of 40 percent. Your goal is to reach 100 percent kitchen knowledge. A cook with 60 percent knowledge will make many recipe mistakes and most likely deliver inferior food products. It's worth noting that many companies are currently using technology on mobile training apps. I have actually helped develop learning management systems for two companies.

Culinary and Kitchen Training

Back-of-house (BOH; I like to call them the *heart of the house*) team training is based on the same principles I stated so far in this chapter.

The only difference is that you should use recipes, not the Star Dish of the Day manual, for your BOH shift briefing, as per the tenderloin filet example. I prefer to hold two separate pre-shift meetings: one for back-of-house employees and another for the front-of-house team.

Take one recipe in your hands, Country Gravy Prep, for example. Discuss the right steps and dos and don'ts. As mentioned before, this will be a highly valuable cross-training exercise because you are discussing a prep station item while your fry cook, butcher, sauce station cook, and baker are also present. They will learn about the prep station. Many restaurant managers complain about not having time to train others. A good pre-shift briefing takes care of that issue. As mentioned before, use the acronym RTTY. **R**ecipe, **T**raining tip of the day, **T**arget of this shift, and **Yesterday's** successes and challenges. You can, of course, cover other areas such as waste and leftovers, any repair and maintenance, etc. But keep your shift briefing to a maximum of fifteen minutes.

One common mistake to avoid is having your food servers learn recipes or train in the kitchen because they end up using kitchen terms and describing a dish to customers with extreme levels of detail and technicality. You want to avoid servers saying stuff like, "We put one ounce of mayonnaise on our burger bun." Front-of-house training should be built around romancing the food—describing it in an appealing way, not a technical way. No customer wants to know that you sprinkle exactly two shakes of seasoning salt on your burger patties, or that you ladle exactly one ounce of dressing on your salad. That's why the front-of-house team must use the Star Dish of the Day manual, not the recipes for the shift briefing below.

Shift Briefing - BOH

Date ____________________ Day ____________________

RECIPE: *Caesar salad prep (Key Notes)*

- Spin-dry lettuce properly and cut lettuce as close to service time as possible.
- Shock lettuce with ice water. This will make the lettuce crispy.
- Weigh chopped lettuce before portioning to ensure portion size consistency.
- For croutons, bake them in the oven, lubricate during baking with garlic herb butter every three minutes, and move around during baking to ensure even cooking. Then, put them on a sheet tray to cool.
- Wash the salad mixing bowl after each use and keep it refrigerated. If you don't, you end up with excess dressing and a food-safety risk if you keep the mixing bowl at room temperature. Choose a big bowl so you'll have plenty of room to toss and mix your ingredients.

TARGET: All appetizers must be served within 8 to 12 minutes
TRAINING TIP: A sharp knife is safer than a dull knife. Why? ____________________
YESTERDAY'S SUCCESSES AND CHALLENGES: (to be discussed)

____

OTHER INFO:
Number of bookings ____________________
86 items ____________________
Waste ____________________
Roster ____________________

Never stop training your team!

Make training part of your business strategy. The biggest mistake restaurant owners make is giving up on training because of high staff turnover or because they know hourly employees may soon leave the organization. Training your team, even though you know they might leave one day, improves your business reputation and customer loyalty. If you do not train daily or weekly, you end up having problems such as low productivity, recurring mistakes, and mediocre food and customer service.

Use a variety of training methods.

Training can be delivered in different forms and should be dependent on the subject and time availability.

There are several training methods for individuals and for groups. Examples of group training methods include:

- Lecture
- Demonstration
- Role-playing
- Research and case studies
- Projects
- Mock training
- On-the-job training

The biggest mistake restaurant owners make is giving up on training because of high staff turnover or because they know hourly employees may soon leave the organization.

I've used different methods throughout my career. I have found that lecture/Zoom presentations are the least effective because attendants' information retention is very low. People learn and retain more information when they participate, engage, and perform hands-on tasks.

I also randomly pick attendees to share their feedback during the session; this way everyone stays alert.

Here is an example of a case study or research kind of learning. I wanted my employees (eighty-five of them) to learn mouthwatering words, so I asked each of them to Google one restaurant menu, and choose and write down ten mouthwatering words from their menu (such as crunchy, smothered with cheese, fresh, crispy, marinated, or hand-scooped). I then asked them to present their words. In each pre-shift briefing, one employee presented their mouthwatering words. After that, we compiled all the words in one file. The team learned a lot about our competitors, the use of mouthwatering words, and how to use words to "romanticize the food." We improved our style of communication with our guests, and most importantly, the team felt that they were developing and learning new skills. It was an exciting project for everyone.

Whatever method you decide to use, keep the following notes in mind for conducting successful individual or group-training sessions:

1. Set clear goals. Set specific expectations and communicate the desired outcomes by describing favorable behaviors and actions after the training. Start each training session by outlining the goals of the training before you begin. For example, say, "Today we are going to train you on salad prep and salad recipes. We will make all the salads together." This step will prepare the trainees mentally. You can also share the objectives one day before the training starts, which will give the trainees ample time to prepare and read about the salad recipes.

2. Make sure trainers are not using shortcuts and that they are qualified and trained on how to train others. I would like to repeat this again: **Trainers need to be trained on the art and science of training others.** Unqualified trainers can pass on bad habits to trainees.

3. Engaging the trainees' five senses—touch, sight, hearing, taste, and smell—increases information retention and keeps the training real. Train the employees at the same station they will be working at. Be practical and relate training sessions to real-life situations. While some training can be theoretical and conceptual, you should try to find ways to connect it to how it can be applied on the floor.

4. Prepare yourself. Bring all the training tools and materials to the station before the employees arrive. Don't start looking for tools while the employees are waiting for you.
5. Praise the trainees when they perform tasks correctly, and don't try to teach everything in one day. Don't overwhelm your trainees with a lot of information. Break down the training into reasonable chunks every day.
6. Ask for trainees' feedback on the training and your approach. (If you are a manager, ask the trainees to give you five minutes of feedback on the training from their trainer. Assess training effectiveness after training sessions and address noncompliance if necessary.)
7. Leverage a blended-learning approach to cater to different learning styles. Example: some people are more visual learners while others prefer to rely on handouts. Use technology: with the new era of technology, capitalize on the use of online games and mobile apps to bring learning to the team, and lastly, make the training fun and engaging.

In the next section, we will cover the importance of team motivation and inspirational leadership.

Team Motivation

Several studies show the link between motivated employees and lower absenteeism, lower staff turnover, higher productivity, and better guest service and satisfaction. It's relatively easy to motivate an employee or to make them feel better with a gesture of kindness, by expressing your appreciation or offering monetary rewards, but one of the hardest tasks in management is keeping motivated staff motivated.

Consider various ways to motivate your team:

1. Use personalized thank you cards. Place them on your team's notice board. (Encourage team members to write thank you cards to other team members. It creates an amazing, positive teamwork environment.)

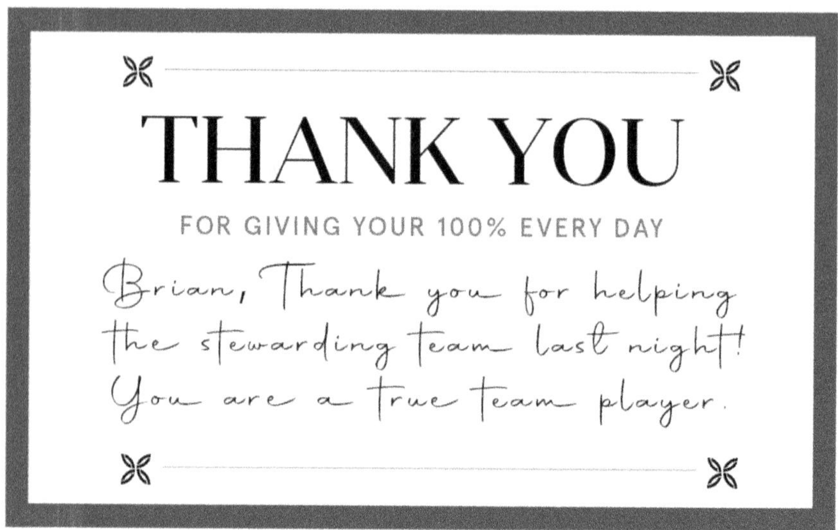

2. Celebrate employee birthdays.
3. Offer a career path. Let your new hire know that when they join you as a food server, they will have a career path similar to this: Food Server → Food Server Trainer → Supervisor or Training Manager → Restaurant Manager → Operations Manager.
4. Use staff surveys to increase participation in leading your restaurant (reward). (Read more about this in Chapter Six: Cost Discipline, section: Team Engagement and Contribution.)
5. Know your team members individually and what motivates them. Ask them about their lives and families. Each person is motivated differently. For example, one employee might be motivated by a simple thank you card, while another will thrive if they are assigned a challenging task.
6. Recognize and reward employees both publicly and privately. Not all rewards have to be monetary. Sometimes a simple "thank you" or "I appreciate your efforts" makes a huge difference in an employee's day.
7. Organize team-building activities to promote team camaraderie.

When you thank an employee, it will be more effective if you are specific. For example, you can say to your grill cook, "Great grill marks on the steak, John," rather than, "Great job, John." When you are generic, John will not know what he did to deserve the thank you. Also, when other employees hear, "Great grill marks on the steak," they will understand the importance of grill marks to you and the restaurant.

Lastly, if your employees feel that your thanks, rewards, or appreciation are not genuine, they are not likely to be motivated. Your honesty, transparency, and consistency go a long way toward earning your team's trust and presenting you as a genuine leader.

Your Leadership

There are thousands of books, seminars, and YouTube videos on the topic of leadership. In this section, I want to highlight the essential aspects of great leadership.

One of the best descriptions I have heard about leadership is this: You could be great at what you do, such as an accountant who is amazing with accuracy and analysis, or a sushi chef who is the best at making sushi, i.e., you have great skills. However, as we know from respected restaurateur Danny Meyer, your skills will only get you 49 percent of the way to success. The other 51 percent is how you make people feel. That's your leadership. In other words, the skill will only get you to the forty-ninth yard, but how you make people feel will get you the touchdown.

> Management is directing people to get stuff done, while leadership is about inspiring people, building effective and motivated teams, and being a role model.

It's important to draw a distinction between management and leadership. Management is directing people to get stuff done, while leadership is about inspiring people, building effective and motivated teams, and being a role model. Some examples of daily management practices include placing a food order to a vendor, hiring a new employee, and conducting a table visit. But leadership is more about inspiring an entire team, resolving conflicts successfully, performing acts of kindness, and developing others to grow their career.

Management includes planning your work; establishing goals, standards, and budgets; organizing your activities; organizing your team and the structure of the organization; coordinating between managers, team members, or departments; delegating work to others; recruiting; training; communicating; giving direction to the team; daily supervision; rewarding and disciplining; managing costs, time, systems, procedures, and objectives; and lastly, evaluating whether targets have been met.

It's important to note that all managers have different amounts of the same resources: money, people, time, energy, products, equipment, and systems/procedures. No manager will have enough of all of them. That's why it's called "management": *we have to work—and succeed—with what we've got.* Once I asked a group of about 120 managers if they needed more staff members. They all said yes. But the reality is that our job is to *manage* labor cost and labor hours. A good manager notices the labor issue, but a great manager addresses it using resources already at hand, without hiring more people and increasing labor cost.

There are many activities that each manager must do to run a successful restaurant company, such as making sure their team has great menu knowledge, making and serving food according to company standards, and delivering a high-quality experience. But here are four ways of thinking that might surprise you. I learned these from a book titled *First, Break all the Rules* by Marcus Buckingham and Curt Coffman.

When motivating and training someone, great managers must focus on strengths, not on weaknesses.

This thought has totally changed how I approach training. For example, if you have a food server who is good at remembering guests' names and their favorite foods, but speed of service is not their area of strength, you should pair them with a quick food server and encourage them to teach others how to remember guests' names.

Make them your guest-service ambassador. Do not waste your resources trying to make them a quick food server. You can try to train them on speed of service, and they might become faster but not fast enough, and it probably won't become their strength.

It would be better to capitalize on the strengths they already have (remembering guest names) and manage around speed of service. This allows you to maximize your staff's strengths without wasting time and efforts on fixing their weaknesses.

When hiring and selecting someone, great managers select for attitude and talent, not simply experience, intelligence, or determination.

When it comes to hiring restaurant and hospitality staff, it all boils down to hiring people who are friendly, outgoing team players, and most importantly, "trainable." Once hiring is complete, skills training becomes the name of the game. While interviewing, I always ask more behavioral- and personality-based questions rather than experience-based questions. For example: "What are the things that your friends like about you?" After they answer, I ask, "What are the top three things that they don't like about you?" Such questions reveal a lot of information about the candidate's personality, attitude, principles, and mindset. More examples: "What are your top personality strengths?" After that, "What are your top three personality weaknesses? In your last performance review, what did your manager say you need to improve?"

Experience can be taught, but it's more challenging to change attitudes and habits.

When setting expectations, great managers define the right outcomes, not the right steps.

In the past, I used to ask my front-of-house team to follow a standard set of service steps for every guest. But the above notion has changed my approach. Every guest is different and may require a different angle or approach depending on their situation. It doesn't matter how and when your food servers use suggestive selling or perform a table visit, as long as they upsell, achieve a good check average, and their guests leave happy because of them.

When thinking of promoting or developing someone, great managers help them find the "right fit," not simply the next available position.

For example, consider a sushi chef who has been working exceptionally. Is the right fit for them a promotion to restaurant manager? Maybe not. It's probably better to cross-train them or give them a salary raise for their exceptional sushi creations. If you make them a manager, you will take their most important strength away and throw them into the world of management, which requires a completely different skill set. The same would apply to a great food server or hostess. Lastly, not every great employee wants to become a manager.

Other Key Criteria of Great Leadership

Be positive and optimistic. Positivity and optimism are contagious. When you focus on the good, the good gets better. Create an environment for people to feel good about themselves in the workplace. Be passionate—people appreciate it.

When you are calm, your team will be calm. Don't try to control everything. Accept the fact that some things will be out of your control. Don't be intimidated by obstacles. There is no need to be upset when things don't go your way. Don't show feelings of anger and disappointment.

Take care of your mental health. Switch off from thinking about work every now and then. Have a hobby. It's important to avoid burnout and refresh your energy. Take care of your physical health too. Our industry requires long hours of work, but your strategy for making your restaurant function should work just as well when you are not there.

Be a role model. "Be the leader you would follow."

Set high standards, but don't be mean. Be tough on standards, not on people.

Listen, listen, listen. This might sound like a given, but listening to your team will enhance your relationship with them and, in turn, influence their performance positively. Listening shows respect and builds trust.

Empower them to make decisions and solve guests' concerns. This is what I call mission critical. Empowerment is key to success.

Empower your team by creating a safe environment where they can learn and aspire to be better. Empower them to make decisions and solve guests' concerns. This is what I call mission critical. Empowerment is key to success.

Genuinely care about your employees. Let them know it's not only a work relationship. Ask about their families. Show interest in what they do. *Don't be task driven; be people driven.* It's easy to get caught up with your to-do list and lose the human touch. Every now and then put your to-do list on the side and have a conversation with your people.

Be humble and open-minded. Be willing to learn from even your entry-level employees.

Lastly, as you know, a *restaurant is a business of endless moving parts.* You must be organized. Using a daily routine checklist will keep you focused on the important tasks. At the same time, do your best to simplify and remove complexities from your team's work. If checklists are too many, try to consolidate them; if policies, steps of service, procedures, or recipes are way too complex, make it easier for your team.

Measure results, but don't get obsessed with measurement, as it takes time away from the business fundamentals: great food, great service, great atmosphere. Don't turn your team into accountants or administration people. I once worked with a senior executive who wanted to measure *every single action.* I, in turn, asked our three-hundred-plus restaurants to do the same, which created a lot of resentment, tick-the-box approaches, and complaints. Being open-minded and listening to the field is key. With all my corporate jobs, I always stayed connected to the field. I spent time in kitchens, dining rooms, and host stations even though I had a senior corporate office position. Such immersion made me think twice before rolling out new programs and gave me valuable insights into what really matters and what is really needed for the business. Later, I reduced the entire program to 12 points and stayed on the program for three years. It became part of our language, and we continually fine-tuned it. Everyone appreciated it, and three years later, people still talk about and use the 12-point program.

Strategy: Vision, Mission, and Values

One of the key elements for leading your team is to have/build a common, shared goal, which is generally represented through vision and mission statements and culture and behavior statements. (Check out the final section of the book to read more.)

Next, I will share a tool that will keep you organized and efficient to avoid the firefighter approach to management.

Daily Routine Checklist (Restaurant Manager/Supervisor)

This is just a sample daily routine, and it will be different from one restaurant to another. Having a routine in place and using it every day will keep you in control of what's known to be "the business of a thousand details!"

Task	Manager (Morning Shift)
Walk outside the building and check for broken windows and doors.	
Walk inside the building and check for last night's closing.	
Read the manager's logbook.	
Master prep list is completed/station prep list; check walk-in cooler and freezer: last night closing/organization/cleanliness, including dry storage area and dining room.	
Check the team roster.	
Count petty cash and check safe audit report.	
Prepare for shift meetings (FOH and BOH).	
Oversee employee arrivals.	
Conduct shift meetings (FOH & BOH) and discuss Star Dish of the Day/recipe.	
Update both communication boards (FOH and BOH).	
Place food orders.	
Receive orders.	
Walk through and follow up daily cleaning report for FOH.	
Check for prep, zoning, walk-in cooler, freezer, and dry store.	
Conduct kitchen line check.	

Doors open, walk through (check window ledges, host stand, awnings, parking lot).	
Check that TVs and music are on, HVAC is working, restrooms are well-stocked and clean.	
All servers' stations are clean, organized, and stocked.	
Start table visits and travel path.	
Write notes in the manager's logbook or a pocket-size writing pad.	
Shift handover to night manager.	

Now, let's take the lessons from this chapter and put them to work.

Training

Question	Comments
I use pre-shift briefings to teach my team something new every day.	
I come to the pre-shift briefings prepared to share a new tip. I pre-read and write what I will discuss.	
Once a month, we conduct an in-depth classroom training session.	
We have an excellent train-the-trainer program. My trainers are trained on how to train and motivate others.	
Our training sessions are based on guest feedback and concerns and are not just generic sessions.	
We conduct a menu knowledge and standards quiz every month.	
A Star Dish of the Day manual exists and is used in pre-shift meetings. For FOH, recipes are used for BOH shift briefing.	
My team knows which menu item will be discussed during pre-shift briefings (from the calendar) and come fully prepared to discuss it.	
I use a variety of training methods.	

Team Motivation and Leadership

I am a calm leader, even under stress.	
I don't micromanage my team.	
I encourage suggestions and creativity. I am a great listener.	
I inspire my team.	
I take care of my physical and mental health.	
I empower my team to solve guest concerns.	
We celebrate our team's birthdays. We reward our team members.	
We organize team-building outings and activities.	
I show interest in my team. I ask about their families.	
I am organized; I use a daily routine checklist.	

CHAPTER FIVE

MARKETING AND REVENUE (SALES) GROWTH

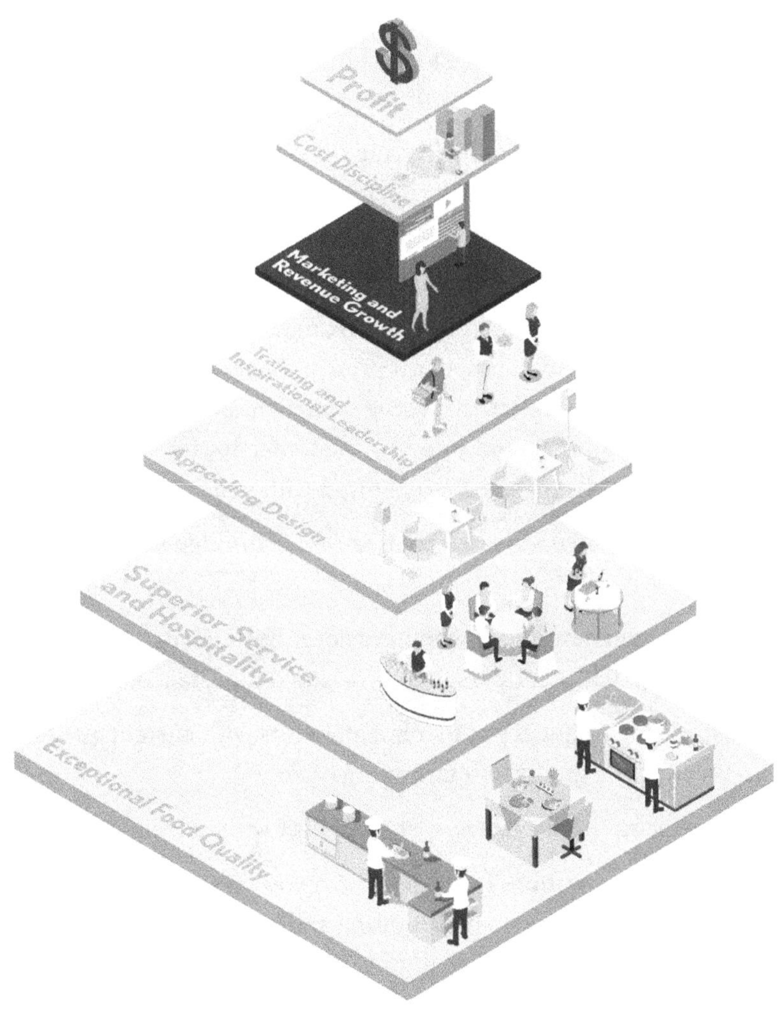

Marketing is one of the most important elements of a business strategy. It can make the difference between success and failure. Through marketing, you are connecting with your guests, building loyalty, creating brand experiences, and most importantly, attracting high-value clientele .

However, marketing can only be effective if you consistently deliver great food and great service. *Marketing is a byproduct of hospitality.* One bad post on social media by an unsatisfied customer can go viral and cause major damage to your restaurant's reputation for a long time. It doesn't matter how much marketing you do, you still need to make sure your operational excellence and everything within your "four walls" is in order, and consider your brand and position in the marketplace as compared to your competitors. Know the answer to this question: what is your point of differentiation?

You must always focus on delivering on your brand promise. There are two key elements that will help: 1. operational excellence (great food, great service, well-trained team, and great atmosphere); and 2. ongoing marketing (consistent messaging, targeted, timely).

The top 5 percent of guests drive approximately 30 percent of sales. Based on this fact alone, it is vital that you prioritize increasing your customers' lifetime value through targeted marketing campaigns. Marketing is the nonstop engine for earning profit and building customer loyalty in the restaurant business. It's about always being top of mind with your customers.

There are only three ways to increase revenue through marketing for your restaurant:

- Bringing in new guests who have never been to your restaurant (first timers), whether in-person or ordering online, takeout or delivery.
- Increasing frequency of incremental visits with current guests, i.e., encouraging guests to return more often.
- Increasing check average/spend per visit with current guests.

In the following section, I will share with you several tactics and tools to get your marketing engine up and running and advise how to optimize your restaurant's sales growth. This chapter is divided into two parts: marketing tactics and revenue-generation tools.

I will start with the most important marketing asset and tool—your guest database.

Database Building

It all starts with building your database.

It is important to build a large and up-to-date customer database while adhering to your local privacy laws. The larger your database, the easier it will be to reach your guests with promotions and low- and, in some cases, zero-cost marketing. A well-built, up-to-date, and accurate database helps you in many ways, such as promoting your loyalty program, sending birthday messages, thanking guests for joining your email list, announcing new menu items, email marketing, telephone marketing, direct mail, and many more. And if you are like many restaurants and have a small marketing budget, your database will be the best tool to use. But if you build a database, you must have consistent communication and something to say.

Your database sign-up forms should include:

1. Guest names
2. Birthdays
3. Phone numbers
4. Email addresses
5. Postal Code
6. Favorite sports teams (optional) or favorite dish/cuisine (optional)
7. Instagram or Facebook accounts (optional)

Remember to ask for the bare minimum, as people are not going to give away unnecessary personal information.

One of the best ways to collect guest information for your database is by using bounce-back cards and comment cards, collecting business cards, holding raffles and contests that are designed to capture customer data, or using digital programs such as web forms and surveys that require sign-up.

Your customer database will help you with all your "in-restaurant" and local store marketing tactics, which are typically inexpensive, highly targeted, and highly effective. Such tools are ideal for restaurants with low marketing budgets.

When you design marketing programs with your database, it is important to know:

1. Where do your customers come from? What area?
2. Age brackets.
3. Genders: the split between male and female (in regard to eating trends).
4. Professions.
5. Which meal period seems to be the slowest based on guest count or check average.
6. Ask yourself: am I trying to increase check average, gain new customers (first timers), or make existing customers return more often?

Bounce-Back Cards (Digital or Paper)

The goal of **bounce-back** cards is to entice customers to "**bounce back**" or return for an additional visit, or to make their next visit sooner and to build your database. Here is an example of a bounce-back card.

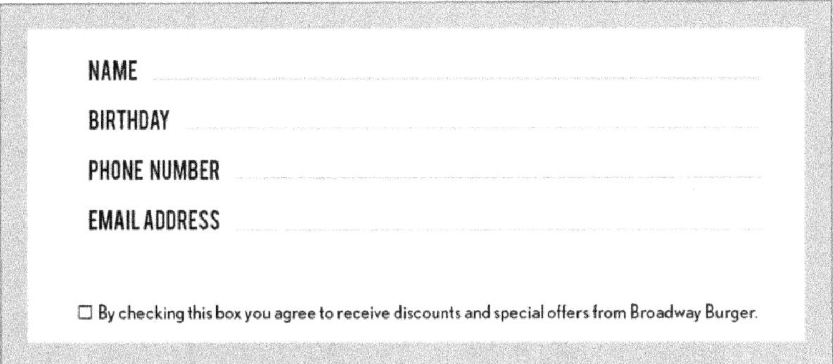

Here are the benefits and key notes for having a bounce-back card program in place:

- Bounce-back cards make your customers return more often.
- They are a good tool for obtaining guests' data and increasing your database.

The bounce-back cards that I designed have a foldable section with space for guests to write their name, email, and phone number, as well as an opt-in tick box for receiving a marketing newsletter. The guest's data was cut off and stayed with us, and the guests kept the offer section. Make sure the bounce-back card is the same size as a business card, so guests can carry them in their pockets. Any larger and your guests will leave it at home. No one wants to walk around with a large sheet of paper. Leave enough space for writing an email address and phone number on the section that you will cut off and keep for populating your database, or it can be on the back of the card.

- Bounce-back cards are inexpensive to produce.
- Make sure you have an expiration date, preferably within two weeks of issuing the card, to encourage guests to return soon. That being said, we used to accept expired bounce-back cards because our goal was to make our guests happy. After all, disappointed guests are far less likely to return to your restaurant than happy guests.
- Try different offers, such as a complimentary dessert or appetizer on your next visit or a redeemable $10 off. Keep trying different offers until you have an offer that has a high repeat-visit ratio.

Loyalty Punch Cards (Digital or Paper)

Here is a sample:

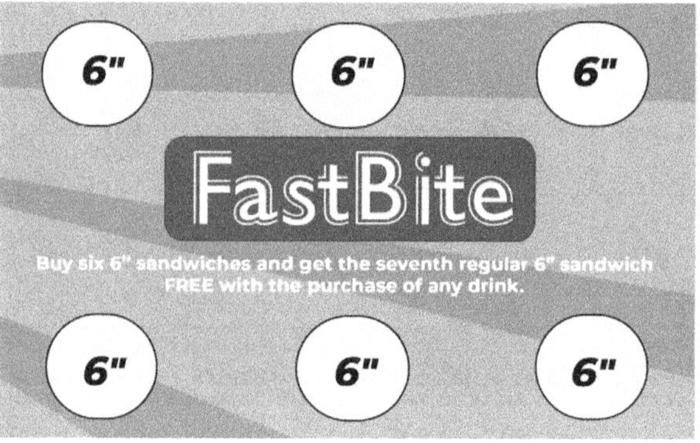

Here is another example:

When designing loyalty cards, make the number of visits required to redeem a free meal eight or less. If the number of visits required is more than eight, customers end up taking the card but not using it. Offering your guests rewards that are perceived as valuable in their minds is the name of the game.

Some people may find this tool outdated and would say it's easier to use technology for loyalty-card programs. Apps are great, but they come with many challenges, such as the high cost to produce and maintain them and the marketing efforts needed to convince customers to download them. However, the advantage of going digital is that you can collect guests' purchase data and ordering behavior and use them to gain insights for future targeted marketing initiatives.

So: As mentioned before, if you want your guests or potential guests to carry around your bounce-back cards, loyalty cards, or direct-mail coupons, **make sure they are small enough to fit in a wallet.** If the coupons are larger than that, guests are likely to leave them at home.

Social Media Marketing

Social media transformed the world of marketing, and now is the time to capitalize on it and to connect with your followers online and turn them into lifelong customers. Social media has become one of the most powerful marketing tools with platforms like Facebook, Instagram, Twitter, and LinkedIn, as well as the trendier options used by younger audiences, like TikTok and Snapchat.

Let's talk about some fundamentals and key tips for Instagram and Facebook. Whichever social media platform you decide to use, make sure you **engage before you sell.** Your social media posts shouldn't only inform customers about a new dish or service—they should engage them, talk to them, excite them, and *eventually* sell to them. It's not enough to say, "Check out our new organic roasted chicken." Show a video of how you roast it. Show energy and action. You can even film your chef demonstrating part of the process. Finally, create an enticing offer and measure your customers' response with book-now codes or a special password.

Your restaurant's social media pages should have engaging and high-quality visual content—both photos and videos. One good approach is to take about thirty photos of different menu items, the restaurant décor, and the atmosphere, and aim to post twice per week. Just like that, you have fifteen weeks of social media content prepared. Engagement leads to sales. Engagement keeps your brand "top of mind." Direct selling is a turnoff for many people. Also, don't expect that by posting a photo of your food people will act.

Once you add followers, consider messaging them directly via Instagram (customers seem to be willing to respond to and receive messages via Instagram and less through Facebook). You can send your posts to thousands of people (current followers). If you aim to send messages to fifty followers a day, you can do that in less than five minutes, but message them only once every fifteen days. An excess of messages causes followers to unfollow you and is annoying to many people. Here are some screenshots from my account that will show you how to send messages to customers.

People don't buy from businesses, they buy from people—so give your business a human touch and think of adding value for your followers instead of spamming them with calls to action, offers, or messaging. Add value by sharing recipes or blogs, or providing entertainment. People go to social media to be entertained, or to learn, or to stay up-to-date on news and happenings.

In summary:

- Make sure your posts are eye-catching or entertaining.
- Post at least twice a week (once before the weekend and once at the beginning of the week).
- Every day, for at least ten minutes, read what your guests write about your restaurant. If you see a negative comment, deal with it quickly before it goes viral.

Consider some key points to succeed:

1. Make sure your handle is easy to find. If your restaurant's name is Marvin's Burgers, make sure it has the same name on Instagram and Facebook. The handle on Instagram should not be "Marvin's Burgers 67" or "Marvin's-Burgers" or "Marvin's Amazing Burgers."

Be easily searchable. Make your name easy to find or tag. People who visit your restaurant may want to tag you in their Instagram stories or any other social media posts. This will allow others to easily find you and know what you have to offer.

2. Choose clarity over creativity. Marketers tend to create unique names for campaigns to generate curiosity and interest, such as naming a fish promotion "Fishtastic" or naming brunch "Funch." Instead of this, I recommend simplicity and clarity. If your restaurant is named Tomo, I would opt for "Tomo's Brunch."

> Choose clarity over creativity.

3. Integrate Instagram with other platforms. As you probably know, you can share the same post with the click of a button on Instagram, Facebook, and Twitter.
4. Keep social media captions under 280 characters. Any caption longer than that will be cut off if someone shares one of your images on Twitter. Tell a story, but strive to keep it close to the length of a tweet.
5. Put your Instagram handle on your menu, but make sure you keep your Instagram updated. This way you drive your guests to your Instagram page while they are at the restaurant, and you gain real followers—especially if you run contests and give away prizes.
6. Engage and interact with followers and reward them with some of the following offers, or come up with your own. Here are some options:
    a. Tag us for a chance to win a complimentary meal.
    b. Ask for customers' opinions on your new menu.
    c. Encourage Instagram users with 1,000+ followers (as long they are popular, effective, and well-known in your city) to post about your restaurant.
    d. If you are adding a new dish to your menu, consider asking your customers to help you name it. By involving customers in the

process, they'll feel compelled to continue following you to learn the result of the contest.

e. Hold photo challenges. Encourage customers to share photos and add your restaurant tag. Ask followers to post an image of your restaurant or an image of their meal with your business name tagged in the photo. If they are dining in, make sure to give out a business-card-sized note with the correct handle name so they don't have to search for it.

f. Tagged photos by users: directly message each user about how you're glad they enjoyed their meal, how you love their picture, and how you'll tag them for photo credit if they give you permission to repost their photo to your page or story. Check the "tagged pictures" tab in your profile and see all the content your customers have shared while eating at your restaurant. If the content is of great quality, you can easily add them to your library for free.

g. Remember to post your Instagram handle everywhere you can: on your menus, table tents, business cards, and guest checks. Or, even better, have a card with your handle on it or QR code ready and encourage your food servers to share it with your guests. We did exactly that at my restaurants and it worked superbly. After we welcomed our guests and sat them at their tables, we told them we were running a contest. "If you post a photo and tag us or follow us, you might win a free meal for two." We made it easy for them to find our handle; we gave them a small card with the handle printed on it.

Remember to post your Instagram handle everywhere you can: on your menus, table tents, business cards, and guest checks.

h. Boost your posts; it can cost as low as $5 per day, and you can choose the targeted demographics, location, age, gender, and interests. You can also decide your budget based on the number of people you want to reach.

7. Use the right hashtags to drive organic impressions and increase your reach. Narrow your target audience: It does you little good to target people across the country or even one county over. They're not likely to visit. If you're an establishment that appeals to young professionals, then showing the ad to every age group doesn't make much sense and will cost you a lot of wasted advertising money. Specify your hashtags by location, e.g., #NYCfood rather than #food.
8. Consistency is key. Your patrons will trust your brand more and feel fulfilled if you continue to share and post what they have grown to expect of you. If your concept is about whiskey and cigars, your followers will expect luxury-based images, earthy tones, elegant images, and people in suits, not casual or sports-themed posts. Staying on-brand is essential for clear and easy-to-understand brand positioning.

Facebook

Facebook is an in-the-moment social network. If a follower comments or shares your post, you want to reply within a reasonable amount of time. Put someone in charge of managing your Facebook marketing and all social media platforms so it's always taken care of.

Create a marketing plan with a clear budget. Plan out your posts and your marketing ideas. Avoid posting random stuff. Break your plan up by creating a weekly post schedule. (The same is applicable to Instagram.)

Consistency and interaction are the keys to making Facebook marketing work for your restaurant. Here are tips and ideas for a successful Facebook page:

1. Target your catchment/trading area/neighborhood toward your local community. As I pointed out before, people on the other side of the country are unlikely to come to your restaurant. Show your support and care for your community by considering initiatives like creating a promotion where customers can donate meals to say thanks for all the hard work of your town's firefighters, doctors, nurses, cleaners, and town heroes.

2. Encourage customers to visit you on Facebook on their cell phones while they are physically in the restaurant. Let them know about special offers on Facebook. This way you will gain more likes and followers. This is applicable to Instagram as well.
3. Create the crave. Take advantage of Facebook's news feed by using tasteful, interesting, and eye-catching imagery of your food that will make users comment, like, and share your posts as they scroll through their feeds. Generate awareness and demand by sharing amazing images and videos.
4. Your brand positioning should match the tone of your Facebook page. Whatever your niche, find your tone—playful, classic, fine dining, or entertaining.
5. The best way to gain and maintain followers is to provide them with content they find valuable. Value can come in several forms. Discounts and promotions are the obvious options, but consider sharing recipes or entertaining and fun content as well.

Try different ideas to drive engagement:

a. Facebook Fan of the Week/Month: Invite the fan to your restaurant, showcase their favorite dish, take photos with them, or ask them if they would like to do a short video about your restaurant. You can also see if they'd like to cook with your chef.

b. Ask your fans for their opinion or post quizzes.

   For example:

   - What would you like to see on our menu?
   - What toppings do you add to your burger?
   - What's your favorite dessert at our restaurant?

c. Share interesting facts about your restaurant, your city, or your recipes.

d. Host contests for your followers. These could take many forms. Maybe you can offer a prize to whoever posts the best image of a recipe or drink. Alternatively, you could challenge your followers to name all your desserts.

e. Share great reviews and mentions. If you get a great review on Tripadvisor, Yelp, or Google reviews, share it. This will highlight your restaurant's success and acknowledge the reviewer. Many guests enjoy social media attention. For similar reasons, be sure to track your mentions. If someone shares a great photo of your food, share it on your page and story on all your social media platforms. Not only does it make that guest feel special, but it also inspires more social media users to share photos from your restaurant.

f. Try to embed the question, **"How did you hear about us?" in several areas. It is so critical to know which marketing methods are working and which are not.**

g. Invite an exclusive group of Facebook fans to meet up at your restaurant once a week.

h. Facebook ads for restaurants are a great way to attract new customers and turn them into regulars, so investing in them is a must.

i. Post at the right time. If you want to target dinner customers, post from 1 to 4 p.m. If you're a coffee or breakfast restaurant, posting before the shop opens in the morning will remind the early crowd to get their morning fix. Another ideal time to post is on the morning of the first day of the weekend (Saturday morning for most people). Many people will be on social media, and seeing an ad for your restaurant could help them decide where to take their family for a weekend dinner out.

Great Photography Tips for Your Online Content

- Shoot photos in natural light next to a large window that doesn't get much direct sunlight.
- Avoid fluorescent and other indoor lighting, as this tends to change colors and tones.
- Try different angles in order to portray the attractive and characteristic components of varying types of food. A plate with a flat arrangement of food might be best shot overhead, while taller dishes, such as a burger or stack of pancakes, tend to look best at a 45-degree or straight-on angle so that you can see the layers, making it look more appealing and abundant.

- Highlight "action" in your photos, like pouring maple syrup or dusting powdered sugar on pancakes; a hand sprinkling on a garnish or liquid pouring into a bowl; a hand holding a spoonful of a dip about to be placed; or hands holding finger-food items.
- When it comes to presentation, include ingredients, flowers, tablecloths, unique dinnerware and flatware, or colored items that accentuate the food. But remember, less is more when it comes to these presentational elements. Don't overdo it with garnishes on a dish—if you do, all that will appear in a photo is the garnish. Elegant dishes typically have fewer garnishes (two to three maximum). A crème brûlée with four garnishes looks less attractive than a crème brûlée with two garnishes. Too many garnishes make the dish secondary and not the center of attention. Not to mention, the more garnishes there are, the harder the dish is to reproduce.
- It's also recommended to show your restaurant's atmosphere and vibe, as opposed to strictly shots of food.

Guests' Touchpoints

Your guests' journey to your restaurant (and their eyes' movement during that journey) plays an important role in their purchasing decisions and presents several opportunities to upsell, increase check average, or drive awareness.

You can also use the journey for potential guests who have never visited your restaurant before to make them choose your outlet. (Read more about this topic under Customer Relationship Management [CRM] in the following pages.)

Touchpoints

A touchpoint is any interaction a customer has with your restaurant. This includes encountering your social media posts, not only when they're in the restaurant interacting with your staff. I encourage you to find all the possible touchpoints a guest might have with your restaurant before, during, and after visiting your restaurant. This can include billboards, banners, posters, social media posts, third-party websites, apps, ads, and all interactions in real life (food servers, hostesses, and managers) or online.

Here are some examples of guest touchpoints:

1. Elevator advertising.
2. Your menu, whether it is printed, on a tablet, or accessed online via a QR code. (There is a section on menu design later in this chapter.)
3. Table tents/table talkers.
4. In-restaurant wall-mounted posters.
5. Building exterior.
6. Billboards.
7. Other areas: door handles, trash cans, digital screens, restrooms (washrooms), and flags.
8. Interactions with your team.

Elevator Advertising

Elevator advertising is a great tool to market to a targeted and captive audience who lives in apartment buildings or works in office towers. It is the first out-of-home advertising opportunity when people leave home, and it is the last marketing/touchpoint opportunity before they return home.

At the end of the workday, elevator occupants are starting to relax and think about what they are going to have for dinner or what their plans are for after work or the weekend. They are tired from the day and are looking for a positive experience. Another reason to use elevator screens or interior, wall-mounted posters is the fact that they capture attention by relieving the social awkwardness of elevators, particularly when strangers meet in an elevator.

Elevator riders appreciate the entertainment value or information it brings to an otherwise uneventful experience. Information such as daily news updates, building notices from the property managers, or sports and weather updates for the day may stick with them, but once the occupants leave the elevator and go about their business, they might forget about the ads they saw. You need to make your ads memorable, so make them entertaining or humorous. If you plan to show images of your food, I recommend featuring one hero image rather than two or three, due to the size of the displays.

There are three types of elevator advertising:

- Digital display.
- Display frames.
- Elevator wraps: advertisers have the freedom to exercise high levels of creativity with wraps and often produce optical illusions or humorous ad displays that leave a lasting impression on riders.

When using elevator advertising, make sure you match the profile of the building. If your elevators are in a building that is occupied by families with children, you need to think about "value" and pricing that meet their budgets, or the entertainment you offer their children while parents are dining.

Table Tents

Before I talk about the reasons for using table tents, I would like to start by talking about the importance of good design, because I often see restaurants with poorly designed or low-quality table tents. The best table tents are not too large, are placed at the side of the table instead of the center, and are mostly placed on larger tables. I do not recommend having them on smaller tables because they take up a lot of space and the customer experience is always the most important factor for restaurant success. I particularly like those that have frames where you can insert your marketing POP and remove it whenever you want to change your messaging. These frames are often made of good quality wood, are easy to clean, and keep the table tidy. In contrast, paper table tents can sometimes look cheap and messy.

Table tents are very effective in capturing your guests' attention.

Table tents are not suitable for every brand. If you are running a fine-dining restaurant, I probably wouldn't recommend using them. If you do, make sure they are unobtrusive. Keep them small, and stick to high-quality materials like wood so that they match the décor and atmosphere of the restaurant.

Table tents are very effective in capturing your guests' attention. Your audience is at your fingertips, especially when guests are waiting for their food. Table tents are less intrusive and not too pushy.

Key Tips

- You can display images of new dishes (no more than one or two, less is more), your preferred charity organizations, your social media handles, awards, or any upcoming events. Your goals are to inspire repeat visits, educate customers, increase check averages, or sell new products.
- Keep your message short and focused. One mouthwatering food image is far better than two or three. Marketers would tell you that more than seven words on a billboard are wasted. The same is applicable to table tents. Get your message across in as few words as

possible. Your guests probably won't give your table tents more than a quick glance, so you want to make sure that they can get all the information you want them to in that moment.

- Make your message eye-catching, use humor if appropriate, or add a call to action. Present an offer. Advertise. Upsell. Encourage repeat visits.

In-Restaurant Wall-Mounted Posters

Your building's exterior can be a great place to hang posters that attract the attention of potential customers in high-foot-traffic or high-car-traffic areas where posters are easily seen and read by large numbers of prospective customers. Posters are always visible and have a long shelf life, meaning you don't have to replace them often. Posters give you additional exposure for your brand and will positively influence potential guests. In comparison to digital marketing, where spam filters and ad blockers allow us to turn off advertisements, wall-mounted posters are an "in-your-face" type of advertising, making it difficult for people to avoid them.

Posters are always visible and have a long shelf life, meaning you don't have to replace them often.

Here are some tips for creating effective posters:

- Place them at eye level in high-foot-traffic areas, but don't hang them in areas that take away from the beauty of your façade (exterior) or atrium. Don't hang too many posters, as it takes away from the image of the restaurant, especially for fine-dining restaurants.
- Make sure the design of your poster is alluring and eye-catching. When highlighting a new product, the graphic design must be mesmerizing. Don't make your poster too busy by using too many colors or different fonts. Keep it simple. Your main goal is to attract attention.

- Use one big image, visual, or graphic. One large photo is far better than featuring two or three. Having a dominant image that's visible from a distance is key. If your poster is near your front door, don't waste space by adding your phone number, email, or website, as your guests are already near the door. This is prime real estate, so make sure you keep text to a minimum. Think elegance and less clutter.
- Revise your poster design and messaging every four to six months. If the same poster hangs on the same wall for more than six months, people will tune it out, the colors fade, and passersby find it boring.
- Hang posters near your front door, on your exterior wall, and on restaurant windows (sparingly; you don't want these to detract from your customers' dining experiences), bathroom stalls, indoor walls, and doors.

Other Touchpoints

- **Building's exterior, awnings (canopies), exterior walls, and windows**. All of these are additional marketing opportunities. Your building's exterior signage and awnings are very helpful, especially if you are located in a high-traffic area. Don't just mount your backlit logo and expect people to know your brand and offering—your logo alone is not enough to draw customers to your restaurant unless you operate a large chain or well-known international brand. I see this mistake often: mounting a logo and expecting people to know what you offer. If you mount a logo and awnings/canopies, add a tagline or a couple of words to educate potential customers.

  I use awnings to highlight our core menu offering. We designed them with words like:

  First awning: Steaks

  Second awning: Pasta

  Third awning: Gelato

- **Billboards.**
- **Door handles:** Every customer will look at the handle as they open the door. Because of this, some restaurants place a small poster (8" x 8") that says, "Free Wi-Fi" or "Kids Eat Free."
- **Vehicle branding/wrapping.**
- **Outdoor trash cans**: McDonald's uses the tops of the trash cans to write "Open 24 Hours" in order to educate their guests about their operating hours.
- **Digital screens**: in hotel lobbies or near restaurants' front desk/ foyer.
- **Flags.**
- **Guest receipts** are a good place for zero-cost marketing. The auto print could contain advertisements for upcoming or recurring events.
- **Washrooms stalls.**
- **More touchpoints:**
    - Interactions with food servers.
    - Interactions with the front desk/reception/hostess.
    - Interactions with the valet team.
    - Your menu (there is a section on menu design later in this chapter).

Brand Positioning and Guest Touchpoints

Always ask yourself how well your touchpoints and marketing vehicles blend in with your brand positioning. If you operate a fine-dining restaurant, it's not advisable to have banners on your windows, bathroom stalls, or trash cans, but you can take advantage of every opportunity for a QSR brand.

Business Cards

Business cards tell you a lot about your customers and where they come from. From a business card, you can learn a customer's name, email, phone number, what their profession is, and where they work.

Companies pay massive amounts of money to get the data above, but collecting business cards gathers the information for free. Consider running a contest among your employees to collect business cards. This works especially well if customers who offer you their business cards are entered into a raffle for a complimentary meal. When you build a relevant database from guests who visited your restaurant and gave you their business cards, you will be able to send personalized messages as opposed to mass marketing. Personalized marketing messages are powerful, less expensive, and have the highest guest-engagement rate!

Personalized marketing messages are powerful, less expensive, and have the highest guest-engagement rate!

Direct mail, telephone marketing, email marketing, and thank you letters are examples of highly effective personalized marketing tools, and collecting business card data gives you what you need in order to personalize your marketing efforts and laser focus your approach. **But please remember to adhere to your country's privacy laws. In some countries it could be illegal to directly contact guests or collect business cards unless they gave you written permission.**

Direct Mail

Direct mail is a marketing tool that involves sending a physical letter, gift card, package, mailer, merchandise, or postcard to your potential and current customers.

I have personally used direct mail in several restaurant companies that I managed. At first, I built my database by collecting guests' business cards (all cards have PO boxes or zip codes on them). I also searched online for businesses that I wanted to market to via direct mail and added their PO box data to my database. I always made sure the campaigns were measured. If a guest received mail with a coupon from my restaurant, the guests would need to bring the coupon with them for me to be able to measure the effectiveness of the campaign. There were times when I sent items such as fridge magnets designed with our restaurant name and number on them. I didn't want to measure these. Rather, they were to keep our business top of mind (fridge magnets stay on your guests' fridges day in and day out, and they're seen frequently because people go to their fridge when they are hungry).

Another positive aspect of direct mail is the fact that it is measurable, tangible, and can be personalized. When you personalize your message, your return on investment (ROI) is far higher and your guest appreciation is much better. With direct mail, you effectively cut through all the marketing noise of social media and receive your customers' undivided attention. Depending on how well you design the mail, gift card, or item, direct mail can create memorable experiences. Lastly, direct mail can be used for highly targeted audience segments, as you choose them by zip code, age, and income level.

Sales Tip: Many guests order gift cards online to be mailed to them or their loved ones.

I love selling gift cards because they don't have 100 percent redemption rates. Some people buy them and end up not using them, so if you sell a gift card at $50, you sometimes make $49 in profit and are only out the cost of the card. If they do redeem the gift card, they end up spending either more money at your restaurant or less than the value of the card. In other words, you always win!

Tips for executing a successful direct-mail campaign:

1. Design: You need to design a piece of mail that stands out. Homeowners receive many direct-mail messages, most of which end up in the trash. Because of this, your direct mail has to be visually striking and immediately engaging, and you can also include or mail swag. For restaurants, some examples of swag include spices, coffee, marinades, sauces, and cookies.
2. Size matters! If you want your guests or potential guests to carry around your direct-mail coupon, make sure the coupon is small enough to fit in a wallet. If the coupons are larger than that, guests are likely to leave them at home.
3. Call to action: Mail recipients must feel a true sense of urgency to respond to your offer. Limit the offer to a specific time period, so your guests feel compelled to visit your restaurant before the offer expires. Include offers they can't refuse. Try different calls to action in order to decide on the best option with the highest redemption rate and favorable results.
4. Follow up: some businesses opt for following up on direct mailings with digital marketing campaigns or emails to make it more effective.
5. Make it targeted: Select a target market based on demographics (gender, income, and location) that are well-suited to your brand. If your country doesn't provide that info, database building becomes even more essential. In general, there are two types of direct mail. Addressed mail is sent to a database of people, and unaddressed mail is sent to postal codes in your area.
6. Combine direct mail and email: if done correctly, combining both could result in higher response rates and redemption of offers.

Direct mail is still one of the most efficient and cost-effective forms of targeted advertising available to business owners. It's a great tool for launching a new menu or announcing the rollout of new dishes.

One of the largest benefits of direct mail is that even when guests unsubscribe or opt out of your email marketing offers, and you have lost contact with them through digital marketing, you will still be able to communicate with them and possibly win them back by sending compelling direct-mail offers, as long as you have their PO box/mailing information.

Developing patience and trust in your direct-mail campaigns can lead to great success in drumming up new business and engaging repeat customers.

Telephone Marketing

Telemarketing is a great example of personalized communication that gives you the opportunity to reach your current and potential guests. It is cost-effective and a great tool for growing your business.

Ideas for Telephone Marketing

- **Birthday Messages**: I personally used this tool for many years. We first used customer relationship management (CRM) software (sometimes a simple MS Excel sheet) and collected guests' birthday data. Here's how it works. We sorted guests' birthdays by date. If we had the time and capacity, we would call all of them. Otherwise, we would stick to a target of calling ten guests a day to wish them a happy birthday. We assigned one employee for this task. Here is a sample script:

  Food Server: Good morning, Mr. Smith. I am calling from Coyo restaurant.

  Guest: Good morning.

  Food Server: Our team would like to wish you a very happy birthday! We wish you happiness and great health.

  Guest: Thank you.

  Food Server: You are welcome. Have a wonderful day!

As you can see, we didn't offer any free desserts, discount offers, or invitations to dine with us. We just wanted to create **a sincere emotional**

connection. Many customers were blown away by the fact that we remembered their birthdays. But if you would like to monetize the birthday program, my advice is to call your guests at least two weeks before their birthday with an offer they can't refuse. Don't do the standard, "Your cake is on us." Be creative, such as, "We will beautifully decorate your table at no charge, and the birthday celebrant gets a gift card worth $100."

We just wanted to create a sincere emotional connection.

There are plenty of birthdays every day of the year. No matter the size of your catchment area/neighborhood, people always have birthdays. Entice them to celebrate at your restaurant instead of somewhere else. Offer a deal that includes food, decorations, and birthday cards. Birthdays often attract large groups—larger than the typical group that goes out to eat together.

Other reasons to use telemarketing:

- Launching a new menu that you want your guests to know about.
- Launching a new event, theme night, or entertainment, such as a new live band.
- Collecting guests' data, reaching out to past customers, and improving customer relationships.

Here are tips for executing an effective telephone marketing program:

- Have a script, but don't sound like a robot or a telemarketer.
- Smile—guests can hear the smile in your voice.
- Make sure you have a conversational tone and natural speed. When you speak naturally and slowly, you speak to people rather than *at* people; you build trust and sincerity.
- Set a target number of calls your team should make in a day, and measure the ratio of successful to rejected calls.
- Role-play with your team members or record the calls to pinpoint areas for improvement.
- Take action after your calls. If you tell a guest you're going to do something, do it right away. If you told them you would make a

reservation or send out a menu via email, don't wait until the next day to do so.

- Empower your team to answer customer questions. Call recipients may have complaints or need solutions to previous problems. Empower your team to offer solutions.
- Connect your CRM software to your telemarketing program so your team can have guest preferences, past visits, and other information to prepare them for a successful call.
- Don't start a call by saying, "I am sorry to disturb you," or, "Sorry to call," but ask if they have a free minute to talk.
- Respect and adhere to your local privacy laws. Check with your legal team before beginning telemarketing (cold calling or call recording).
- **Text Messaging** is another great tool and a cost-effective method for telephone marketing. It works well as long as you include a call to action, a great offer, and a link to your website or reservation platforms.

Online Reservations and Guest Review Platforms

Online booking platforms are important when it comes to your restaurant's reputation. Some examples of these platforms include Yelp, Tripadvisor, Google reviews, and TheFork.

People rely on reviews to select a restaurant. According to research by KPMG, these platforms are the second most-used channel to choose a restaurant after personal recommendations. (When a friend or colleague recommends a restaurant, the likelihood of you visiting that restaurant becomes very high in comparison to watching a TV ad or seeing an Instagram post.)

Nowadays, many people do a little bit of research before they decide to spend their money at a particular restaurant, especially if the restaurant is slightly above their budget or if they want to invite others.

It's very important to make sure that:

- Your restaurant has high ratings. Aim for between 4.5 and 5 stars. No one wants to spend their money in a 3.2 star restaurant.
- Add great photos of your food, your interior, and your exterior. These platforms have high traffic, so take advantage of this free marketing opportunity.
- Make sure your restaurant's name, phone number, menu, website, online ordering platform, social media, hours of operation, and other services are up-to-date and accurate online.

There should be no surprises for your guests when they visit. That's why your information and photos must be relevant and up-to-date.

- Train one of your hosts to scan these booking engines on a daily basis in order to flag any negative comments. One negative comment about food safety or cleanliness can go viral and damage your restaurant's reputation. I encourage you to respond to both negative and positive comments. When people go out of their way to talk positively about your restaurant, you should respond by saying something like, "Thank you! We are glad you enjoyed your meal and we hope to see you again." But don't create a standard, robotic type of answer that you copy and paste everywhere. Keep it personalized. Thank guests for great reviews and manage bad reviews. Managing reviews is a great opportunity to engage with your guests.

- Log on to Google Maps, Waze, and other popular navigation tools and type in your restaurant's name to make sure the GPS is accurate. Many new customers will do just that before driving to your restaurant.
- If you run a Chinese restaurant, Google "best Chinese restaurant near me" or "Chinese restaurant near me." If your restaurant name doesn't come up, you need to work on Google reviews scores and update Google Business Profile. Not only does Google Business Profile help boost your online presence, but it also increases your visibility on Google Maps.
- Create FAQs. Google Business Profile has a built-in FAQ section. Compose a list of questions that your customers frequently ask you on the phone, in your restaurant, or on social media, and provide clear answers. It will save you and your customers time.

Your Restaurant's Website

Your website is your digital front door. It is where your future guests get their first impression of your restaurant. It is a sales tool that operates 24/7, and you must take full advantage of it. It provides information and, more importantly, it's a revenue-generating tool. Your website is a branding tool. **Remember, you are building a brand, not just running a restaurant**. People connect with brands in different ways, and your goal is to make them fall in love with your brand. The images and colors, the design of the page, and any music, logos, and typefaces give readers an impression of your restaurant. The same is applicable to social media.

Key tips for building and maintaining an effective website:

1. **Key Information:** Your website's visitors must be able to find key information easily. The reader must not have to hunt or click several times to find your contact information, menu, hours of operation, address, and table bookings. I recommend some of these be placed at the top of your page. Customers spend less than sixty seconds on a website if they don't find what they are looking for, so you don't want them to leave too quickly because they couldn't find the info they needed.
2. **Mobile-Friendly:** Most of your customers will search for your restaurant on their cell phones. Make sure the colors, typefaces, and website overall are mobile-friendly.
3. **Clean and Simple:** Don't try to add too many things to the website. Declutter; keep it clean. I have mentioned below several items to include, but you need to pick and choose the most important aspects for your particular restaurant. White space is important to give the content room to breathe and to declutter the site.
4. **Your Story:** Your story is the soul of your brand—what makes you unique, what steps you take to cook different and distinctive food, and how you source your food. What differentiates you from your competition not only in terms of great service and hospitality but also in what food and drinks you offer?
5. **Homogenized Presence:** your website, your staff uniforms, menu, service, music, and everything else must blend and result in one homogenized brand positioning that is consistent and clear to consumers.
6. **Look and Feel:** Make sure you feature photos of your food and atmosphere (having fun, family dining, etc.) on your landing page. You don't need thirty photos. Six food images of your best-selling signature dishes and five to six photos of the ambience/interior will be enough.

7. **Social Media:** don't forget to integrate your website with your social media handles.
8. **Sell:** Add these services if you have them: online ordering, gift card sales, business catering (banks, offices), social catering (weddings, birthday parties), home meal kits, and merchandise (hats, mugs, T-shirts).
9. **Search Engine Optimization (SEO):** This is key for your restaurant to appear at the top of the list when people search for your outlet on Google/Yahoo/MS Edge. Let's say you're a restaurant that makes Arabic food and you're located in Dallas, Texas. Go to Google and search for "best Arabic restaurants in Dallas." If your restaurant doesn't come up, then you have a lot of work to do in terms of content strategy.
10. **Other Items:** Here are other items you can include on your website, but please remember: don't try to include everything. Don't make your website overwhelming and overloaded with information.
    - Collect email addresses for marketing.
    - Online ordering.
    - Charity that you endorse.
    - Loyalty program and app download.
    - Media: press releases and blogs.
    - Sustainability programs and actions.
    - Virtual classes (culinary/wine tasting).
    - Upcoming events.
    - Contests.
    - Recipes.
    - Other services: jobs, franchising, events, and catering.
    - Awards.
    - How you engage and support your local community.

Note: Check your country's laws regarding creating websites that are user friendly for visually- or hearing-impaired people.

Nothing is more persuasive than great photos and videos that make guests crave what you are offering. Pictures are more powerful than words and should make up an integral part of your content strategy, paid media advertising, and search engine optimization, which will significantly help you when people search for the type of food you serve and your location.

Your biggest challenge will be how fast and at what cost you update your website. You shouldn't be at the mercy of your website developer. You should learn how to make simple updates, such as pricing, removing or adding new menu items, changing your hours of operation, and adding new events or announcements. You also need to make sure that whatever changes you make are aligned with Twitter, Facebook, Instagram, Google Business Profile, OpenTable, and all other online platforms. This is critical in order to avoid confusion. Keep a list of all your online platforms and Google the name of your restaurant to see where else your restaurant is mentioned or being promoted. Sometimes you'll find platforms that you have never heard of before displaying your restaurant's information.

Guest Relations, CRM, and Sales Growth

Guest relations has a huge impact on sales growth. In this section I will cover two important elements: Guest Relations and Customer Relationship Management Software (CRMs).

Guest relations is about incorporating a guest-centric culture into the organization and building lasting and genuine relationships with your customers by remembering guest names, being friendly and outgoing, taking the time to send greetings cards, handling guest complaints effectively and empowering your team members to do so, remembering guests' favorite foods, remembering guests' birthdays and children's names, being part of the community, and showing genuine interest in your guests. All of these things make guests want to return to your restaurant.

Over the course of my career, it has been proven to me time and again that customers return to a restaurant that cares about them. Are you a role model when it comes to building long-lasting relationships with your customers?

One of my best experiences was when I worked with a restaurant general manager who knew *every* guest by name, spoke to every table, and welcomed and bid farewell in person to every guest! We had many superstars when it came to service, but every guest asked about him. Now that's great guest-relations management.

Customer Relationship Management Software (CRMs)

Customer relationship management (CRM) is about using technology to facilitate and provide data for building lifetime guest relations. It's a business strategy to retain guests and compel them to come back more often, while relying on data that shows purchasing habits, history, gender, address, preference, income, age, and profession. It's built on learning more about customers' needs and behaviors to develop stronger relationships with them.

It is much less expensive for a restaurant to retain an existing customer than to acquire a new one. Your goal is to build a base of loyal guests who will come back more often and may influence other potential customers.

Building positive relationships with loyal customers requires reviewing every step of your guest journey:

Review your marketing posts, messages, websites, banners, press releases, and all other marketing vehicles
1
Guests become aware of your restaurant
Review your online presence: pictures, information, hours of operation, guest reviews
2
Research
Arrival experience, parking, and welcoming process
3
Arrive at your restaurant
Menu design, readability, variety, pricing, menu item descriptions, clarity
4
Read the menu
Food server knowledge, uniform, attitude
5
Order food
6
Wait for the order
7
Have food
8
Interact with the food server or restaurant manager
9
Ask for the payment
10
Leave the restaurant
11
Leave feedback
12
Return

- First, guests become aware of your restaurant (they review your marketing posts, messages, websites, banners, press releases, and all other marketing vehicles).
- Research (They review your online presence: pictures, information, hours of operation, guest reviews).
- Arrive at your restaurant (examine your arrival experience, parking, and welcoming process).
- Read the menu (menu design, readability, variety, pricing, menu item descriptions, clarity).
- Order food (food server knowledge, uniform, attitude).
- Wait for the order.
- Have food.
- Interact with the food server or restaurant manager.
- Ask for the payment.
- Leave the restaurant.
- Leave feedback (not always).
- Return.

Identify the gaps, the weaknesses, and areas of improvement from the exercise above. At one company that I worked for, 80 percent of the 445 restaurants had old photos, complex table-booking steps, missing or wrong operating hours, and lots of negative reviews without any response. We were able to improve our online presence and provide better images and accurate information.

Menu Design

When I graduated from hotel management college, I chose menu design as my graduation project because I believe that the menu decides everything: your restaurant's theme, image, equipment selection, pricing, positioning, restaurant design—the list goes on. It is the profit maker of the operation. **The menu is your number one marketing strategy**. It places your restaurant's image in the market and stimulates your customers.

The menu is your number one marketing strategy.

Regardless of whether the menu is printed or digital, keep these design tips in mind:

- **Tell a story**: A short story about your restaurant and its unique methods of food preparation will help you to stand out from the competition. Graphics, typefaces, and materials must also fit with your restaurant's theme.
- **The sweet spot (also known as prime real estate):** There are numerous conflicting studies on how readers' eyes move when they are reading a menu. The most-reported finding is that for a single-page menu, readers' eyes focus on the upper middle section. For a two-page folded menu, the eyes focus most on the upper right-hand side of page two. For a three-fold menu, the eyes focus most on the middle section of the middle page. Having said that, you can still draw attention to certain dishes—even if they are not placed as mentioned above—by placing them in a box or by using a star, icon, or image.
- **Psychology and friendly manipulation:** eye-movement studies, description, placement, photos, add-ons, stars, boxes, and mouthwatering words are all part of menu design and psychology.

Focal Point of Single-Sheet Menu

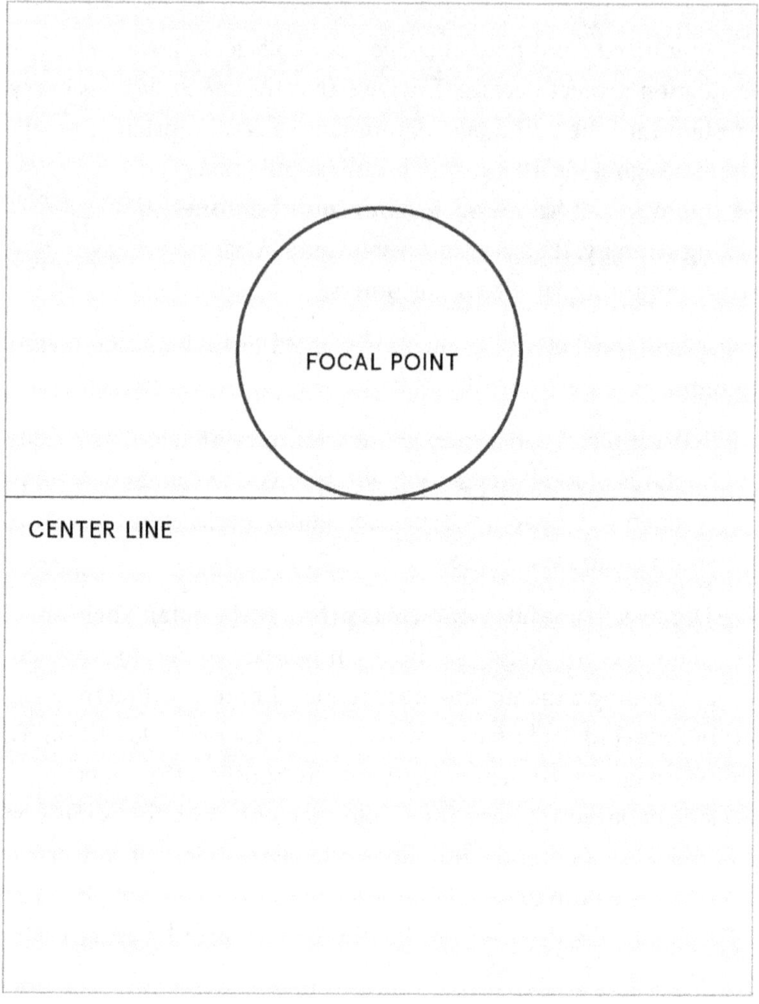

Focal Point of Single-Fold Menu

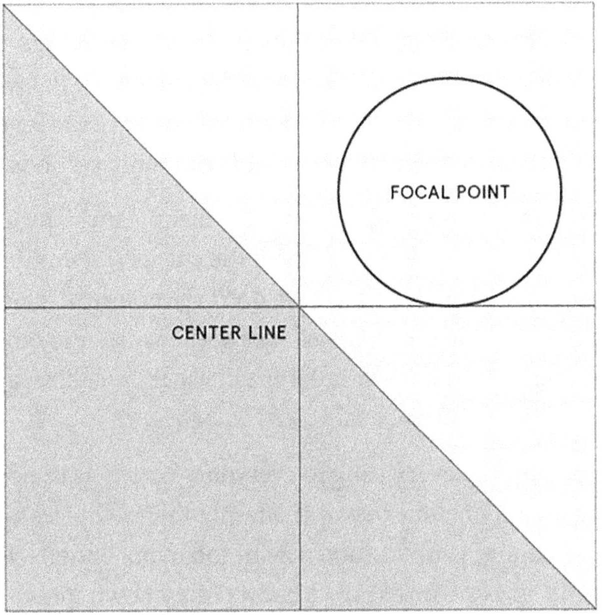

Focal Point of Two-Fold Menu

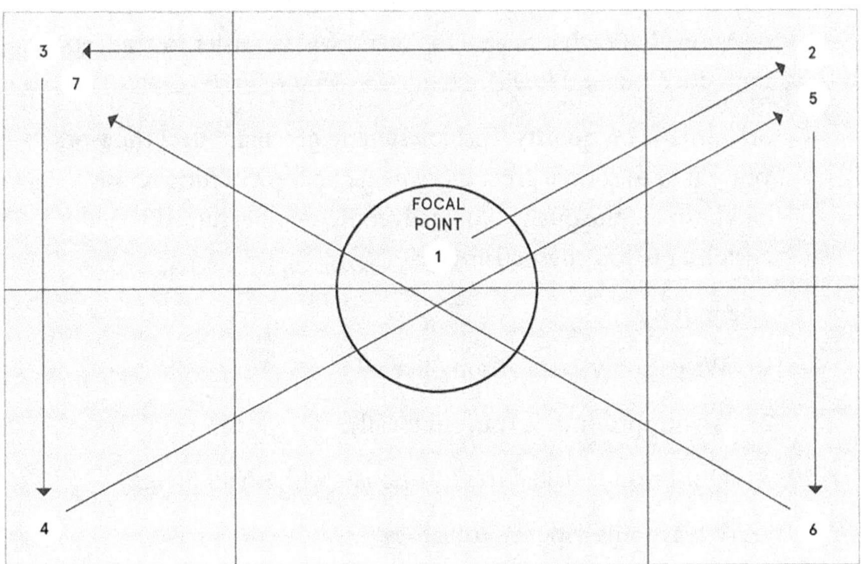

- **Material:** The material you decide to use for your menu must blend in with your brand positioning. Leather folders go well with high-end restaurants. Some other restaurants use tablets, laminated paper, or a digital menu with QR codes at the table. I am in favor of printed menus, as they are user friendly and guests have the tendency to order more with printed menus and read more sections.
- **Menu item sequencing**: The way the menu item sequencing appears on your menu shouldn't start with the cheapest items. For example, under the heading for Breakfast, don't show several single croissants with different flavors, followed by eggs benedict and omelets. Cost-conscious customers will order the cheaper croissants, a missed opportunity to increase sales.
- **Focus**: Don't be everything to everyone. Variety is important, but there is a fine line between offering varied choices and overwhelming your customers with too many options. If you cross that line, guests won't know what you are known for.
- **Include subcategories**: For example, instead of listing everything under Breakfast, break it down into omelets, sandwiches, and specialty breakfast dishes. This will help your guests come to a decision about what to eat. The menu will be easier to read, appear more focused, and it will actually show more variety.
- **Statements on quality**: Include statements that reflect the work you put in to source great ingredients or cook in unique ways, emphasizing the quality you deliver. Remember: an educated customer is your best customer!

  Examples:

  1. We use only extra virgin olive oil.
  2. All our produce is sourced locally.
  3. Our bread is baked fresh in-house, with no additives.
  4. We use vine-ripened tomatoes.
  5. Our coffee is made with single-origin beans.

6. We only use Angus beef.
7. All our burger patties are made to order.

- **Well-written food descriptions**: Descriptions of menu items must generate both interest and sales. Readability and ensuring the menu flows naturally and smoothly are key in making the menu more reader friendly. Mouthwatering words that excite readers are one way to make it appealing without wordy descriptions and too many graphics. You may also consider the opposite approach by stripping down descriptions to help build your guests' imagination; the only possible drawback to the latter is any gap between guest expectations and what they end up receiving, which causes disappointment.
- **Add-ons statement**: In order to increase check average, consider placing an add-ons statement in the menu. Example:

 The Original Burger: Our burger patties are made with 100% pure beef, grilled to your liking, and served with iceberg lettuce, locally sourced vine-ripened tomatoes, and a fresh homemade bun.

 Add cheddar cheese $1
 Add grilled bacon $1

In the above example, even if food servers forget to upsell, the menu will do the job for you.

Another example:

 Southwestern Salad: Mix of greens with corn relish, beans, cilantro, bell pepper, red onion, and chopped tomatoes tossed in our homemade dressing $16

 Make it even better and top it off with a scoop of guacamole $2

Don't use the above method (shown in italics) with all your menu items, only your highest-selling items. If you add it everywhere on the menu, it will look busy and overcrowded.

- **Blending price with description:** There are many articles and consultants who are currently recommending blending the price with food description (see the Southwestern Salad example on the previous page). When I've tried this in the past, our restaurants received several complaints about lack of clarity. Because of this, I personally don't recommend it. Ideally, you want your customers to choose what they are going to eat according to what sounds and looks good, not according to price. You can do the above by showing the pricing and dollar signs clearly.

Also, make sure that all your statements (allergies, sourcing, etc.) are accurate.

My best advice is to use a hybrid model: provide a QR code menu but also offer printed menus, as some customers seem to read more of the menu, and it's a better experience versus a smartphone with a small screen. In my career, I used printed/physical menus, but I made sure they were designed in a way that if I needed to delete an item or increase price, I was able to do so by removing one page and not changing the entire menu. I have recently started seeing physical menus coming back to restaurants.

Printed or digital, your menu makes the strongest impression on your guests, helping establish the personality of a restaurant. Guests may skip menu items if they are price-conscious and looking for lower-priced dishes. This happens when the menu is designed like a list from highest to lowest, which is not the best approach from a sales standpoint (you can mix pricing throughout the menu). Using photos, shades, boxes, or graphic design can help draw the attention of your guests to certain items that you want to sell more.

White space is necessary—don't cram everything in and make it look busy. Graphics, typeface, and font must complement the restaurant's look, feel, and market positioning.

Digital Menu Boards

Digital menu boards are typically used for behind-the-counter, wall-mounted menus. They are useful for updating pricing, placement, short videos, images, and menu items quickly and easily. It positions your brand better, especially for millennials and Gen Z. Plus, they are pleasant to read. Here are some tips for setting up an effective digital menu board.

First off, focus on readability. *Put clarity ahead of art and design.* Use easy-to-read fonts. **Keep it simple. Don't overwhelm people with a lot of text, animations, and graphics.** Use colors and fonts that are high contrast.

Keep in mind that too many menu choices can lead to no choices at all.

Loyalty Programs and Apps

A good customer loyalty program tracks the spending of repeat customers and then rewards that loyalty with points that can be exchanged for rewards.

Reward loyalty on each visit. Keep the program simple and make sure it is easy to sign up for with only a few questions. Establish both digital and mobile strategies for your restaurant loyalty program and drive enrollment while guests are dining with you with initiatives such as offering 10 percent off the bill for any customer who signs up.

Consider a tiered restaurant loyalty program with different rewards for each tier.

Reward ideas:

- Free menu item once customer reaches X number of points.
- Welcome drink or complimentary dessert.
- Free valet parking.
- Preferred seating.
- Chef's table (a table is reserved for the guests of the chef. The chef cooks a special curated menu for those guests).
- Celebrate your customers' special days.
- Invite-only events, live music, concerts, and theme nights.

Sales/Revenue Generation Tactics

In this section I will focus on revenue-generation tools, ideas, and tactics to maximize sales.

I will offer my perspective on discounting and briefly highlight different and nontraditional revenue streams that might be beneficial to your restaurant.

Add-Ons and Upselling

Upselling is the main job of your food servers. They should do it every day without you offering them an incentive to do so. However, the main goal of upselling should be to maximize your **customers' enjoyment of their meals**, and the secondary goal is to increase sales. Suggesting shrimp as an add-on to a burger is not the best way to make the meal better. Suggesting a slice of cheese, bacon, or mushrooms is more likely to elevate a burger, thus increasing enjoyment.

As mentioned in Superior Service and Hospitality (Chapter Two), restaurant managers often make the mistake of pushing food servers to upsell in a way that leads guests to *pay far more than they expected* in terms of check average. Though a higher check average seems good in theory, if customers are dissatisfied with the price, your restaurant will end up trading short-term gains for long-term customer losses. Once again, upselling should be about making the guest's experience better, which will keep them coming back for more. In other words, it's about suggestions that make the meal taste even better while increasing the check average.

One way to make upselling an exciting task for your team is by creating a league table and posting it on the staff notice board, as you know no one wants to be at the bottom of the list. Here is an example showing how many adds-on were sold per food server:

Server's Name	Sun	Mon	Tue	Wed	Thu	Fri	Sat	Total
John	6	5	3	7	6	4	OFF	**31**
Mike	3	4	3	2	OFF	2	5	**19**
Rita	8	10	6	OFF	9	10	7	**50**
Joan	4	3	OFF	0	4	2	3	**16**

Key notes from the table above:

1. You will notice that the check average in your restaurant is improving.
2. You can pinpoint and retrain food servers who are not excelling at upselling.
3. Sometimes food servers over-upsell and upset their guests, as they become pushy in order for them to lead with upselling. Table visits and supervision are key (I have encountered this issue at one of the restaurants that I managed).
4. My advice is to use this tool on and off or on an as-needed basis.

Pop-up Events

One way to drive revenue and create interest and curiosity in the market is with pop-up events and four-hands dinners (two chefs develop a one-time menu jointly; they work closely to create a special menu and express their skills and innovation).

Pop-ups are growing in popularity and proving to be very successful, but as I mentioned before, marketing these events needs to take place at least three weeks before the kickoff date, and you should consider possibly partnering with a great PR company.

The events can last for a few hours or a few days, and they can take place in nontraditional locations—or perhaps in the form of one whole restaurant pop-up opening for a few hours in a new area or two chefs creating a pop-up at an existing restaurant.

Pop-ups are great for testing whether new dishes will be very successful or not. Since the events are based on a limited time period, they create interest and encourage customers to act faster. Pop-ups have limited—not full-fledged—menus. If you hold a pop-up at your existing restaurant, let your patrons know that only a few dishes from your current menu will be served. In some cases, none of your current dishes will be served. One particular thing I appreciate about pop-ups is the excitement it creates for the kitchen teams—it really helps them learn new techniques and ideas. It's also amazing for their career and skill development.

Succeeding with the Lunch Period

The lunch period is an important revenue generator for many restaurant concepts. In this section, I will lay out several ways to improve lunch service that will make your restaurant successful.

Lunch guests are often pressed for time and on a limited budget, so convenience and pricing are important.

Customers who frequent restaurants for lunch have different wants and needs than dinner or breakfast guests. They are often pressed for time and on a limited budget, so convenience and pricing are important. Because of this, making sure that parking is available and investing in delivery, curbside pickup, and grab-and-go options can help drive topline sales/lunchtime traffic.

But before you make a lunch menu, consider whether it is the right step for your restaurant. Do you have the right trade area/neighborhood to start a lunch business? Would it be better to close the restaurant during lunch and operate only during dinner? Whether it's because of your location or your market position, if few people come to your restaurant for lunch, you may save more money by skipping lunch service and opening later.

If you decide to start a lunch offering, consider these notes:

Research First: Go to the busiest lunch restaurants in your area that are comparable to your brand. Understand why customers prefer them. What are their most popular dishes? What is their price point? What type of food do they sell? Go deep and wide with visiting nearby businesses to understand who lives in the area, who the potential customers are, and what your competition will be.

Wants and Needs: Meet your guests needs when it comes to speed of service, price, type of food, and convenience. Know your service ticket time (duration from ordering to serving the food) and stick to it. (See Chapter Two: Superior Service and Hospitality/Pace of Service.) Many lunch customers prefer to order ahead of time due to time constraints, so make that option available via online ordering or WhatsApp.

Service and Hospitality: Recognize regulars, know them by name, and remember their order modifications. If the same customers are coming to your restaurant for lunch several times a week, building a relationship will help turn them into committed regulars.

Variety and Lunch-Friendly Food: Rotating menu items will help keep your menu fresh and exciting for lunch customers who return frequently. Consider offering some items only on certain days of the week and try to have a daily special. Otherwise, repeat visitors may get bored by your menu and move on to a different restaurant for lunch. Similarly, consider offering shared meals for larger groups. Here are more examples of options for lunch offering:

- Bento Japanese-style boxes with several components, reasonable price point, and variety. State calories, and avoid too many modifiers on the menu.
- Provide hot prepared lunch and home cooking—not just sandwiches.
- Offer light lunches so workers will feel energized and avoid facing an energy slump later in the day. *You want people to equate eating at your restaurant to finding a wholesome energy boost that will help them through their busy afternoon.*
- Add flavor and spice it up slightly. Asian food and Asian fusion are very popular lunch options. Don't be afraid to serve slightly spicy lunch offers.

- Soup and half-sandwich combos or soup-and-salad combos are popular with lunch crowds because they tend to be inexpensive and healthy.
- Provide entrée salads and "small" portions of desserts (the dessert can be packaged to go). Lunch guests opt for ordering dessert as long as it's in a small portion and not too heavy.
- Supply superfoods, like salads.
- Include rich smoothies.

Offer Desserts: Many people talk about wanting chocolate or a sugary product right after lunch. Give it to them. Here is the science: Sugar cravings that strike after a meal may be due to serotonin, a feel-good brain chemical that is associated with an elevated mood. Eating a sugary dessert causes serotonin levels to rise in the brain, which can make you feel calmer and happier. Keep portion sizes small, otherwise customers avoid ordering dessert at lunchtime.

The Need for Speed: Consider self-checkout. Avoid making customers wait too long for the check, as this is a common complaint among restaurant goers. Offer fresh salads that are packaged to go for the diners who just want to pick up. Once guests place their order, keep the guest informed of cooking time. For example, your steak will take ten more minutes.

Encourage regular guests to pre-order before they leave their offices to come to your restaurant. And for prebooking/dine-in guests, know the exact time of guests' arrivals.

Create a menu with food items that can be ready in five to seven minutes. Don't make the menu complex. Don't make it a Michelin star–type menu. (unless you operate a Michelin star restaurant). Offer quick, convenient meals. In one of the restaurants that I oversaw, the team would bring an hourglass to each table with a limit of twenty minutes. If the sand in the hourglass ran out, the table's food was free. By doing this, they wanted to show customers that their time was important to them.

Create a menu with food items that can be ready in five to seven minutes.

If customers are having a business lunch meeting, give them space. Don't interrupt them with too many questions.

The lunch crowd is more demanding than the dinner crowd; they have a limited amount of time to spend at your restaurant and are, in general, more stressed out. Your customer service cannot be lacking. Train your staff to be ready for the lunch rush hour. Friendly and speedy service will win over loyal lunch-crowd customers.

Avoid a complex ordering procedure. If customers take too long to order, your table turnover will slow down. Let them customize their orders, but not too much with too many options, as customization slows the ordering and ticket time.

For business meetings for four or more, consider offering prefixed, preset menus where the price is known. These will be easier to order and easier to execute.

Profit and Cost: Know your cost after adding in packaging/delivery fees for takeout orders and delivery.

Branding: Use eco-friendly containers and locally sourced food with minimal additives and zero hormones. Highlight this accomplishment on your menu so that customers are aware.

Marketing: Market the heck out of it. For example:

- Go to businesses and offer free lunch as a form of shock advertising. Build your database; offer bounce-back cards. Plenty of restaurants fail because they do not market their new changes. How can you expect customers to know about your new prefixed lunch menu if you don't tell them? Create a lunch loyalty program that is based on earning rewards on every dollar spent, not discount-based. If you have no parking or easy access, opt for delivery. Market around the problem.

Branding: I like the term Express Lunch.

If you have lunch specials, food servers must inform every table of what they are.

If they aren't coming to you, you should go to them.

Aim for creating one hundred superfans. You should know them by name, and they should know you. You should know their orders and preferences.

Offer sampling, but don't do it on the cheap. Send them samples of your best food. For example, your best pizza, pie, or cake.

Offer group specials.

Offer staggered portion sizes, like small, medium, and large.

Don't let lunch customers break the bank. Habit and affordability are the key to a successful lunch business.

Meet customers where they are. *If they aren't coming to you, you should go to them*. Consider delivery on foot that is done by your team.

Offer free Wi-Fi.

Choose your target audience: office employees, hospitals, banks, call centers, etc.

Have a goal to visit three businesses every day.

Remember you will serve different customers: working from home, working in-office, online ordering, groups, business meetings, and pickup.

How Do I Measure My Success?

Measure the number of customers one month after launching your business lunch offerings. Count how many repeat customers you see. If your goal is to increase check average, check if it has increased after two weeks. See how your guest satisfaction scores are trending.

Understand how your food waste increases or decreases as you implement these changes.

Succeeding with the Breakfast Meal Period

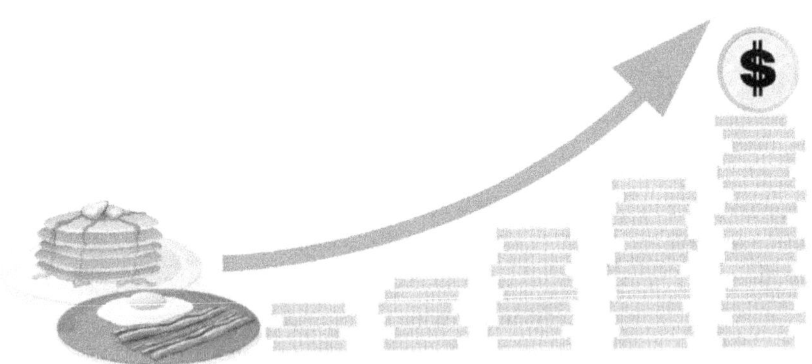

Offering breakfast has many benefits; it definitely increases the overall awareness of your restaurant, traffic, and sales. At one of the brands that I led, breakfast was extremely busy, so we took advantage of such exposure to promote lunch and dinner offerings. We made sure that our breakfast menu was combined with our lunch and dinner in order to educate customers on the other meal periods (we intentionally placed the breakfast dishes at the end of the menu) and supported that with table tents that promoted lunch and dinner dishes.

Demand is increasing for convenient breakfast, so be sure to include several quick breakfast options. But all-day breakfast can be risky depending on your restaurant concept. While it sounds appealing, it runs the risk of cannibalizing sales from lunch and dinner if the prices and margins are low.

Here are some tips and thoughts:

- Differentiation and culinary innovation are important. You can be creative with egg dishes and sides; don't just copy exactly what other restaurants are serving.
- You must have a great coffee program to support a great breakfast program.
- Coffee and eggs have huge profit margins.
- Cater your offerings according to guests' needs:
- Add ethnic dishes like shakshuka.

One of the fundamental rules of breakfast service, is that great coffee is the cornerstone of an outstanding breakfast.

Weekday breakfast guests' needs are: fast meal, affordable, healthy, and filling.

Weekend breakfast guests' needs: Many guests opt for brunch or menus with a large breakfast variety. They appreciate the coffee variety; be playful. One very popular breakfast restaurant in Vancouver, Canada, had lavender-flavored cappuccino and people loved it!

Weekend customers don't want a rushed atmosphere.

Lastly, remember to be creative and offer Instagram-able dishes, as guests on weekends use social media far more than weekdays.

Seven-Day Business Activation and Dinner Revenue

As you know, **the most expensive thing in a restaurant is an empty seat.** You're paying rent, water and electric bills, food cost, and labor cost for every minute the restaurant is operational. Your expenses are always accruing, so you want to counter this by optimizing your revenue generation. Sales per square foot can be a good indicator of how you optimized your revenue.

Analyze each day of the week and create more reasons for people to visit your restaurant. If Tuesdays tend to be slow, consider offering special menu items that are only available on Tuesdays. The food offered **must be so good,** so unique, that it will make people want to come to your restaurant, even on Tuesdays. This requires a serious look at your menu development.

Another way to drive revenue on Tuesday evening is through value offers (see ribeye example below). Or consider a promotion like Taco Tuesday. Perhaps the regular price for tacos is $9, but on Tuesday it's only $3.99. Just make sure you have at least 5 percent profit per taco sold on Tuesday.

Consider this weeklong schedule for Jerry's Steakhouse:

Monday: No offers—staff break day.

Tuesday: Let's say the most popular dish on the menu is the ribeye. The regular menu price for ribeye is $65, but on Tuesday the price drops to $49. This way you attract people on Tuesday, when the restaurant is normally only one-third full. Everything else on the menu remains at normal price. Customers will come with their friends or families, and you will make your sales from add-ons, drinks, appetizers, and all other menu items that are not discounted. As you can see, lowering the price of one dish only once a week can help generate revenue on a day when business is typically slow.

Wednesdays: Beef Wellington (unique and craveable dish that's only available on Wednesdays).

Thursday: Live entertainment.

Friday: No offers. You don't want to discount your menu on Friday when people go out to dinner anyway. This will cannibalize your sales. *(If Friday nights or Saturday lunches are not busy at your restaurant, it's an indication of having serious problems and lack of consumer trust/affinity; you need to do deep analysis. It could be your food, service, pricing, convenience, and the list goes on.)*

Saturday: Offer a special brunch menu or consider pop-up events where you collaborate with chefs from other restaurants. (*I created a program called chef exchange for a large company with more than 700 restaurants in 28 countries. For example, I would send a chef from India to Dubai for a three-day Indian night, which made it very authentic. I sent a Lebanese chef to Muscat, Oman, to start a Lebanese night and train the team. Everyone loved it. The chef did something new in a new country, the team learned from the new chef, and our guests got to experience authentic food by great chefs. Everyone won!*)

Sunday: Offer another special menu or homestyle cooked food.

Create an organized schedule for your restaurant:

Day of the Week	Activation
Monday	No offers, regular menu (most staff members take off days).
Tuesday	Ribeye Tuesday.
Wednesday	Beef Wellington (unique and craveable dish that's only available on Wednesdays).
Thursday	Live entertainment.
Friday	(No offers.)
Saturday	Saturday brunch or pop-up event.
Sunday	Sunday lunch: homestyle cooked food. In the afternoon, offer unique desserts and creative coffee and tea offerings.

Non-Traditional Revenue Streams:

A variety of revenue streams will help you drive revenue. I could write an entire book on each of these, but for now, a simple list:

- Delivery
- Takeout
- Business catering (schools, banks, hospitals)
- Social catering (weddings, birthdays, etc.)
- Ghost/dark/virtual kitchens

A Note on Restaurant Concepts and Partnering with Celebrity Chefs

In the hotel industry there is a belief that success or failure will boil down to the type of concept you have: its design, menu offering, theme, and all other aspects. It is typically design-led. We often see hotels changing their restaurant concepts with the hope of driving better revenue or improving image.

But, most of the time, the problem lies not in the concept or its design but in the way it has been operated and managed. I often say a great restaurant concept without operational excellence equals a total waste of money.

> A great restaurant concept without operational excellence equals a total waste of money.

I would like to offer some advice on this matter: changing your concept is costly. Think about your return on investment and payback period.

If you have reached a conclusion that your restaurant concept needs to change, make sure you do in-depth research to know what your trading area needs, what will fit with your hotel positioning, what kind of caliber your head chef needs to be, and whether you can afford it.

You are basically opening a new restaurant from scratch. Don't be passive when dealing with your project consultant—understand what they want to do, the budget, the menu, the kitchen layout, equipment specifications, and the list goes on.

I have seen disasters when it comes to back-of-the-house kitchen layout. I have seen a four-hundred-seat restaurant with a small, twenty-four-inch flat grill. I have entered dry storerooms with plates, smallware, and decorative items that have enough for six more years than the consultant asked the hotel to buy. I have seen all-day dining with two Chinese duck ovens (Peking duck ovens) where there are no Chinese customers, and a super-expensive ice cream machine that was never used!

In general, consultants seem to do a great job with the front-of-the-house design look and feel and an average or even poor job with kitchen layout. The problem with the hotel industry is that orders for buying equipment are placed before even the chef or director of F&B are hired. Instead, these orders are approved by the hotel's GM, who might not have an F&B background.

Partnering with Celebrity Chefs

Some hotels or restaurateurs partner with celebrity chefs to launch a new concept; my advice is as follows: as long as your agreement/commercial contract with celebrity chefs is financially viable and built on a win-win understanding, then you are good to move forward. But here is what happens most of the time: celebrity chefs ask for a sign-up fee, which is high, and they also ask for a percentage of your topline sales and bottom line and business-class flights whenever they visit your restaurant. Some ask for payment for every day they spend at your restaurant, and they mandate that you airship certain ingredients, which makes your food cost skyrocket. They also keep control of the restaurant management as they bring their own restaurant manager and outlet chef, who are typically highly paid. I know for a fact that two of the best chefs in the world shut down their restaurants in five-star hotels due to high costs and because there were no sales except for the initial stage.

If you manage to negotiate a win-win deal, then go ahead and partner with a celebrity chef. I have seen such partnerships work well for hotels and increase their room rates and improve their overall image in the market.

A Thought on Discounting

If your restaurant is struggling, resist the temptation to start pulling every trick out of the book in a desperate attempt: fifty percent discount, free wine on Mondays, family dinner deals on Sundays, or coupons. They all seem like good ideas, but the truth is that **marketing is much more effective than discounting.**

Your customers can sense desperation and will avoid it like the plague. Special events and thoughtful extras can add some pizzazz to your place, but they can't rescue a sinking ship.

You can't build loyalty in the restaurant business with discount-based marketing. Discount-driven customers are fickle. The only true route to building loyalty is by delivering incredible, memorable experiences. When people finish their meal, they only remember how tasty it was and how welcoming your team was—not the discount or points they received.

> Discount-driven customers are fickle.

Having said that, QSR and fast-casual brands use discounts and deals to drive sales extensively and are not perceived as "desperate." Discounting may work for certain categories of the industry, but not all.

In Conclusion

In this chapter I've shared many marketing ideas and tactics. Pick the tactics that will create the most value for your business, because your time and budget are both limited.

Watch your expenses and ROI on signing up with third parties such as loyalty apps, marketing apps, and magazines. Don't overspend and overcommit. Avoid loading your Profit and Loss Statement (P&L) with unnecessary marketing expenses. Be careful with deceptive marketers: salesmen who walk in the door and offer another app or another bank discount with fake data and estimates.

I really love what Mike Ferretti said in my interview with him (Chapter Ten): "Stop-and-start advertising is close to a waste of money. To achieve regular and compounded growth requires consistent and steady advertising."

Develop and use a marketing calendar and content strategy. A well-planned annual marketing calendar puts you in control and gives you ample time to plan. The one I developed shows twelve months and states each important event, public holiday, and sporting event, such as the Super Bowl, Valentine's Day, Fourth of July—and the list goes on. We capitalized on all events, including the International Day of Coffee! The worst thing in marketing is to kick off your activities only one week before the promotion or event. Last-minute marketing is ineffective and results in a waste of money. With a marketing calendar, we can start marketing at least two to three weeks, even months, before the event. We can also budget and plan all our spending and choose the right holiday/public event to take full advantage of it.

Lastly, be strategic and think long-term. Use marketing to build a great, long-lasting brand!

Evaluate Your Marketing

Question	Comments
1. Are your operations, food, and services in the best condition before you start marketing your restaurant?	
2. Do you grow your database every day?	
3. Do you have a loyalty program that is attractive to your guests?	
4. Do you measure your team's upselling and add-on efforts?	
5. Do you engage with customers on social media? Remember: engage before you sell. Do you boost your posts on Instagram?	
6. Do you take advantage of guest touchpoints to market your restaurant?	
7. Do you use direct mail, bounce-back cards, or telephone marketing?	
8. Do you have an outstanding online reputation, photography, and food photos? Do you review guest comments and respond on a daily basis?	
9. Do you have a guest-relations program in place?	
10. Is your menu designed efficiently?	
11. Do you activate your space and sales per square meter seven days a week? Do you create events and promotions to drive sales during slow days?	

CHAPTER SIX
COST DISCIPLINE

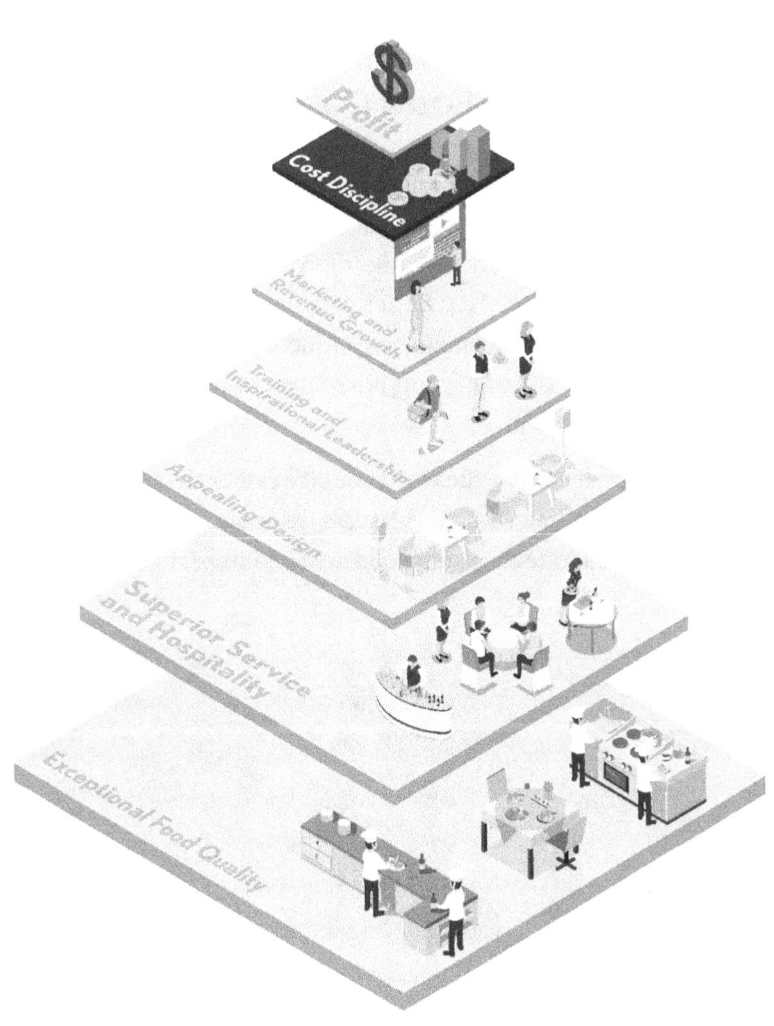

I am a quality- and sales-driven professional. However, I also pay close attention to cost management. Because of this, I often find massive savings opportunities without negatively impacting guest experience or food quality.

Too many restaurant owners don't realize that a restaurant is more than a fun place that serves food and provides hospitality. It's a business with commercial needs, and if not treated as such, it is doomed to fail.

What follows are some key ways to save, streamline, and manage or reduce your costs.

Food Cost

The following actions will help in managing your food cost; indirectly reduce your labor, waste, and energy costs (electricity, natural gas); and improve your profitability and cash flow while delivering better food quality due to simplifying your menu. Yes. Better food and better guest experience. My approach to cost management is unique. Ninety percent of the cost-management programs I see end up hurting food quality or service levels. My approach improves both.

In general, I prefer to use the word manage rather than reduce your food cost. If food cost is in line with your budget, recipe costs, and product/menu mix, there is no need to reduce your food cost and impact quality negatively.

Food and labor are the largest controllable areas of any restaurant, and that's where most restaurant owners must focus. Rent is another high expense, but it's only a percentage of sales, so you can counter that by driving revenue. Let's begin.

Cross-Utilize Your Ingredients

This means using the same ingredients in multiple dishes. For example, offering shrimp in a pasta, a salad, and as an add-on to grilled steak. Please note that the shrimp must have the same prep procedures for all three dishes.

When you make sure your most expensive or perishable ingredients are cross-utilized, you will reap many benefits:

1. Lower labor cost: as seen in the above example, shrimp has the same prep steps/procedures for all three dishes.
2. Smoother kitchen operation: same procedures for the same ingredients (shrimp) for three different dishes.
3. Less spoilage of products: shrimp will have higher turnover.

I cannot emphasize enough the importance of implementing cross-utilization for smoother kitchen operation, lower costs, and increased profits.

Make sure your ten most expensive, sensitive, or highly perishable ingredients are cross-utilized, but be careful not to overdo it. Be aware that going too far with cross-utilization can result in overly similar dishes and a boring menu.

Reduce Your Single-Use, Single-Prep Ingredients

Single-use, single-prep ingredient examples include spinach that you buy and prepare only for a spinach pizza, or fresh blueberries as a garnish for crème brûlée. The problem with these ingredients is that they require labor hours, increase the number of steps in preparing and finishing dishes, use up storage space, and often expire and go to waste. You will still need to have some single-use ingredients to keep your menu exciting and unique. My advice is to make sure single-prep, single-use ingredients do not exceed five to ten percent of your total purchasing list. Here is a good exercise that will help you determine how many single-use ingredients you currently have.

Take your purchasing list and analyze it as follows:

Ingredient	Used in Dishes	Action	Comment
Shrimp	Shrimp Pasta Surf and Turf Shrimp Salad	Keep shrimp.	Shrimp is cross-utilized well, as it's used in three dishes.
Blueberries, fresh	Crème Brûlée	Remove or cross-utilize blueberries.	Crème brûlée sales are less than 0.5 percent of your menu and only 1 percent of the desserts category. Alternatively, use blueberries in other desserts/dishes.
Swiss cheese, sliced	Burger topping	Remove Swiss cheese.	Sold only four burgers in one month with Swiss cheese.

Notice that Swiss cheese wasn't selling, but you were purchasing and stocking Swiss cheese instead of cheddar cheese, which is selling well. By doing the exercise above you will eliminate many unnecessary ingredients and improve your cash flow while reducing waste and menu complexity.

Complete the above exercise for *all* your items in inventory. Knowing what ingredients are purchased and prepared for only one dish, and evaluating whether their direct and indirect costs are worth it, is essential for running a successful restaurant.

Revise Total Number of Dishes

Unless you operate an ethnic restaurant, the ideal number of menu items should be between twenty-five and thirty-five dishes (side items included). A menu with the correct number of dishes (core items, smaller menu) will result in better consistency, better quality, and fewer errors.

Remember the old adage: less is more. Focus on quality, taste, and serving excellent food. There are many successful restaurants with only ten to twelve menu items, such as Chipotle, Five Guys Burgers, and Shake Shack from the QSR/fast-casual sectors. On the other end of the spectrum, I worked with a Michelin-starred chef who operated high-volume restaurants with only twenty-eight dishes and generated millions of dollars.

Remember the old adage: less is more. Focus on quality, taste, and serving excellent food.

Reducing your total number of dishes means:

1. More focus on quality and taste (greater ability to execute the menu flawlessly).
2. Lower labor cost.
3. Simpler training.
4. Fewer ingredients expiring.
5. Better profitability and cash flow (less inventory stacked up on shelves).
6. Clear restaurant positioning.

Conduct Menu Engineering

Menu engineering must take place every three months, not every six months. If you do it every six months, you have waited 180 days to remove menu items that are going to waste every day.

Remove non-moving items. Analyze your product mix from the last three months and historical sales data for each category. If you have four desserts, find out which one is the lowest selling in the dessert category and make a decision accordingly. Slightly increase the prices of the highest-selling items. For an item that sells well and is priced at $24, you can increase the price to $25. (Price increases can take place twice a year or depending on inflation.)

Such an increase will further reduce your food cost and improve your margins. A $1 increase will not make your customers upset. Please remember that price turns into value at the end of the dining experience.

Price turns into value at the end of the dining experience.

Restaurant consultants and managers often advise restaurant owners to sell food with high profit percentage. In their opinion that will mean lower food cost and higher profit, which is half-accurate advice. Let me explain.

If you sell a slice of cheese on a burger as an add-on for $1, and your cost is 10 cents, your profit percentage is 90 percent and your contribution margin (dollar profit) is 90 cents.

If you sell a steak for $60, and your cost is $30, your profit percentage is 50 percent and your contribution margin (dollar profit) is $30.

Based on the misguided advice of the restaurant consultant, it looks like it's better that you sell more add-on cheese, as it gives you 90 percent profit. But **remember that you don't take percentages to the bank**—you take dollars to the bank.

I will surely sell more steaks, as I get more profits in dollars and, yes, less percentage.

Now make sure your menu is balanced and doesn't have many dishes with a high price but a low-contribution margin.

Another common mistake in product mix analysis is how we look at percentages. For example, if you are looking at the sales of brownie cakes, don't take into account the complete menu and say it's only 1 percent of the entire menu. You need to look at the brownie sales from the desserts category, such as brownie cake is 30 percent of the *desserts category*, not the entire menu.

Garnishes and Food Decoration: Do Not Exceed Three per Dish

One of the most common problems in the culinary world is when chefs overdecorate dishes. Here are the implications:

- It slows down your kitchen.
- Dishes look less elegant when they are overdecorated.
- It costs you more money.
- It impacts consistency.
- It impacts food temperature: the longer you take to decorate a dish, the colder it becomes.
- More steps = more labor cost.
- More garnishes = more purchasing = more spoilage.

My experience of working with celebrity and successful chefs taught me that they add a maximum of two to three garnishes per dish, which makes their food elegant.

Use Prep Leftovers and Trimmings

Most dishes involve some level of trim and byproduct from meat, produce, and other items. For example, potato and sweet potato skins, garlic clove trimmings and skins, tomato trims, mushroom trims, onion skins, carrot tops, chicken bones, and celery leaves, bottoms, and tops can be saved to make an incredible broth or stock. Some chefs use leftover bread for bread pudding or pico de gallo for salsa, and the internet is full of recipes for leftover food and/or ingredients. Determine ways to use prep leftovers or trimmings to either create new dishes or be put to use in existing dishes. One tactic I used is to run a contest among chefs to come up with recipes for leftovers and reward them accordingly. It was a fun and useful exercise.

Use Waste Sheets *Every Day*

Waste sheets must be in place. The restaurant manager should **ask daily** about the highest wasted items from the day before. If you don't track or measure it, you won't know what or where the waste or the increase in cost is coming from. Also, **discuss it daily** during the pre-shift briefing in order to keep this topic top of mind.

Food Waste Log

MONTH: ____________

Date	Time	Food Product	Amount Disposed of	Cost	Reason for Waste

Reduce Your Market List/Purchasing List and Manage Your Inventory

If your restaurant purchases 350 ingredients, challenge your team to reduce them by 20 percent. You can use the single prep/use method, removing non-selling or high expiry items. This will directly impact cash flow, storage, and food expiry.

Invest in an inventory-management system/software so you don't overorder; you will see your inventory movement, and you can view an analysis with the click of a button.

The inventory-management system also helps establish PAR levels, so you can forecast your exact stock requirements and ordering based on the consumption trends of your restaurant. As a result, you will reduce any undue wastage due to over-ordering.

Negotiate with Vendors

Renegotiate your current contracts with all vendors. For the best approach, add up all purchases from one supplier for the past three to five years as follows. Say to your vendor, "We bought $750,000 worth of NY steaks from you during the last three years. We would like to reduce the purchase price." Adding up three years of purchasing makes your argument stronger and shows your value to the vendor.

Review your contracted deals by consistently surveying the market, current price trends, and what is newly introduced. This could include asking new suppliers to send samples for new product testing and evaluation.

Make sure your contracts are sealed with a quick and flexible termination clause.

Sort and Rank Your Purchasing, Market List, or Inventory Sheets from Highest to Lowest in Terms of Cost

For example: You can see the top twenty ingredients that you buy in the sheet on the following page. This will help you focus on which exact items you need to negotiate the pricing and reduce the cost of purchasing or increase your sales price for. Most restaurants will have a sheet with more than one hundred ingredients. Sorting it this way will help you quickly see where you are spending most of your money and where you should focus.

Market List (Purchasing List Sorted from Highest to Lowest in Consumption)				
Item Name	**Cost in Dollars**	**Unit**	**Three Months Consumption Quantity**	**Total Consumption in Dollars**
NY Steak	8	Each	2,250	18,000
Ribeye	5	Each	2,880	14,400
Tomatoes	4	Pound	2,250	9,000
Sliced Bread	3.5	Basket	450	1,575

Reduce Immediate and Sudden Cash Purchases of Ingredients

This happens when you run out of ingredients due to under-ordering and poor forecasting and send a team member to dash to a nearby supermarket or grocery store. When this happens, you pay a high retail price, so it should be avoided as much as possible.

Inform Your Staff About Food Cost Results Every Month

I used to write the monthly food-cost goal on our team's notice board and then talk about it in pre-shift briefings. I would ask the team to share their ideas on reducing cost (but never by way of reducing quality). For example: "Good morning team, last month's food cost was 33.5 percent. For this month we want to achieve 32 percent. Let's talk about ways to reduce it." Listen to their suggestions. The best ideas often come from the team. I always rewarded the team when we achieved the target. (I'll discuss incentive ideas later on in this chapter.)

Sort and Rank Your Purchasing Sheet from Highest to Lowest in Terms of Volume

This action will help you see the thirty to fifty items you buy the most and make decisions depending on profit margins and popularity.

Stop Freebies

Such as free chips and salsa and/or a large bread basket. These reduce your appetizers sales and overall check average. You can use this tactic only if you struggle with appetizers ticket time—i.e., appetizers take a long time to be served—to counter any guest complaint. Please note, once your guests get accustomed to freebies, it will be extremely difficult to take them away without losing guests or making them upset.

Portion Control and Adhering to Recipes

Use scales and pre-portioned ingredients during prep and while building/finishing dishes. This is extremely important. Profit per plate is calculated based on certain portioning and measurement; if your team overportions, you underdeliver on profits. This is critical and requires close supervision, creating a culture of adhering to recipes and conducting daily training during pre-shift. See Training and Inspirational Leadership (Chapter Four) for a more detailed discussion on BOH training and ways to consistently adhere to recipes.

Point of Sale (POS) Use and Abuse (Comp and Void)

This is one area that can negatively affect your food cost. It's crucial to review which items were voided, discounted, or given as complimentary (comp) each day and why. If this task is left unattended, your food cost will increase dramatically. Managers need to have a sign-in sheet in place for voids and discounts to maintain accountability. Using the void option presents a theft opportunity, as managers could pocket the cash sales. It's difficult to control theft by managers because they have total control over POS totals. That's why daily or weekly review of the comp/void report is key.

Unfortunately, we had a situation at one of my previous jobs where a restaurant manager was caught voiding items at the end of the night to pocket cash, in addition to giving away food to his friends and voiding the items. I used to review the void, discount, and comp reports daily to control and reduce overuse. Most POS software has such reports readily available. Still, I also gave my managers a budget and target to give them the option to treat loyal customers, solve guest complaints, or surprise some with complimentary desserts. Managers needed to write a brief explanation for voiding items or for giving complimentary food.

I believe we have to be generous in this industry, and we have to surprise and delight our guests, but this P&L line item should stay under control. As I said before, unfortunately I had situations where I had to fire an employee for abusing the "void" option in the point of sale. They used to void the item and pocket the money after the guest had paid.

Sensitive Items Count

Steaks, lobsters, oysters, and wagyu beef are high-cost items (sensitive items). You especially don't want theft or waste of your sensitive items, as it significantly impacts your cost. Count prepped steaks before and after a shift and compare it to your sales mix for that shift. Investigate variances.

Give only managers the keys to the alcohol supply room. Conduct frequent spot checks and keep counts of alcohol and an inventory logbook on hand. This will also help managers make better decisions when placing alcohol orders. Some restaurants ask their bartenders to bring all empty alcohol bottles to their managers instead of throwing them away. Such control procedures and close supervision can create a culture of accountability and awareness. AM and PM shift managers must communicate the results of the bar spot check during shift handover.

Use Jiggers and Portioning Bar Tools

Free pour can erase profits. Make sure that your staff is measuring each drink. I know some bartenders hate it because it prevents showmanship when pouring drinks, but there are several other ways to showcase creativity and bar flair.

If you use jiggers and proper portioning tools, you'll maintain your high profit margins—and reduce overall costs.

Spot-Check Your Trash

Use clear trash bags and spot-check your trash to spot waste. Your trash tells you a lot about what's going in your restaurant (leftovers, unfinished food, and sometimes you will find forks, knives, and ramekins). For instance, if you see a lot of lettuce, it could mean your prep employee is not trained well enough. Or, if you see a large quantity of french fries, it could mean the staff is overcooking them. Lastly, if you see a large number of half-eaten salmon dishes return from the dining room, it means guests didn't love it and the recipe or ingredients need to be revised. As I said before, **if you want to know what your guests don't like, check your garbage.**

Team Engagement and Contribution

At some of the restaurants I managed, I used to seek suggestions from the team for the four items below *every quarter (I encourage you to try this exercise):*

1. Please share your top three ideas to reduce cost.
2. Please share your top three ideas to drive sales.
3. Please share your top challenges at work.
4. Please share any suggestions about anything you wish to change at our restaurant.

One of our cooks reminded us of the importance of installing curtains in each walk-in cooler and freezer. His idea helped our twenty-three restaurants with:

a. Reducing energy/electricity cost, as curtains keep walk-in coolers and freezers cool without forcing the compressor to work harder when the door is open.

b. Preventing flies and other insects from entering the cooler.

c. Extending the shelf life of food, as it is not exposed to temperature abuse.

This employee won the contest of great ideas. We issued him a check worth $100 and acknowledged him in front of all his teammates. Not only was he motivated to share more ideas in the next quarter but he also always cleaned and checked the curtains. Plus, it inspired and encouraged everyone else on the team to share more ideas. (We started receiving many great ideas and valuable suggestions/feedback.) T**his action turns your employees into partners and drives engagement.**

The best culinary ideas come from the frontline employees. The highest-selling sandwich in the world, the Big Mac at McDonald's, is the perfect example of an employee or franchisee making a dish suggestion to the corporate office that then became a huge success.

The next three points are revenue related, but they are critical for reducing costs. Please remember that food cost is just a percentage of food sales.

You can't manage costs with poor-quality food, low check average, or without targets; let me explain.

Each Dish Is a Star! Food Craveability Is a Must

As mentioned in Exceptional Food Quality and Kitchen Management (Chapter One), when we develop menu items, we should develop them with the following goal: "Each dish will be the best in my city." The dish must be developed with a concise and clear recipe. Kitchen teams must challenge themselves to continually look for better recipes compared to the existing ones. This is about cultivating a mindset; menu development must be part of quality obsession and craveability. You can try recipes from famous chefs or from culinary cookbooks, culinary websites, or even from your team's suggestions. **But no matter how you find recipes, they must result in dishes that become the talk of the town.** The reason I have added this note on food taste is because it will result in higher sales, which also helps your profits.

Higher Check Average Means Lower Food Cost

We always hear restaurant owners talk about upselling. For it to work, keep these three key things in mind:

1. Create competition among your food servers. Display the names of top performers with add-ons and upselling on your communication board. For example, who sold the largest amount of cheese on burgers or mushrooms on steaks yesterday?

   Such competition will fuel your team to upsell. No one wants to be at the bottom of the list.

2. Keep in mind, upselling is about making the meal taste better (as mentioned in Chapter Two: Superior Service and Hospitality). A burger with bacon and cheese tastes better for many people than a plain burger. A taco salad with a scoop of guacamole on top makes it look and taste better. It's not about selling the most expensive items on the menu and losing your guests for good. It's about making suggestions that enhance the experience. A glass of white wine will surely make your fish dish better than suggesting an expensive strong cocktail that might take away from the taste of delicate white fish.

   When a guest asks your food servers about menu suggestions, food servers must not try to sell the most expensive dish. Instead, they should recommend the most popular dish and upsell it with add-ons such as salads, sides, and drinks that go well with the food.

3. Establish an incentive plan to reward employees on their achievements. The core purpose of a smart incentive plan is to be a win-win to all parties. It should drive employees' productivity, creativity, ownership, and upselling.

See Marketing and Revenue (Sales) Growth (Chapter Five) for more information on upselling.

Cost Management and Revenue Tip: Price your menu on what customers are willing to pay, not based on industry food-cost averages. If you do the latter, you could end up underpricing your food.

Set Targets During Pre-Shift Briefing

Give your food servers targets each shift. Follow up during the shift and see the results at the end of the shift. This action will totally change your team's dynamics and will impact your overall sales, which results in a reduction in food cost. For example: today, each food server must try to sell ten add-ons, such as grilled bacon on each burger, or each food server must sell ten NY steaks. Add-ons such as bacon, mushrooms, cheese, and guacamole have low food cost and high margins. I used this method for both counter-service restaurants and full table service, and it worked well. Key note here: you will need to check in and follow up on the targets during the shift; don't wait until the end of the shift, as it will be too late to save the day.

Labor Cost

Here are several tactics for better labor cost/payroll management:

1. When you prepare the team's schedule, **schedule just enough people so that you won't be short-staffed**. This will create a feel of urgency, focus, and seriousness. In operations, most problems happen when restaurants are overstaffed and business is slow. Slacking takes over. I believe in Parkinson's Law: "Work expands so as to fill the time available for its completion." This means that when your staff is given less time for a task, they will work faster and get more work done than they are presently doing. Analyze the first and last fifteen to thirty minutes of each shift. If the staff is easygoing, relaxed, casual, or slow-paced during these times, it may mean that they could get the same amount of work done on their shift with fewer hours on your clock.

2. **Understand the labor cost percentage** formula as a percentage of total sales: Total Labor Cost divided by Total Sales. But labor cost is not just salaries; it also includes vacation, overtime, visa cost (in some countries), benefits, and bonuses. Additionally, look at labor cost compared to the number of guests served rather than total sales, as the latter is influenced by the average check and can be misleading.

   Moreover, I would link the labor to efficiency level by calculating the number of guests served by each server.

3. **Reduce operating hours,** understand your low sales hours, and do the math. If there is no demand and no viable business opportunity, you'd be better off closing earlier or opening later in the morning.

4. **Improve employee training with on-the-job training (OJT).** Refer to Training and Inspirational Leadership (Chapter Four) of this book for an in-depth explanation. To make sure your team is productive and your labor cost is reasonable, conduct refresher training and reinforce good habits, standards, and procedures. Bad habits can always sneak back in. Also, hold regular performance reviews and set the right expectations. Cross-train your team on different stations.

5. **Conduct productivity analysis.** For example, analyze how many times food servers have to leave the dining room to go to back-of-house areas. The most common reasons would be to bring additional sauce (ketchup, ranch, mayo) or to bring extra forks and knives. Reduce or eliminate the reasons for them to leave the dining room. Put enough forks and knives at the server's station. Keep mayo and ketchup at the server station. Another example: Ask two food servers to punch the same menu item into the point of sale (POS) and time both. Make the order a bit complex, like NY steak, rare, add mushrooms, no salt, add steam veggies. This exercise will show you whether some food servers need more training on POS functionality. Reducing the time it takes for food servers to punch orders in reduces the meal period per guest, improves table turnover, and saves labor minutes.

6. **Add prep recipes' recommended time**. For example, time how long it takes to prep mashed potatoes. If it's twenty minutes, add that timing on the recipe. This way, you will be able to calculate your entire prep time required and how many people you need to schedule. Set standards for the team. If the recipe says it takes twenty minutes to dice a box of heads of lettuce, your team knows they don't have forty minutes to finish prep.
7. **Reduce turnover**. Keep your team motivated and engaged. Celebrate their birthdays, organize outings, and create a recognition card that you can post on the team's notice board. These things will all increase employee retention. When your employees stay with you for a long time, you save money on expenses like recruiting and training. Treating your employees well may not seem like a way to save money—unless you take the long-term view and consider your staff an investment in your business.
8. **Keep your kitchen organized:** an organized kitchen means less labor cost and a smoother operation. When your team members have to look for products, that means labor minutes wasted. Organization means a faster process. I encourage you to take a look at Exceptional Food Quality and Kitchen Management (Chapter One) where I explained the importance of "zoning," the use of the labeling machine, and operating like a blindfolded bartender.

Various Cost-Management Ideas

- Buy fewer varieties of chinaware. I understand the need to have a variety of plate-ware, but having too many service pieces will mean more inventory is needed. It can complicate service and speed of service, and you will need to replenish the inventory of dishes and silverware more often.
- Make sure you do a weekly inventory of all your plates and silverware for two key reasons:

1. Running out of teaspoons and water glasses, for example, means slower service and might indirectly make you think you need more employees to manage the work when the actual issue is lack of tools, not staff.
2. When your team sees that you count your plates and silverware every week, they will be more careful. You will need to post the results every week so that your staff is aware of the inventory. This step will help you avoid suddenly learning that you are out of many tools and needing to place an urgent order (more details in Chapter Two: Superior Service and Hospitality).

- Remember to place rubber mats on the floor in the dishwashing area to prevent slips and falls that can lead to injuries and broken dishes.
- Energy cost: Cooks and chefs turn on all equipment as soon as they enter the kitchen, but you only need the equipment on full blast during rush hours. If you open at eleven o'clock for lunch, why would you keep all your equipment—ovens, salamanders, cheese melters, flattops, fryers—on full power from 7 a.m.? You can save a huge amount of money by simply turning most of your equipment down during slow periods. Turn them up only twenty minutes before rush hours. You will save eight hours a day of electricity—that's 2,880 hours of savings per year for only one piece of equipment!

  One more tip here: wait to run the dishwasher until the racks are fully loaded.
- Break down your cost-management efforts into two or three tasks per week. This way, you can make sure you have the time to analyze the information properly, decide how best to address any issues, and implement solutions without overwhelming your team.
- Be careful if you ask suppliers to train your team. At one of the restaurants I managed, we invited our cleaning supplies vendor to train our team on how to use the products best. The supplier wound up teaching them to use more chemical supplies for him to sell us more

Be careful if you ask suppliers to train your team.

of his product, which resulted in the restaurant paying for more supplies in the long run.

- Ask your suppliers for bulk discounts on products with high turnover rates.
- Make sure the ladles, scoops, and cups you use on the kitchen line are the exact measurement you need for recipes. Don't use a four-ounce ladle for a three-ounce ramekin. If you have a three-ounce ladle, your team will be more consistent.
- Don't allow staff to take home or eat leftover food, as they will have the tendency to cook more than needed to take food home or eat it during staff lunch break.

Don't allow staff to take home or eat leftover food.

- Build a waste-reduction team to embed a culture of low or no waste in your organization.
- Keeping a careful eye on your dish area can tell you a lot about your menu. Let's say you notice that sides of rice are often brought back from the dining room on cleared dishes. This could have a few causes: maybe you're overportioning the rice, or maybe the recipe needs to be reworked, as guests don't like the rice. Either way, observing these trends in returning dishes brought the problem to your attention.
- Always review prices from your suppliers to make sure they match your contract. If there are any differences, bring them up and ask for a credit.
- Be sure to measure like for like: food sales against food cost, beverage sales against beverage cost. This is better than measuring total F&B sales against F&B cost.
- Make sure someone is supervising delivery of supplies from vendors. The cases should be counted carefully to make sure you're receiving everything you paid for.
- Cost out every menu item and recipe. Use inventory management

software (not MS Excel sheets) in order to track and update cost instantly.

- Know your daily break-even point (the required sales every day in order to not lose money).
- Establish daily prep level PARs. (See Chapter One: Exceptional Food Quality and Kitchen Management for more information.)
- Track shrink and waste on in-house cut fish and meats. Shrinkage, waste, and trim are significant factors that can hurt your bottom line. If you cut your own steaks, seafood, or poultry or offer cooked meats such as prime rib, smoked brisket, ribs, roast beef, or pulled pork, then it is a certainty that the true cost per pound of the finished product will be significantly greater than the original purchase price.

Profit and Loss Management

Your profit and loss statement (P&L) functions as a bank statement for your restaurant to monitor your company's financial health. In this section, I will cover tactics and tips to manage your P&L in an effective way.

Take a look at this image (this will vary from one country to another):

For 1 dollar you have:

Every dollar you make breaks down as:

- 30% food cost = 30 cents
- 28% labor cost = 28 cents
- 18% non-controllable cost = 18 cents
- 15% controllable cost = 15 cents
- 9% net profit = 9 cents

Educate your team, show them the image opposite. Another way to think about expenses and teach your team the importance of cost management is to show it like a pipe of water that is leaking from different areas.

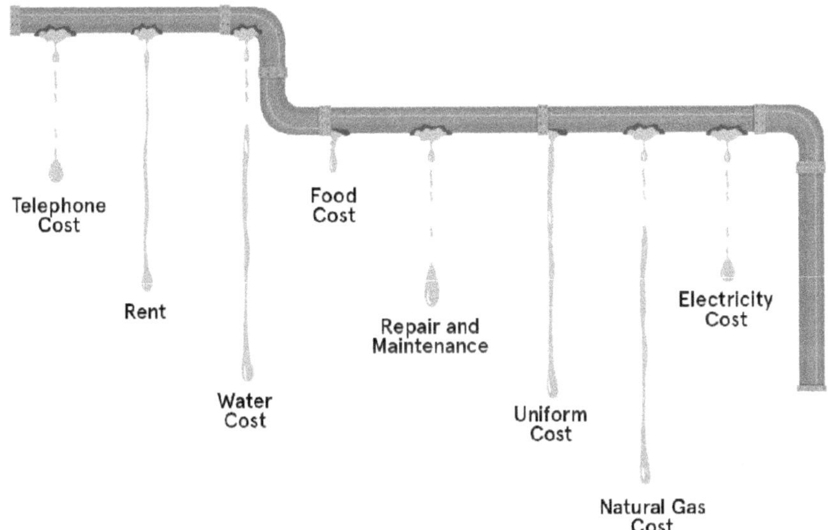

Imagine that your revenue is a constant flow of water in a pipe. The more holes you close, the less water you lose, and the more water you get to keep.

Telephone costs, uniform costs, natural gas, food cost, lights left on overnight, broken plates—these are all ways that water leaks out of the pipe. That is, this is all money out of your pocket. When you train your team, you should coach them how to avoid many of the little incidental costs that add up over time. Teach them to patch the holes in the pipe, and you'll lose less water. It's as simple as that.

A Tip for P&L Analysis

When I analyze my P&L, I always look at monthly and, more importantly, phased P&L—that is, over a three-to-five month period, as shown below. I also ask our accountant to produce graphs to show increases or decreases of certain expenses as per this example:

Expense	Jan	Feb	Mar	Apr	May
Electricity and Water	$525	$540	$620	$530	$529
Repair and Maintenance	$650	$589	$596	$1,520	$620

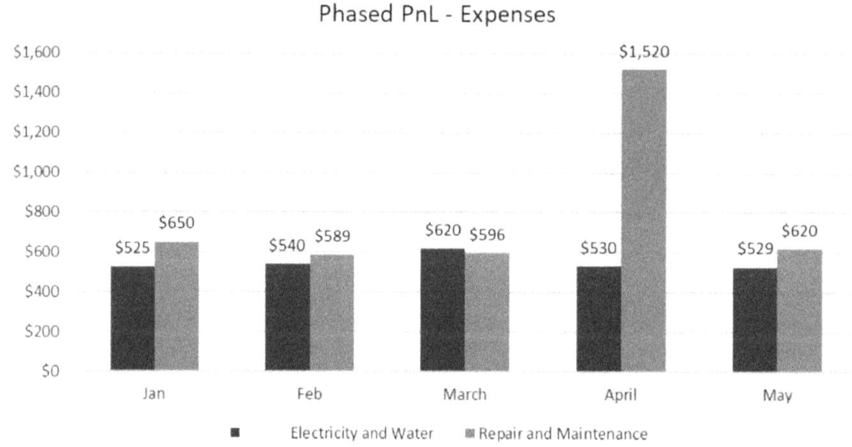

I can quickly spot issues with cost fluctuations from the above and figure out how to address them. I would ask questions about the reason for the increase in April in repair and maintenance and in March in electricity and water and ways to keep these expenses under control. If I have no historical data or trends, I wouldn't know if the expense is high, average, or low.

Here's another way to look at it:

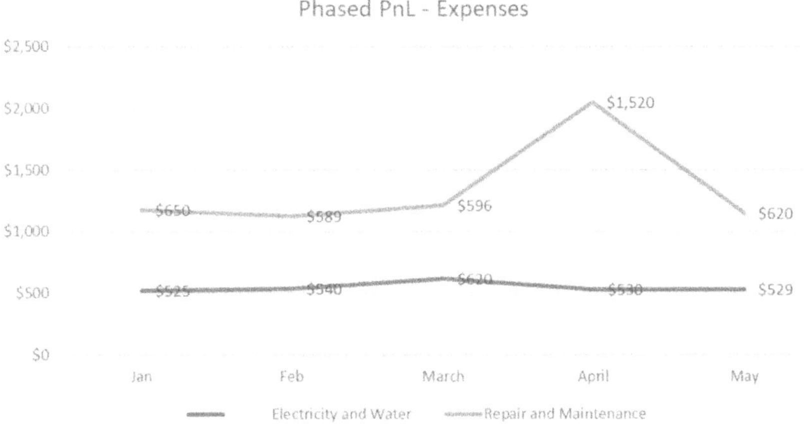

P&L Analysis:

When you are reviewing your P&L, ensure that you break down your review between topline and expenses.

Topline to include all items below:

1. Revenue breakdown by revenue source (food, beverage, and other income).
2. Revenue breakdown by meal period.
3. Review your guests' profile source (Are they tourists? In-house guests [for hotels]? Groups/locals from the neighborhood?); where do they come from?
4. Review total guests against monthly items sold and see what your percent of customers coming to your restaurant and having three-course meals is. This way, you will be able to find out which category is selling less, and you can pass this information to your waiters to encourage them to upsell whatever is selling less.
5. Ensure that you have a clear breakdown of discounts and value offers given within the month. This allows you to review the performance of each discount and how much value it added to your business.

Expenses (Cost of Sales, Payroll, and Other Expenses)

One key element in the P&L review is to be able to break down your expenses between variable and fixed expenses. This way, you can set clear targets and goals for your managers and hold them responsible for all variable expenses variances. Also, it will give you a clear idea of your monthly fixed cost and prepare you to better handle this and your cash flow in the future.

Conduct payroll reviews to be able to understand how many employees you need to provide consistent and effective service without scheduling too many people.

Forecast and Break-Even Analysis

It's important that you don't wait until the end of the month to review your P&L. Since P&L is historical data, any decision you make based on it will take time to implement. Because of this, depending on only P&L reviews will cost your business a lot of money you may not notice. To counteract this, you should create a forecast analysis for a month/quarter ahead and plan your operations accordingly.

Another important tool to keep in mind is break-even analysis. Break-even analysis should be conducted before starting any new project/marketing initiative in your restaurant, such as launching brunch or a themed night with live music, so you can understand all direct and indirect costs and what is required from topline. If you want your restaurant business to be successful, these tools are essential.

Monthly bonuses change everything!

One of the best practices to control costs is to involve your restaurant manager, head chef, sous chef, and supervisors. At one of the companies that I managed, I changed the bonus program as follows:

- Bonus to be paid monthly upon reviewing the P&L with the restaurant general managers and finance team. (I don't believe in annual bonuses because the motivation and engagement are typically low.)
- The bonus was divided into three parts. Restaurant managers receive one-third of their bonus if they achieve the budgeted sales, one-third if they achieve the budgeted profit, and one-third if they achieve the guest stratification ratings targets (quality of experience). So, one-third sales + one-third on profit + one-third guests ratings = 100 percent bonus. If a restaurant manager achieves only the profit target, they will still receive a one-third bonus.
- Notice that this plan wasn't based on food cost or labor cost. If you want to achieve your profit target, you naturally need to keep your expenses in line, including food and labor cost.
- I had eight restaurant managers who reported to me at the time. **They knew their P&L more than the finance team for three reasons:**

Firstly, they wanted to show me during our monthly meeting that they knew their numbers. Secondly, they wanted to achieve the bonus. This plan took their ownership to another level. And thirdly, they were always looking for ways to drive sales and lower costs so they could hit their targets. Since one-third of the bonus is based on guest satisfaction ratings and quality, they couldn't sacrifice quality or service standards to cut costs.

- Since it was monthly, they were far more engaged. They didn't have to wait for twelve months. We issued bonus checks right after the P&L meeting. They left my office with bonus checks in their hands! This bonus plan helped turn around the entire company's performance.

A Note on Theft and/or Lack of Training and Accountability

No one likes to think that their employees steal, but the reality is that employee theft is common. Theft is a different consideration than lack of accountability and carelessness (seen in the form of a lot of food waste during prep). Here are some tips to manage theft and/or carelessness.

- One common place that staff theft occurs is in walk-in coolers. In Philadelphia, I once saw a walk-in cooler with an interior camera and a large glass panel on the door.
- Theft happens while receiving orders. Vendors can take back cases and put them in their trucks. Because of this, someone should be there to receive the order and make sure everything you paid for is there.
- It's good to have a camera in the dumpster area to supervise trash removal. Most thefts happen when staff put supplies in trash bags and take them home later.
- No rings is another major issue for counter-service restaurants. The customer orders coffee and the employee doesn't ring in the order, instead pocketing the money. Void and Comp is another issue as we mentioned earlier in this chapter.

Unfortunately, there are several ways for employee theft to occur. Consider hiring an auditing company to review your practices and give you the right control procedures.

Final Thoughts

Restaurant Rule #1: Quality before Cost.

The shortest route to profit is revenue growth. Yes, it's important to watch your cost and manage your expenses, but always remember that cash flow and revenue growth are the lifeblood of your business. There are times when you reach 100 percent savings and you can't cut expenses anymore. If your revenue is low, your business is in danger. So manage your expenses, but take time to drive revenue growth every day. Check out Marketing and Revenue (Sales) Growth (Chapter Five) for more than thirty tips and tools to drive revenue.

Now, let's put the learning to action. If you answer with a No to any of the questions below, it means you might have a gap or an opportunity in that area.

Evaluate Your Cost Management

Question	Comments
1. Do we cross-utilize our most expensive and/or fast-expiring ingredients?	
2. Do we reduce single-use, single-prep ingredients to no more than 5 percent of the menu?	
3. Have we revised the total number of dishes? Is our menu too large?	
4. Do we conduct menu engineering every three months?	

5. Are our garnishes and food decorations no more than two or three maximum per dish?	
6. Do we use prep leftovers and trimmings?	
7. Do we use and discuss waste sheets *every day?*	
8. Have we reduced our market/ purchasing list?	
9. Do we negotiate with vendors?	
10. Do we know our top twenty highest cost ingredients?	
11. Do we inform and engage our staff on a monthly basis with our food cost targets?	
12. Do we have great portion-control practices in place?	
13. Do we monitor comp and void every day?	
14. Do we conduct sensitive items count every shift?	
15. Do we conduct monthly team-engagement surveys? Do we reward them for the best ideas?	
16. Do we keep in mind Parkinson's Law when we create our team's work schedule?	

17. How do we improve employee training? How often?	
18. Have we analyzed our operating hours?	
19. Do we conduct quarterly productivity analysis?	
20. Do we have prep recipes' recommended time?	
21. Do we have an action plan to manage employee turnover?	
22. Is our kitchen/restaurant highly organized? Is zoning/labeling in place?	
23. Do we conduct forecast and break-even analysis?	
24. Do we have an engaging and rewarding monthly bonus program?	
25. Do we conduct monthly P&L analysis using phased P&L and showing trends and percentages?	
26. Do we have a program in place to manage electricity- and water-consumption costs?	

CHAPTER SEVEN
SUSTAINED PROFITS: A NATURAL OUTCOME

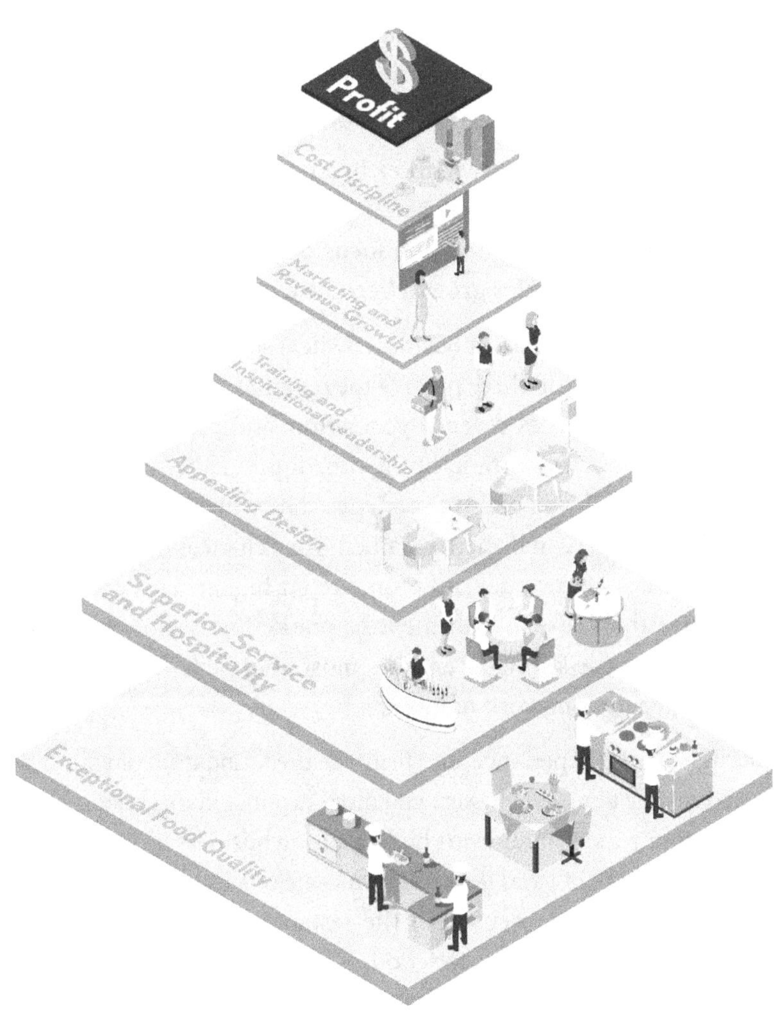

As I mentioned in the beginning of the book, if you excel at the first six sections of the success pyramid, sustained profits and sales/revenue will be a natural outcome.

Focus your efforts on enacting the first six sections of the pyramid as successfully as you can while putting huge emphasis, time, and effort on the first four categories: Food, Service, Atmosphere, and Training. Your food's taste, quality, culinary innovation, and consistency should be your number one priority. Support that priority with great hospitality, a well-designed and well-maintained, squeaky-clean restaurant, effective team training, operational excellence, and smart marketing initiatives. If you turn your restaurant into a place guests will love to visit, profits and sales growth are sure to come. This is key for forming the right business strategy!

I want to repeat what I wrote earlier, because **this is really the core of this book: when you serve great food by well-trained and motivated food servers in a fun atmosphere—with ongoing focus on marketing and operational excellence—profit and sales growth become a natural outcome**.

> Experience builds the strongest and the most affordable form of marketing and revenue generation: **word of mouth**.

Most business owners spend too much time on the top three parts of the pyramid: cost cutting, marketing, sales/revenue generation, and profit. These things are important, but if your food quality can be improved, your guest experience can be heightened, or your team can be better trained, your chances of generating more revenue and profit are far higher. This approach is far more effective than cost management or marketing, simply because great experience builds the strongest and the most affordable form of marketing and revenue generation: word of mouth.

Your food, guest experience, and team are the foundation of your business. Cutting costs may temporarily earn you more profit, and increasing marketing may draw more guests, but it won't build a strong business model. It's better to create a smaller base of loyal guests than a cycle of single-visit guests. Failing to attend to these fundamentals of the restaurant business has led many restaurants to close their doors for good.

As a reader, you may expect a long chapter on sustained profits and sales, but in fact, the tools, ideas, and tactics presented in chapters one through six are all you need to drive your profits and sales.

My goal with this chapter is to present a different way of thinking for restaurant management strategy, to help you build a new mindset and spend your time and resources on initiatives that will make your restaurant more successful. Build a culture that is focused on craveable food, great service, and great training. Be obsessed with table visits, product freshness, and team training. Stay on top of cost management and marketing. Above all, focus on what can improve your guests' experience at your restaurant.

My goal with this chapter is to present a different way of thinking for restaurant management strategy, to help you build a new mindset.

This book has shown you tools and *tricks* to apply in every area of your business, but the through line is that, at the end of the day, they are all geared toward improving the guest's experience at your restaurant. Making this experience as great as can be is the most important factor in the financial success of your restaurant.

CHAPTER EIGHT
OPERATIONAL EXCELLENCE

All the tactics, philosophies, and advice that I have shared with you in this book so far won't help you if you are not laser focused on operational excellence.

Operational excellence is the cumulative result of all your consistent efforts to excel in every aspect of restaurant management: service, hospitality, food, cleanliness, training, kitchen management, restaurant upkeep, and repair and maintenance. **It's when your restaurant runs like a Swiss watch: with precision, accuracy, and reliability**.

As you can see from the image above, operational excellence is primarily built around **consistently** executing fundamental *systems* and *procedures* while focusing on the *details*. Some examples of systems include table visits for service, line checks, recipe use for food, travel paths for shift management, and shift briefings for daily training.

Consider the following:

- How would guests feel if they arrived at a restaurant and the parking lot had litter and bottles lying around? What would their impression be?
- How does a guest or host feel if the food (all of the starters or all of the mains) does not arrive at the table all at the same time? Or if it's served cold?
- How would a guest feel if the restrooms/toilets were dirty and had tissue paper scattered around? Or the food server is not neat?

These are just examples of when operational excellence is not present!

Details Matter!

The food and beverage industry has always been and always will be about the little details. Having an out-of-order plate warmer could destroy an entire meal period. One server with an old and torn uniform could tarnish your restaurant's reputation. One bad review could be monumental. Because of this, it is essential to manage the details.

When restaurant executives become out of touch with the details of their operations and spend most of their time building unnecessary strategies, long spreadsheets, or PowerPoint presentations (I call that fluff), their business begins to falter.

All global restaurant companies that have enjoyed operational excellence, success, and loyalty were obsessed with details like the temperature of the food, the exact execution of recipes, the service team's menu knowledge, hostess grooming, pace of service, washroom cleanliness, lighting in the dining room, and the list goes on. All of these are examples of operational excellence.

For some executives, these are "small" things. For others, they are *everything*. I am from the latter school of thought. **Attention to detail is one of the most essential parts of my strategic thinking**.

In 1999, our restaurant was visited by the global VP of an international franchise for a Fortune 500 restaurant company. I was a restaurant manager trainee then. The VP went through the entire kitchen line and checked every single ingredient. That company operated twelve hundred casual-dining restaurants worldwide and had one of the highest average unit revenue volumes in its category.

The attention to the little details was incredible from the highest levels in the organization. Such leadership behavior doesn't make a leader tactical, a micromanager, or detail-driven as opposed to a strategic leader. This assumption is totally wrong. **Such focus on details is the core of sound restaurant business leadership strategy.**

As another example, think of Chipotle, a company worth $5.5 billion. During its heyday, CEO Steve Ells declared a strategy that was built on removing unnecessary complexities from the company's operations. His belief was that Chipotle is based on the simple idea of using great ingredients, preparing them using classic cooking techniques, and to serve good food quickly. These are examples of operational excellence.

Whether a restaurant company's strategy is based on innovation, expansion, acquisitions, or retention, it must also embed operational excellence as part of the same strategy. **The more companies move away from these fundamentals, the further they get from guest loyalty and success.**

Strategies, plans, visions, and missions reach nowhere if restaurant executives don't stay close to the field and take care of the details in a precise way.

Great operators consider every aspect of their business. They feel accomplished when they have mulled over the details and repeatedly ensured the quality of their craft. Repetition is no chore when it comes to getting every detail correct.

The best operators focus on guests, doing all they can to go above and beyond for their customers. The name of the game is clean restaurants, great service, and great food at a good price.

Great operators hire the right people and create a culture of only accepting exceptional work. Great operators have high standards for themselves and demand high standards from their team. Operators who take care of their restaurants take care of their guests. Operators who neglect maintenance and do only the bare minimum when it comes to cleaning are risking guest loyalty. Not only this, but it can lead to a spiral whereby even mediocre standards eventually become too costly to maintain. Embrace proactivity.

> Great operators have high standards for themselves and demand high standards from their team and create a culture of only accepting exceptional work.

Never let your standards slip. Invest in maintaining and upkeep, rather than waiting for an avoidable problem to arise to address it. Great operators are obsessed with quality and make sure their kitchen team follows each recipe to the dot.

I would like to share what one of my mentors—hospitality leader, executive chef, and head of operations of dozens of restaurants—wrote to me:

My family and I go once a week to a small mom-and-pop cafe (twenty-four seats inside and twelve outside; often there's a waitlist: the largest I've seen is sixteen), sometimes more often. They serve only home-cooked food, which can lack finesse at times, but it's fully in keeping with their brand. However, there is always a great welcome, the food is always delivered together and piping hot and consistently to recipe. If you order something and ask for an element of the dish to be removed, they make up for it and add some more of another ingredient, e.g., breakfast no beans, they add sausage or bacon. They always check back to confirm satisfaction and make any changes if necessary. And then there is always a great farewell. The owner is often there, his wife is in the kitchen, and at least one of his two daughters leads the service. It absolutely epitomizes the running of a restaurant/cafe. This cafe attracts people in suits and ties, manual workers, tourists, families, locals, and all age groups.

I ask myself why, as outlets/restaurant companies get bigger, do they lose that personal and genuine touch? Why do managers believe that they have to sit in an office with a computer? Sayings I always believe in are, "Lead by example," "It's the manager who sets the standards and the pace of the service," and, "You only get one chance of a first impression."

Restaurant Manager Operational Excellence Journey and Critical Control Points

One way to observe your restaurant's operational status is by dining at your restaurant as a guest.

Start from the reservation step. How is the tone of the reservation team when you call? How detailed were they when asking about your food preferences, table preference, the occasion, and allergy concerns?

What's your impression of the restaurant's exterior as you arrive? Is it clean and well painted? Does it have proper lighting? What about the parking lot? If you have valets, how is the welcome experience? Are the valets and hostesses welcoming and outgoing?

Did the host welcome you with a smile? Did she walk with you to the table (not ahead of you)? Did she mention the name of your server? How did the server welcome you? Are the staff's uniforms neat? Is the table clean and comfortable?

Did your food server make recommendations that made a difference? Was the server attentive, friendly, and knowledgeable about the menu?

Was the food served at the right temperature, with the right portions, fresh, and matching the menu description? Was the food exceptional and craveable to the point that it makes you a loyal fan? Did a manager perform a genuine table visit?

Was the payment processed in a timely manner?

On your way out, did the hostess invite you back and wish you a great day?

By taking the place of a customer and answering the above questions, you can evaluate strengths and weaknesses in your operational excellence program.

Another way to look at operational excellence is to embed it in the manager's daily routine checklist. Let me explain further. (Some of these topics were also discussed in Chapter Four: Training and Inspirational Leadership, section: Daily Manager's Routine.)

If you are a restaurant manager or shift leader, the following journey will show you what a restaurant manager that values operational excellence would do:

From the moment you arrive to your restaurant:

- Walk outside the building and check for broken windows and doors. Check the cleanliness of the building as well.
- Walk inside the building: dining room, hostesses' station, washrooms, pass window, kitchen, dry storage, walk-in coolers, and freezers. Check that everything was done properly at closing the night before. It's important to set expectations on how to close the restaurant. If you find a piece of equipment that wasn't cleaned well, note that in the management communication log. If food containers were left open, note that as well. It's important to keep track of what is wrong so that you can communicate that to staff and other managers.
- Read the manager's logbook so that you know what happened during the previous shift. Look for incidents, needs, and observations.

- Fill out the master prep list and station prep list, and check your walk-in cooler to make sure everything is correct from closing the previous night (this is for restaurants that have no kitchen manager or head chef).
- Fill out the employee roster and assign stations.
- If your restaurant accepts reservations, review it, check special requests, identify regulars, and learn about first timers.
- Count and verify the petty cash and check safe audit report.
- Prepare for the pre-shift meeting for the front-of-the-house and back (heart)-of-the-house teams (FOH and BOH). Decide on what the training tip is going to be for front-of-house staff and which Star Dish of the Day (feature of the day) you will train and taste with the team. Decide on the recipe you will discuss with the kitchen team. Print it and highlight key points, steps, and procedures.
- Oversee employee arrival. Say hello to employees who have just arrived. Ask how they are doing.
- Conduct separate shift meetings for BOH and FOH. Discuss the daily feature with the FOH staff, and conduct the daily recipe discussion with the BOH staff.
- Update both communication boards for BOH and FOH. For the dining room team, you can write the upselling goals and post the daily feature, any special guest bookings, and the goal of the day (for example: sell five steaks per food server); share praise for great performers and motivate the entire team.
- For the kitchen team, hang the recipe that you discussed during the pre-shift meeting on the communication board, highlight any out-of-stock items, recognize team members, and write the goal for the shift (for example: our goal today is to serve appetizers within eight minutes).
- Contact suppliers to make food orders. Food orders must be done carefully and thoroughly so you don't overorder and have expiry

issues or underorder and run out of products. Go to the walk-in cooler, walk-in freezer, and dry store, and check what you have on hand. Place orders following established PARs and sales forecasts.

- Make sure someone is there to receive orders from vendors. Don't leave vendors by themselves. Count the cases received to avoid theft. And, more importantly, check to make sure the product matches the specifications and price that your restaurant requires. For example, if you order Hass avocados, make sure you're receiving Hass avocados.
- Walk through the dining room and follow up on the daily cleaning report for FOH. You should deep clean one specific area each day. Breaking cleaning into small chunks helps you keep the restaurant clean without wasting labor hours.
- Do a kitchen walk-through. Check to make sure prep is conduced correctly, cleaning schedule is adhered to, recipes are followed, food is stored and labeled properly, shelf life is adhered to, and that the walk-ins and dry-store room are organized.
- Conduct a line check half an hour before you open for business. (See Chapter One: Exceptional Food Quality and Kitchen Management for more information on conducting a line check.)
- When it's time to open for customers, quickly walk outside the restaurant and check the exterior again, and make sure everything is clean and presentable.
- Check that TVs and music are on, restrooms are stocked and clean, and that the heating, ventilation, and air conditioning (HVAC) is set at the right temperature.
- Make sure all food servers' stations are clean, organized, and stocked.
- Now, begin your table visits at every table. Welcome loyal guests by name and get to know the first timers. Don't delegate these to someone else or skip tables. Do your travel path every forty-five minutes (travel path is further explained later in this chapter). Focus on guest service, pace of service, and serving great food.

- Toward the end of the shift, write notes and shift observations in the manager's log. Don't strictly write mistakes and things to improve. Also note when people are doing things correctly or are doing exceptional work. Use these notes to recognize your staff for excelling and motivate and inspire the team.
- At the end of your shift, perform the shift handover to the night manager. Let the night manager know what went well and what didn't. Wish the night manager and team a great shift.

The Absolute Fundamentals

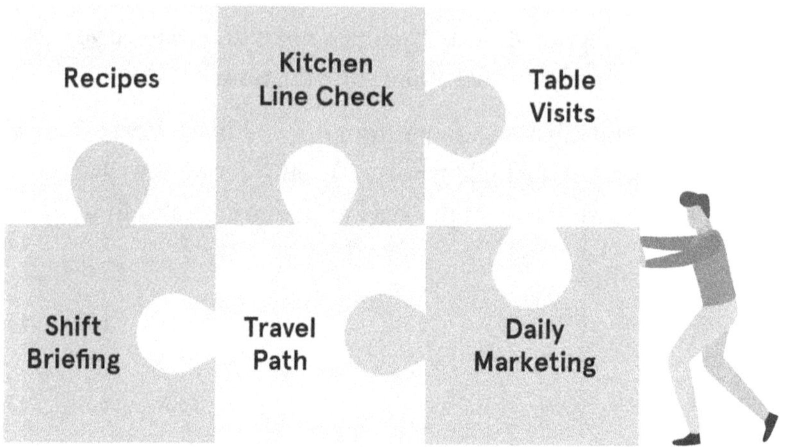

There are six fundamental elements that cannot be missed during any shift. I would also not recommend delegating these tasks to others. **These are the absolute essentials to achieving operational excellence**. Here is how to verify if they are in place or not:

1. **Recipes** are the best way to achieve consistency and should be used and strictly adhered to. **Kitchen line checks** help you confirm that recipes are being followed, as well as ensuring that the kitchen is organized and orders are being placed and received efficiently.
2. Always personally conduct **table visits** with every table. Review **guest comments**/online reviews daily. Monitor the **pace of service** and make sure food is being served on time. **Hospitality** and **friendliness** should be evident.
3. Hold separate **shift briefings** for kitchen and dining room teams. Prepare a **daily training tip** and share it and the **shift goals** at the meeting.
4. Drive **marketing during every shift**. For example, create initiatives like birthday calls, bounce-back cards, and social media posts. Keep an eye on reviews on Tripadvisor, Google, and other websites.

5. Conduct your **travel path** in FOH and BOH every forty-five minutes.
6. Record your **notes** and **observations** on operations throughout the shift.

Don't delegate these tasks to other people. These need to be conducted solely by the restaurant manager. Notice, I did not mention daily breakeven, labor cost per hour, or food cost. This is because I want to keep the focus on operations in this section. It's critical that you look at the numbers every shift and manage cost, especially labor, but numbers are only historical results, and if your operations are strong, revenue and profit will follow.

Avoid the Shiny Objects

Spending time and money on marketing, PR, restaurant decor, and/or changing chefs or launching new menus *often* to drive sales without being laser focused on the first four layers of the pyramid (operational excellence) is like trying to fill a leaky bucket with water. This creates a vicious cycle. You end up having first-time customers who don't come back. You see a slight increase in sales followed by a decline, simply because you are not a strong operating brand. You are not delivering memorable experiences.

What's a Travel Path?

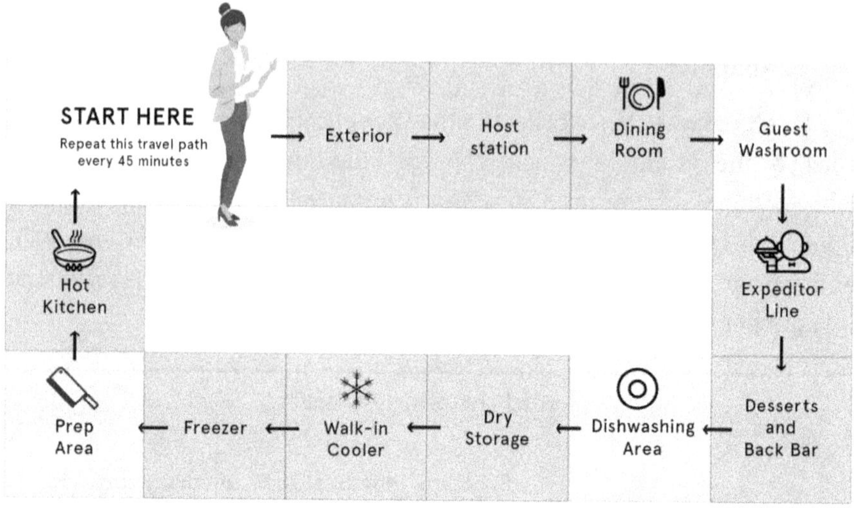

A "travel path" is a forty-five-minute routine that the manager follows. The travel path should take the manager through each part of the restaurant so that they can keep an eye on everything.

Areas: The manager must determine what areas in the restaurant need the most attention. This way, they can make sure those areas aren't left unattended.

Procedures: The following scenario depicts a typical travel path by a manager on duty (MOD).

The MOD decides to start their travel path from the main door and hostess station. They check to make sure the hostess station is organized, that the menus and waiting list are prepared, and that the hostesses are well groomed. They then move to the dining room, conducting table visits, seeing if the tables are being pre-bussed, and checking on customers who are waiting on food. After this, the MOD stops by the guest washrooms to make sure they are clean and well maintained. At the expediter section, they check on the ticket time and pace of service. In the bakery, they perform quality management on dough-rolling procedures and check on the final color of the baked buns. From there, they move on to the prep area to check on the line cooks' work. At the grill, they make sure burgers are being properly seasoned, and at the fry station, they make sure frying procedures are being followed. Finally, the MOD checks on plating and garnishing at the expediter section, and then stops in at the walk-ins and dry storage to make sure everything is properly cleaned and stored. They repeat this tour every forty-five minutes.

Tools: The manager should be using all of their senses. Smell the food, watch the prep and cooking procedures, touch the meat, taste the products for consistency and quality control, and listen to feedback from cooks and food servers about how the shift is going. (Remember to wash your hands between tasks.)

Listen to the volume of the music level. Feel the temperature of the air conditioning. Listen to guest interactions and, when necessary, direct the team without micromanaging. Help your team clear dishes, serve dishes, and welcome guests. That's true leadership.

In this example, you can see that the MOD has completed more than twenty-five observations and actions in the walk-through, has demonstrated their hands-on, team leadership and presence, and has ensured that all staff know the MOD is leading them. They didn't spend most of their time standing by the hostess station or in one corner of the restaurant. They kept everything under their control and supervision.

Death by Meetings

I always stress the importance of having your F&B leaders and restaurant managers on the ground, on the front lines with your team, with their guests, in order to make sure your guest experience is top notch.

When a hotel F&B director or restaurant manager has a meeting schedule like the one below, their "on-the-ground" leadership suffers:

9 a.m. to 10 a.m.: Team briefing

10 a.m. to 11 a.m.: Revenue generation meeting

11 a.m. to 12 p.m.: Capital expense meeting

12 p.m. to 1 p.m.: HR celebration meeting

1 p.m. to 2 p.m.: Marketing meeting

2 p.m. to 4 p.m.: P&L meeting

5 p.m. to 6 p.m.: Supplier meeting

6 p.m. to 7 p.m.: Emails and office work

We interview and hire restaurant managers and F&B leaders for their skills in guest relations, hospitality, service, business management, as well as food and drink knowledge, which is demonstrated mostly through hands-on management (not through office work and meetings).

When I first moved from independent and franchise restaurants to working in the hotel industry, one of the things that surprised me most was the huge difference in the number of meetings and level of hands-on management between the two segments. Hotel F&B has a large number of meetings and less hands-on management.

In my view, every minute spent away from your guests, kitchens, and dining rooms detracts from operational excellence, which is the backbone of success in the restaurant and bar business.

In global franchises and large independent restaurant companies, the focus is always on operational excellence. We had one or two meetings per week. That's all.

Unfortunately, there are times when restaurant managers or executive chefs spend long hours in their offices or behind their laptops. They only show up to the dining room when there is a serious guest complaint. To reduce the amount of time spent in the office, I designed restaurants without a manager's office. We only had a cabinet for files, a PC, a safe deposit box, and one chair. No walls or doors!

One of the most successful hotel general managers that I worked with would never allow his F&B team to book or be in meetings during rush hours.

In my view, every minute spent away from your guests, kitchens, and dining rooms detracts from operational excellence, which is the backbone of success in the restaurant and bar business.

Take a look at your F&B/restaurant leader's schedule, and then ask yourself about the necessity and duration of their meetings before your team's operations become totally ineffective via "death by meetings."

Paralysis by Analysis

If your operations are slowing down, it may be because you are paralyzing them with overanalysis.

I often come across leaders who walk around with calculators and laptops and spend countless hours in their offices on spreadsheets, trying to save every penny or measure and track every action, campaign, and project. Spending this time on taking action instead of analysis will have a significant impact on your revenue.

These paralyzed leaders often think about food cost, other costs, and the bottom line instead of focusing on sustained sales/revenue drivers: great food, great service, and great atmosphere, which requires being on the ground every day with your team and making sure every guest leaves extremely happy.

These paralyzed leaders often think about food cost, other costs, and the bottom line instead of focusing on sustained sales/revenue drivers:

Don't get me wrong; analysis is important. What gets measured gets done, but there are times when business leaders try to fix declining revenue issues by launching multiple promotions and campaigns without knowing or understanding their impact. But there is a fine line between trying to measure everything and hampering your restaurant's progress.

The challenge with operational excellence is the fact that you might do 99 percent of things right and miss just one. You could do table visits at almost every table, but it might be the one you missed that leaves a scathing review on Yelp. That's why your goal should be to keep the team focused 100 percent of the time on operations.

Action makes things happen, but over analysis does not.

Bad Habits and Obstacles to Operational Excellence:

- Holding meetings during operating hours or holding too many meetings (managers, suppliers, staff meetings) overall.
- Restaurant manager lingering by the hostess stand most of the shift.
- Manager/chef spending time on their cell phone and social media during the shift.
- Restaurant manager asking the team to serve guests with a smile but not acting as a role model when it comes to table visits, friendliness (smiling to guests), or hospitality.
- Manager spending hours behind the computer or in the office instead of being a hands-on leader. (Office work and laptops are the enemies of operational excellence. When you see managers occupying a dining table with lots of paperwork and laptops, as a guest you can't help but think you are not a priority to them. Seeing such things also makes the dining room look like an office space—not the relaxing experience you want to project to your guests.)
- Manager creating a lot of checklists or complicated documents.
- Building a business around discounting and marketing, not guest experience and quality.

- Restaurant managers not taking time to train their team.
- Restaurant managers avoiding entering the kitchen. Chef avoiding the dining room.
- No goals given to staff or measured during the shift.
- Excessive changes in menu items or changing them too often and too soon. The team is unable to cope with learning and several consistency problems arise.
- Restaurant manager/director of F&B not knowing how to use the point of sales (POS) system. Additionally, Open Food button/Off Menu on POS is often used.
- Restaurant manager not understanding the Profit and Loss statement (P&L), not accountable for it.
- No clear restaurant positioning. Different employees have different understandings of the positioning, target market, image, branding, or culture.
- Things start to go wrong when business slows down because the team loses focus.

Evaluate Your Operational Excellence and Put the Learning to Work

Question	Comment
Do your managers spend a lot of time in their office instead of with their team and customers?	
Is a line check conducted before and during every shift?	
Are recipes used and strictly adhered to?	

Is receiving and ordering only done by an experienced manager?	
Are table visits conducted at every table by a manager?	
Is a team member assigned to review all comments on Google Reviews, Yelp, and Tripadvisor to flag any negative comments and take action right away to avoid viral negative press?	
Is guest feedback from table visits and online comments taken seriously and discussed during shift handover, shift meetings, and weekly manager meetings?	
Are pace of service and ticket time monitored throughout the shift? Are chefs and servers aware of the pace?	
Are valuable training tips shared during every shift briefing? Are shift goals shared with team members, and do managers walk the talk? Do they follow up on what was said during shift briefings?	
Is marketing active in every shift? For example, are you growing your database? Are you handing out bounce-back cards? Are you calling guests two weeks before their birthdays? Do you post three times a week on social media?	
Do you conduct your travel path every forty-five minutes? Are managers leading the shift?	
Is the shift routine checklist followed 100 percent of the time?	

CHAPTER NINE
IT'S ALL ABOUT THE FOOD

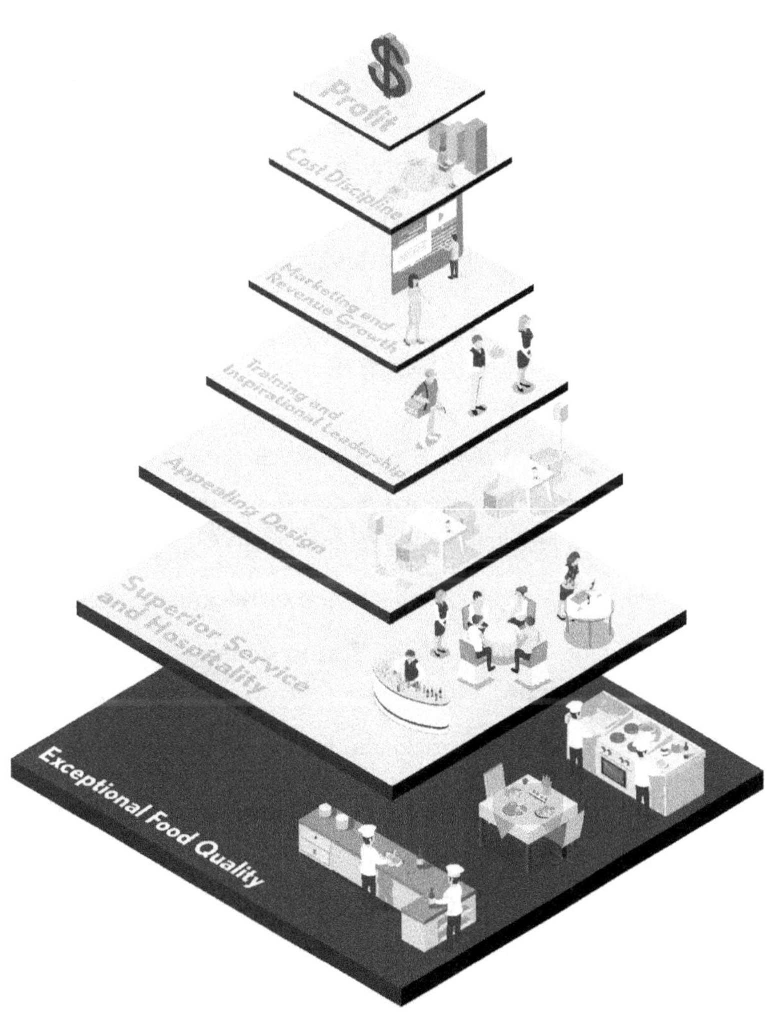

This chapter aims to help you pay attention to the little details that make the difference between average food and great food. It enables you to avoid wrong practices and shows you proper, practical procedures for cooking great food. This chapter also highlights common mistakes in food production and menu execution.

You will notice some sections discuss a specific menu item or ingredient while others cover an entire menu category. For experienced chefs, these tips and practices may sound basic and elementary in nature, but for others, these may be new information. We decided to choose the most popular items or menu categories that are found in restaurants around the world.

Lastly, there are hundreds of ways to make a given dish in the culinary world, so I encourage you to be open-minded, especially if you see tips and procedures with which you are not familiar or not used to doing.

Thank you to chefs Will Stanyer, Nikolaos Tsimidakis, and Mathieu Balbino for their valuable feedback on this chapter.

Soups

Good Practices

- If held in a bain-marie, stir every twenty minutes to avoid skin formation and redistribute the temperature.
- Balanced flavors: not too acidic or too bland, and well-seasoned.
- Fresh vegetables are not mushy. Texture adds an important taste dimension to soups.
- Vegetables are locally sourced and seasonal where applicable.
- Aromatic: you can smell an appealing aroma before you even start eating.

Bad Practices

- Microwaved and way too hot; guests may burn themselves with the first bite, and the actual flavor will never come through. *This happens often in restaurants.*

- Too salty or bland: some chefs don't do line checks or taste tests.
- Some restaurants keep adding water as the soup thickens, as it's kept for a long time in a double boiler, a bain-marie. It's better to discard the product because adding water changes the taste and texture.
- Holding soups on heat for the entire shift. Discard soups after a certain period.
- Lack of variety: offering only creamy soup, only clear soup, or only vegetable- and tomato-based soup will not suffice. Guests should be given at least two options.
- Serving with cold bread or stale crackers.
- Using too many garnishes and toppings or no garnishes at all.
- Using the same soup from the day before. Chefs should be self-disciplined and serve it fresh daily.

Burgers

Good Practices

- Set your flat grill to 365°F (185°C). Any less, and you will not get a proper sear on the patty.
- Make sure sauce is well spread and covers the entirety of both sides of the bun. Many chefs use squeeze bottles. I prefer a spatula for even sauce spreading.
- Lettuce is crisp, dry, and cut/sliced fresh for each service.
- Medium well and well done must still be juicy. Well done doesn't mean dry.
- Scrape the flat grill after each run. Remove excess fat and carbon buildup.
- Fat-percent ratio to lean beef must between 20 and 25 percent fat when using beef chuck.

- If you can, use vine-ripened tomatoes and either slice to order or cut fresh for each service as close as possible to opening to maintain optimum freshness.
- Each ingredient must be great. One bad ingredient can ruin the entire burger. Sometimes chefs use 99 percent great ingredients and only one poor-quality ingredient, such as low-quality, low-grade bacon or pickles, which ruins their work.
- Choose the right bun to suit your own/guests' preference—potato buns and brioche are popular choices nowadays.

Bad Practices

- Pressing the burger patty for faster cooking. This dries out the patty by squeezing out its natural juices.
- Serving the burger with super cold sauce, tomatoes, lettuce, or pickles; it will bring down the temperature of the entire burger. I like to bring items to room temperature for at least thirty minutes before building a burger.
- Serving the burger with a cold bun. Bun toasting with butter must be the last step in the process. The bun is what the customer touches first, and it forms their first impression. Butter is not preferred for the brioche bun because the dough is already enriched with butter.
- Overseasoning the patty. During cooking, or in advance, overseasoning will dry out the patty or take away from the meat's natural taste. Salt is the preferred option to season patties, not a mix of several seasonings.
- Assembling too early because the ingredients will get cold and the burger will get soggy. Make sure you properly time your fries and finishing the burger.
- Using imperfect ingredients: remember that guests will taste every ingredient in one bite. Don't build your burger with many small slices of low-quality tomatoes; don't use an overly large, low-quality, store-bought bun; and don't use an overpowering sauce made from garlic. You need to enhance the flavor of the burger, not overwhelm it.

- One common problem with burgers is carbon buildup on the patty. No black or burned ends must be shown on the patty. Watch closely and time when to flip the patties before burning the edges, and scrape the flat grill after each run.
- A dry and deformed burger bun is another common mistake. Make sure you don't stack more than two sleeves of buns on top of each other to prevent this from happening accidentally. Cut open two to three buns to check freshness before each shift.
- Serving on several types of buns: red, black, brown, and white. Most likely you will complicate the kitchen operation and have expired buns from time to time.
- In general, I am not in favor of adding sausage, breadcrumbs, or eggs to the raw beef mix. Good quality ingredients should be able to shine without distraction.
- For fast-food restaurants: stacking patties in the heat chute. To avoid overcooking and drying out the product, shingle them instead. Don't build burgers and place them in the expeditor window too early. Don't serve expired burger patties; most fast-food restaurants have a thirty-minute hold time. Make sure you adhere to it.

Pizza

Good Practices

- Choose the right tomatoes for the pizza sauce, like San Marzano, which are rich-fleshed and sweet with few seeds, thin skin, and low acidity due to the volcanic soil they are grown in. I prefer freshly made sauce, and I am not a fan of canned tomato sauce, as it's often too sharp with a high level of acidity and vinegar taste unless you find the right quality.
- Use low-gluten dough/flour. Caputo 00 flour is ideal for pizza dough for two reasons. First, it's finely ground, and second, it has a lower gluten content than most flours. (I have seen chefs who use a mix of type one and type zero flour.)

- Keep your pizza simple. Too many toppings can ruin a great pizza. It will wet the middle, and you will lose the flavor. Follow this principle: less is more. Overloading the pizza with too many toppings will weigh down the light crust and prevent it from baking properly.
- Be creative: come up with unique and new, nontraditional toppings. Guests are often wowed with never-before-used toppings. I have seen chefs use non-traditional toppings like flowers, Kimchi, and basil paste instead of basil leaves as toppings.
- Some guests ask for onion as a topping. Bake onions (while you're baking your pizza), as it is far better than oily sautéed onion. Red onion is always better. Half-moon-size cut, not finely chopped, to help ensure the onions do not burn while cooking.
- Allow proper time for fermentation (at least twenty-four hours or longer); the dough must be at room temperature before baking (some chefs believe you can bake from 50 degrees Fahrenheit [10 degrees Celsius]). Slow fermentation gives pizza dough its chewy and crispy texture. (For dough mixing, some chefs don't use electric dough mixers; they believe in folding and mixing the dough by hand as it produces less friction. With mixers/machine mixing it creates too much heat, which changes the dough temperature, which causes chewy texture.)
- If any ingredient is kept in brine, its juices, or water, drain it well before adding it to a pizza.
- The freshest ingredients will always yield the best results. Your mantra must be about choosing to use only prime, raw ingredients. Whenever possible use garden tomatoes (as a topping), fresh-grown basil, oregano, and garlic.
- Some chefs use mozzarella, which is perfectly fine. I recommend using fior di latte, which is a fresh cheese made with cow's milk. It's abundant in flavor with a delicate and sweeter taste and is less fatty than mozzarella.

Bad Practices

- Using canned, sliced olives as a topping—they are too salty. Always use fresh ingredients. Like burger building, one bad ingredient can ruin the whole pizza.
- Allowing even ten seconds under the heat lamp. Serve immediately.
- Using a plastic rolling pin. Roll by hand. Rolling pins take too much air from the dough and affect its elasticity. Rolling pins deflate the pizza's gas pockets and remove the soft and fluffy texture.
- Burning the crust or the bottom of the pizza. Balance top and bottom of oven temp.
- Forgetting to clean the oven—the buildup of excess flour or semolina will burn and transfer to the next pizzas you cook.
- Soggy crust due to adding too much tomato sauce.
- Adding too much cheese; otherwise your pizza will end up greasy or fall apart from the weight.
- Rushing the stages of proofing—it takes time and patience and should not be rushed.

Pasta

Spaghetti Bolognese

A lot of debate surrounds whether this dish is the American version of an Italian classic—in Italy they use tagliatelle and a completely different sauce. This section will provide tips for the type of spaghetti Bolognese that one would find in North America.

Good Practices

- Cook the meat gently and avoid too much evaporation. Make sure there is enough binding between meat and sauce. Cook for two to three hours and add celery, carrots, and a splash of milk. Sufficiently brown the meat to achieve good caramelization.

- When boiling pasta, season the water and add salt to flavor the pasta fully.
- When browning the meat, ensure it is caramelized—not just boiled. It is the caramelization that creates a depth of flavor.
- If you are using ready-made pasta instead of fresh (made-from-scratch pasta), after boiling to al dente, finish cooking it to order. Most chefs boil the pasta again quickly while others finish cooking it as they combine it in the pan with sauce. I prefer the latter option.
- Note: Al dente for some customers in North America might mean undercooked pasta; in Italy al dente is the only acceptable way of cooking and eating pasta.
- Use double-zero pasta flour for fresh pasta, and use good quality eggs for the pasta dough.
- Use high-quality parmesan and extra virgin olive oil to finish.
- Tip: grate parmesan to order and add to finish and top your dish. Aged parmesan in particular is great because it adds amazing flavor.

Bad Practices

- Sacrificing quality for ground meat—the best-quality ingredients will always yield the best flavor.
- Meat that is not flavored enough.
- Meat that is overcooked.
- Serving in a cold bowl, which reduces the temperature of the food.
- Overcooking your pasta.
- Buttering the pasta.
- A common mistake is lack of flavor: not enough garlic, onion.
- Using the microwave to heat pasta, as the product will become chewy and dry.
- For pasta with white cream sauce, a common mistake is making the sauce too creamy by overreducing it or allowing the sauce to split due to adding too much fat or using low-quality cream.

- The main mistake when preparing ragù alla Bolognese (as it's called in Italy) is adding too many tomatoes. Ragù alla Bolognese is a meat preparation and should taste mainly of meat.
- Adding too much sauce. The amount of sauce must not overpower the spaghetti.
- Sauce that is too spicy or too acidic.
- Using coriander and parsley or oregano in your spaghetti Bolognese.
- Using 100 percent lean ground meat instead of choosing meat with a little fat, which is essential not only to keep it from drying out but to provide more flavor as well.
- Not draining excess fat after browning the meat can cause it to be greasy.

French Fries

Good Practices

- Make sure you start the day with fresh oil; never use the french fries fryer vat for any other product.
- The brand of fries and their origin is essential in determining the taste.
- Salt sticks best to fries while they're still hot.
- If you toss and season your fries in a stainless steel mixing bowl, clean it after each use so you don't overseason the next batch.
- Drain excess oil from fried items. Allow enough time to drain and/or use paper cloth.
- For fresh-cut, never frozen fries, I recommend poaching at 285°F (140°C), letting them rest, and cooling in the fryer. Fully cool, and when you have an order, fry at 360°F (180°C).

- If you are using fresh-cut fries, soak for half an hour in cold water (some chefs recommend one hour at room temperature). This is done to remove excess starch, which makes them crisp up and prevents them sticking together. Remove and pat dry to remove excess water.
- Use equal-size cuts for even cooking.
- Use high-starch potatoes like Idaho potatoes or agria (russet potatoes). These varieties are denser and have the least amount of moisture. Avoid waxy potatoes such as red skin, new potatoes, and fingerling potatoes.
- Skim oil often to remove food particles as they break down the oil and negatively affect food presentation.

Bad Practices

- One common problem I see is fryers that have a carbon buildup. Fry baskets can have carbon buildup as well, which negatively affects the taste of the fries.
- The oil isn't hot enough. All fryers must have thermometers to check whether the oil has reached the desired temperature to fry food, which is about 365°F (185°C).
- Frying large amounts at once. Fry fewer items more often, and don't keep them under a heat lamp for more than five minutes.
- Some chefs believe you shouldn't wash cut potatoes with water as it removes starch, but other chefs prefer to wash the fresh potatoes because it draws out the starch.
- Frying from frozen in large quantities. It will reduce the temperature of the oil, resulting in soggy fries.

Grilled Steaks

Good Practices

- Steaks are preferably cooked on a broiler/chargrill or Josper charcoal oven, not a flat grill.
- Apply only a little non-flavored oil to grill grates so the steak doesn't stick. Some chefs believe you should slightly oil the steak instead of the grates, and if the fat content/marbling in the steak is high, you may not need to oil the steak or the grill.
- Turn the steak on a 45-degree angle to create grill marks in a diamond shape. Note that some chefs believe turning your steak too many times defeats the purpose of searing the outside to lock in all the juices. They believe that instead of flipping every few minutes when your steak starts to caramelize, flip it only once. The key here is to achieve the diamond shape without overflipping the steaks and draining the natural juices.
- If steaks are vacuum-packed, take them out of vacuum two hours before cooking.
- Pat steaks dry with a paper towel before seasoning and grilling them in order to develop an even crust. A dry steak (from the outside) will take on caramelization far better than a wet one. No matter how you cook a steak, you must aim to serve a juicy/tender steak.
- Use sea salt or kosher salt to season your steaks. I don't recommend table salt, iodized salt, or other small, fine-grain sea salts, as you may end up overseasoning due to their weight-to-volume ratio. Additionally, they don't provide the same flavor as kosher or sea salt. Season with salt just before cooking (otherwise, if salted too early, the steak will dry out of its natural juices) and add pepper after cooking (if before, it can cause an unpleasant, burnt flavor).
- Some chefs like to finish steak in an oven, preferring to cook it in its own juices.

- Fat in steaks provides flavor. Great raw steaks look plump, bright red, and marbled. Marbling is the fat present in high-quality beef that gives it a marbled appearance. It is also called intramuscular fat, which is the flecks of white fat found within the actual lean muscle. Grain-fed beef will have more marbling than grass-fed beef.
- Take steaks out of the fridge thirty minutes before cooking. Bringing them to room temperature helps ensure even cooking.
- After cooking, let the steak rest instead of cutting straight into it. This gives the collagen in the meat time to thicken the juices, giving you a more flavorful, juicy steak. You should allow your steak to rest for at least five minutes before cutting it. Some chefs cook steaks to five degrees below the desired doneness. The meat will briefly continue to rise in temperature while resting, progressing to the desired temperature. This is called carryover cooking.
- Steak must be served on a hot plate, and food servers must serve it immediately, as it continues to cook. Avoid holding under the heat lamp.

Bad Practices

- Sacrificing on quality—buy the best beef you can afford.
- Pressing steaks to cook them faster. Pressing dries out the steaks.
- Stacking raw steaks on top of each other in the cooler; the one underneath will dry out.
- Taking your steak straight from the cooler to the grill. It makes the outside char while the inside remains undercooked. Also, the inside will require a longer cooking time in order to reach the desired doneness.
- Even if you are an expert, don't stop using a meat thermometer to determine the doneness.
- Dirt, carbon buildup, and debris on the broiler grate make steaks sticky and cause the meat to adhere, tear, and burn. Brush and clean the grill often during the shift. Brush it with a small amount of oil regularly.

- Impatience and trying to skip the resting process—a steak sliced without proper resting will be undercooked and chewy.

Poultry

Good Practices

- Buy the best quality you can afford—a corn-fed/organic bird is far more likely to taste great than its cheaper alternative.
- Grill on skin side first.
- Marinate with flavor—not only the skin but the meat as well. Remember, acidic marinades can toughen meat if you marinate for longer than two hours. Poke small holes in your chicken or cut it into smaller pieces so it can more effectively absorb the marinade. Put chicken in a sealed plastic bag to better distribute the flavors.
- Make sure to give each piece of chicken enough room to cook. Meat needs the heat rising from all sides in order to fully cook.
- Reduce the chicken's overall moisture content by patting the chicken dry prior to cooking. You will get crispier skin.
- For roasting the whole bird: Spread oil or butter on the skin before roasting. You will not only get amazing, crispy skin but also a beautiful golden color.
- Buy fresh, never frozen, chicken. Frozen chicken often results in dry chicken.
- Brine your chicken: Soak it for two hours in a solution of saltwater and herbs in order to season the meat inside out. This way you retain moisture when you cook it and avoid a dry final product.
- If the chicken has taken on an odor, a sour smell of any sort, or if its colors start to fade and turn gray, it's better to discard it. Fresh chicken has a pink and fleshy color.
- Finish chicken in the oven because, with oven cooking, you can reach the internal temperature and prevent the chicken from drying out.

- Remember to rest the bird, just as you would a steak—this helps ensure even cooking and a juicy, mouthwatering texture.

Bad Practices

- Dry chicken is the number one guest complaint.
- Simply buying free-range without checking the other standards—the words are a marketing gimmick. Use chickens that are fed with non-GMO food such as alfalfa, clover, annual rye, kale, turnips, buckwheat, and grain grasses. What the chicken is fed makes a huge difference in how it tastes.
- Removing the skin. The skin keeps the chicken crispy and retains more fat and moisture.
- Cooking with ice-cold chicken. This can lead to uneven and overcooked chicken. Bring your chicken out of the cooler at least thirty minutes before cooking.
- Overcrowding the pan results in a soggy product. If you overcrowd your pan, you end up steaming the chicken instead of searing it.
- Washing or rinsing chicken with water when starting your prep. This can lead to the spread of potentially harmful bacteria everywhere, including sinks and internal parts of the chicken; and if the water splashes, all other areas will be contaminated.
- Wastefulness—be mindful of how you prep and trim your chickens. Items such as the wings or breast filets can be used for bar snacks and kids' food, yielding delicious results and increased profitability.
- Reheating chicken that was cooked the day before will never be as good as cooking it fresh, to order.

Salads

Most, but not all, tips below are applicable to Caesar salad.

Good Practices

- Spin-dry lettuce properly and cut lettuce as close to service time as possible.
- Tear/cut by hand, not with a knife. Cutting lettuce with a knife makes it oxidize and bruise. If using a knife, ensure it is razor sharp.
- Shock lettuce with ice water. This will make the lettuce crispy.
- Use romaine lettuce or little gem lettuce, sometimes called baby gem lettuce.
- For croutons, garlic herb is widely considered the best. Don't deep or shallow fry. Instead, bake them in the oven (some chefs use Salamander), lubricate during baking with garlic herb butter every three minutes, and move around during baking to ensure even cooking. Then, put them on a sheet tray to cool.
- Use good-quality parmesan in the dressing—it makes all the difference.
- Some chefs blanch the garlic in boiling water for thirty seconds to remove its harshness before adding to the dressing.
- A tip for all salads: Cutting ingredients into uniform sizes is key, as salads are supposed to be eaten one bite at a time.
- A tip for all salads: Make sure you have a variety of textures and colors. If you don't, your salad will be boring and bland.
- A tip for all salads: Soak cut onion pieces in ice water for fifteen minutes, and let them rest for five minutes. This will reduce the pungent flavor and sharp taste of freshly cut onions. No ingredient should dominate the taste of the salad.
- For the dressing, aim for Nappe consistency, i.e., not too runny and not too thick. Dressing needs a bit of acidity.

- Mix in the dressing immediately before you serve it. This is applicable to all salads and will prevent a mushy product or finding all the dressing at the bottom of the salad while the top part is flavorless. Adding the dressing too early will also drop the entire greens down, causing the salad to look flat.
- Keep lettuce crisp and cool in the cooler until the moment you have an order.
- Wash the salad mixing bowl after each use. If you don't, you end up with excess dressing and a food-safety risk if you keep the mixing bowl at room temperature. Choose a big bowl so you'll have plenty of room to toss and mix your ingredients.

Bad Practices

- Using croutons that are too big, too dry, or flavorless. The type of bread you choose for croutons makes a huge difference.
- Crispness issue: in some countries, lettuce may not be crispy due to high temperatures.
- Dressing consistency is the number one problem for salads. You must have a recipe in place and measure carefully before prepping your dressing.
- Adding cabbage, avocado, or boiled eggs, as they are not really part of a Caesar salad.
- Overlooking the importance of any single ingredient. A salad dish is the sum of its parts, and any one element can bring the rest of the dish down.
- Neglecting to chill the serving plate.
- Some chefs taste the dressing by itself; that won't provide an accurate final taste of the salad. Keep in mind that guests don't only taste the dressing. Instead, mix the dressing with a small amount of lettuce/salad and taste. This way you will know precisely whether the dressing is correct. I want to stress again the importance of creating and following the dressing recipe, so you don't have to second guess yourself.

Fish (Grilled Salmon)

Good Practices

- Lightly salt your fish right before you use heat to cook it; this way you draw excess water/moisture out and intensify the flavor. Some chefs believe that if you apply salt too early, you end up curing the fish before cooking.
- Well-cooked salmon must have sufficient moisture. It must flake, and when touched, it breaks without damaging the fish.
- Use a digital probe to check doneness.
- If it's skin-on, make sure the scales and pin bones are removed correctly.
- Fresh fish should smell like the sea or river, not fishy or sour.
- Cook skin side down to protect the flesh from overcooking and to achieve a crispy layer.
- Finished salmon should be served slightly pink.
- Make sure it's evenly trimmed. An even cut is extremely important.
- Fish and seafood must be kept in the coolest part of your cooler with ice underneath and on top of it. Use ice bags. Fish can expire quickly and are considered potentially hazardous food (PHF). Change the ice bags often.
- Like meat and poultry, start cooking while your fish is slightly closer to room temperature. You can cook the fish for a shorter amount of time, which means you'll have salmon that is more moist, but make sure it stays at room temperature for no longer than ten minutes.

Bad Practices

- Overcooked and dry: food continues to cook after it's been removed from the heat, so you should remove it slightly below the desired final cooking temperature.

- Overseasoned fish is just as bad as bland fish.
- Taking off the skin before cooking. Don't do it.The skin will help the meat retain its moisture as it cooks.
- If you're using an acidic marinade and submerging your fish for a long time, the fish will cook in the marinade before you put it on the heat.
- Touching the salmon too much while grilling will make it break down.
- Forgetting to trim the fish to an even size will prevent it from cooking evenly. Any trim, such as the belly, can be used to make other delicious dishes like ceviche, tartare, pasta dishes, or fish cakes.

Sautéed Vegetables (Side Item)

Good Practices

- Respect side dishes and cook them to perfection, just like other menu items.
- Provide a great variety and color mix.
- Add butter or extra virgin olive oil to glaze.
- Use fresh, locally sourced ingredients.
- Always use what's in season.
- Provide a generous portion.
- Vegetables should be crispy, not soft.
- Provide interesting flavors and garnishes to elevate the sides.

Bad Practices

- Serving overcooked or undercooked vegetables.
- Overseasoning or underseasoning.

- Too much oil or butter and too much fat.
- Chefs tend to forget tasting sides, even as they come from the pan.
- Cutting vegetables into unequal sizes.
- Plating too early—the dish will not be hot enough when it reaches the guest.
- Serving the dish cramped into a small bowl or other incorrect serving vessel.

Guacamole

Good Practices

- Use fresh, ripe avocado.
- Season well because avocado by itself is bland.
- Wait at least five minutes after seasoning before tasting—this gives the flavors time to develop and meld together.
- Keep it chunky; don't overmix. Mash the guacamole by hand with a fork. Never use a food processor.
- Discoloration: Use tight wrap and store wrapped in plastic cling film to help prevent oxidation. Let the plastic cling film *touch* the guacamole to prevent the air from oxidizing it.
- Use lime instead of lemon. Keep it original.
- Use juicy, ripe tomatoes. There's no need to remove the skins.
- Guacamole must be made fresh every shift or to order.
- If you receive underripe avocados, keep them at room temperature in your dry storage area and they will ripen within two or three days.
- Hass avocados are my favorite variety as they are rich with concentrated flavor.

Bad Practices

- Using avocado premade paste and calling it guacamole. Buying premade, pre-mashed avocado in a tub is a huge no.
- Using unripe avocados—the texture will be unpleasant and unpalatable.
- I don't recommend adding olive oil, peas, bacon, or blue cheese. Keep it original and simple. All you need is avocados, fresh lime juice, fresh cilantro, tomatoes, fresh onion, fresh jalapeno, and salt.
- Prepping guacamole too early will cause it to brown quickly.
- Working slowly will cause browning of the product.
- Overmixing and completely mashing the avocados.
- Bland, under salted is a common mistake.

Desserts

Good Practices

- Create at least one dramatic and Instagram-able showpiece dessert.
- Consider the balance of sweetness, acidity, texture, and richness.
- Use the best quality ingredients throughout your dishes—dairy, chocolate, fruit, and garnishes make the difference.
- Add seasonal desserts using seasonal ingredients.
- Offer at least one option that is simple and small, such as an option of ice cream or sorbet, for those that may not be able to find room for a full dessert. Alternatively, create sharing desserts.
- Do consider those with allergies. Often desserts are full of gluten, dairy, and nuts, which are some of the most common allergies—don't leave your guests feeling unloved. Offer sugar-free desserts.
- Don't make it too heavy—people want to enjoy the whole meal and leave feeling fulfilled but not bloated.

Bad Practices

- Offering only a large portion size.
- Offering only chocolate-based, heavy options. Restaurants should offer fruit-based desserts—for example: grilled pineapple with cinnamon (which also helps in food digestion after a heavy meal)—or a sorbet, for a light dessert option.
- Taking too long to serve—desserts should take five to eight minutes max.
- Serving extremely sugary or extremely sweet desserts.
- Using low-quality cream or chocolate.
- Serving old product, not rotated, left in the cooler for a long time.
- Serving dessert on an extremely hot skillet which burns desserts from the bottom.
- Allowing ice crystals to form on ice cream. Put the lid of an ice-cream container on tightly before putting it back in the freezer. This will help prevent ice crystals from forming on top of your dessert.
- Storing ice cream next to foods with strong odors can make funky-tasting desserts.
- Neglecting to use a dedicated cutting board and knife for fruit to avoid accidentally cross-contaminating flavors from other ingredients, especially onion.
- Forgetting to taste test the desserts—these are often overlooked but can spoil just as easily as your savory menu items.

Common Kitchen Mistakes and Helpful Tips

1. Cold butter is nearly impossible for guests to spread. It must be taken out of the cooler before service so it slightly softens.
2. Avoid cold breadbaskets. Bread should never be cold. Warm bread makes a huge difference.
3. Don't make sandwiches with thick bread. It may look nice, but the taste is all bread. Make à la minute if you can.
4. Avoid bad waste management!
5. A common mistake is no scale and no portioning, which leads to inconsistent food taste, portion size, and cost.
6. Do not ignore local culinary resources, such as buying supermarket bread in a city known for local bakeries or buying store-grade cheese in a town known for great dairy products.
7. Never make a fraudulent menu statement. For example, you cannot list, "We serve organic eggs," when they are not. You cannot write, "We cook with extra virgin olive oil," when you do not. That's a major issue and could cause legal implications and, of course, a PR disaster. Do not make untruthful cooking statements, such as homemade—"We serve homemade ice cream"—when it's not. It's illegal.
8. Mistake: containers in walk-in cooler that are not covered or sealed. This becomes a cross-contamination hazard.
9. Mistake: herbs, salt, and pepper are not rotated and poor rotation exists in storage areas.
10. Always drain fried products for at least twenty seconds before serving.
11. Avoid overdressing dishes, especially with soy sauce.
12. Keep coffee beans rotated and water filters checked.
13. Any protein must be à la minute: steak, pasta, sandwiches, burgers, and fish.

14. Respect customers' choices. If they want ketchup, don't create a no-ketchup policy. Allow them the freedom to add salt and pepper as per their own palate.
15. Avoid prepping large quantities when you prep due to panic or laziness. Instead, prep as close to service time as possible if you really want to impress your guests with the freshness of your food.
16. Avoid shortcuts. Follow recipes to the letter. Do not skip steps.
17. Don't forget to communicate with your front-of-house team about what items need to be upsold or pushed—this helps the flow of service and guest experience and looks after the financials.
18. You must change and wash food containers in your walk-in cooler every day. Don't add new products into a container if an old product is already in there.
19. If a guest wants an extra-well-done steak, chicken, or burger, your chef should say yes.
20. Train your chefs on dietary requirements. Chefs sometimes avoid it due to lack of knowledge.

I hope you found this chapter helpful. As I mentioned in the beginning of the chapter, there are hundreds of ways for cooking a certain dish. You might not agree with some of our suggestions or tips above, or you might have a better way. The intent of this chapter is to help restaurants serve fresher, tastier, better-quality food, and most importantly, to avoid common industry mistakes. **Oftentimes it is a little detail that takes a dish from good to great!**

Let us know your feedback—reach out to me with comments or questions through LinkedIn:

https://www.linkedin.com/in/marvinalballi/.

CHAPTER TEN
INTERVIEWS WITH INDUSTRY LEADERS AND MICHELIN-STARRED CHEFS

I have compiled these interviews to give the reader another perspective and to share valuable business advice from Michelin-starred global chefs, CEOs of restaurant companies, and high-profile industry executives.

Each executive was given four questions to cover key areas, such as best advice for success, mistakes to avoid, critical elements for restaurant success, and overall guidance to help readers enrich their knowledge and learn valuable insights that will set them up for business longevity and career success.

Enjoy learning from the best!

MICHAEL ELLIS

Before founding digital content start-up Passionomy.tv in early 2021, Michael Ellis was the chief culinary officer at Jumeirah Hotels and Resorts from 2018 until 2021, overseeing the food and beverage activities of their twenty-three properties in Europe, Asia, and the Middle East. Before his time at Jumeirah, from 2011 to 2018, Ellis was global director of the world-renowned Michelin Guides, overseeing the Michelin inspection teams around the world and managing the production of Michelin Guides in twenty-seven countries around the globe. This gave Ellis an intimate knowledge of the world's best chefs and restaurateurs as well as a unique understanding of global culinary trends.

As a young man Ellis attended the École Hôtelière Ferrandi in Paris and worked in front-of-the-house positions at Fairmont and Rosewood hotels. Ellis has held senior commercial roles with a number of companies in the Fortune 500. He has spent most of his life in Europe as a dual American and French citizen.

What is the best business advice you can give to chefs?

To run a successful restaurant, you need to understand three things well:

1. What kind of food do my guests want to eat?
2. How much are they willing to pay for their meal?
3. What kind of atmosphere do they want to be in?

If the chef understands these three things and can execute them in the restaurant, then the establishment will be a success.

What are the most important elements for leading a successful restaurant?

The team has to operate as a whole; ensure you align the kitchen crew with the waitstaff in terms of what experience the restaurant aims to deliver. It is easy to say but often hard to do, but it creates a truly memorable guest experience. It would be best if you had the right team in both the front of the house and back of the house.

What are some common mistakes you see restaurant operators or executives make?

The most common and dangerous mistake that restaurateurs make is the failure to understand who their target client base is and to tailor the key elements of the experience (food, price, and atmosphere) to that audience. Unfortunately, this happens all too often in my experience.

Any other advice (wisdom, mantra, daily routine, time management, strategy advice) you would like to share?

I always say a restaurant owner should try to think like a customer and not necessarily like they would think about the guest experience. More often than not, the owner is not representative of the target audience!

GEORGE E. MICHEL

George E. Michel most recently served as CEO of both Friendly's and Johnny Rockets. With more than forty years of experience in the restaurant industry developing and executing global initiatives, Michel is one of the industry's leading experts in turnarounds, effective restaurant operations, and domestic and international development. Before joining Friendly's and Johnny Rockets, Michel served as CEO of Boston Market, where he led a successful turnaround of an ailing brand from 2010 to 2018. He served as CEO of Timothy's Coffee of the World, Inc., based in Toronto, Canada, from 2008 to 2009, until its sale to Green Mountain Coffee Roasters. Before that, Michel spent several years overseeing international operations for Burger King in the Middle East, Asia, and Canada. He served as chief operating officer, global markets, of Brinker International. He was also CEO of A&W Restaurants in the United States from 1991 to 1995. Michel's career began with A&W Canada in 1971 as a kitchen cook and has spanned five decades, with a majority of those years spent at the executive level in various leadership roles. Michel splits his time between the United States and Canada and considers himself a citizen of the world.

What are the most important elements for leading a successful restaurant?

Treat your customers like a guest in your home, enrich the jobs of your employees by delegating responsibility and authority to make decisions, and finally, greet your customers at the entrance to your restaurant by opening the door, helping them with their takeout bags to their car, surprising and delighting your regulars, and celebrating their birthdays.

There are many moving parts and thousands of little details in the restaurant industry. How do you stay in control?

My role as CEO is to be focused on the business rather than just being involved "in" the business. When the mission and vision are clear, team members take care of the moving parts and little details through effective delegation. However, this does not stop me from practicing situational leadership. At times, I spend time in the field with our restaurant GMs and hourly staff to observe the details and ask for valuable feedback on our initiatives and tactics.

What are some work and life habits that made you a successful industry leader?

I believe strongly in the following concepts for success:

- Think from a customer's or restaurant team member's point of view.
- Visit restaurants at nights and on weekends.
- Be very involved in site selection and market visits.
- Internal PR is as valuable as external PR. Team members can spread the brand story just as *effectively* as a TV ad.
- Practice situational leadership, including working in restaurants on hectic days.
- Drop the title "CEO" and use instead "The Big Chicken." It made me more approachable with restaurant team members (while leading Boston Market).
- Get experience working in kitchens when you are in college and developing your career.

Any other advice, work routine, ideas, tips, or wisdom you would like to share for people who just started their career in the restaurant business?

Always stay focused. Never get distracted by fellow team members who enjoy gossiping.... Always exceed expectations by underpromising and overdelivering.

MIKE FERRETTI

I joined Great Harvest Bread Co. in 2001. During my tenure at Great Harvest I have had the honor of working with a great group of people. The only difference is that what is mainstream now with the rise of interest in low-carb diets was not mainstream then. We have had to morph into a cafe from a strict bread store. The public demanded that as we see less demand and more competition for bread but the opposite in the cafe space of our business.

How did I get here? I spent quite a few years as a franchisee of a different system to learn how to operate a small business firsthand. I also consulted for that same franchise company, later acting as their chief financial officer. This combination of franchisee and franchisor experience has allowed me to bring a unique—and hopefully fair—perspective to Great Harvest.

Life before franchising was pretty different. I was a tax accountant with Price Waterhouse, specializing in the financial institutions business. I went to college at the University of Virginia and earned my MBA at the University of North Carolina at Chapel Hill. In my free time, you'll find me hanging out with my wonderful wife, Eadie; our cool kids, Peter and Michael; and our two dogs, Shae and Lana. I love spending time on my bike and crave moments on the open road. I also really love running and hope to reenter the marathon world soon. Triathlons are another passion, even though I haven't done one in quite a while. See you in Montana, the bakeries, or somewhere in between…

What are the top five things you believe restaurant/café operators should do to be successful?

I recently wrote an article summarizing my answer to that question. You can't go wrong following these guidelines:

- Have a phenomenal product.
- Provide an exceptional customer experience.

- Be involved in your community.
- Know your numbers.
- Advertise consistently.

What is your best business advice to restaurant owners and chain leaders?

Remain engaged with the roots of your business. Engage with your operators and customers.

What are some of the common mistakes you see in the industry?

Forgetting who is most important. Not your HQ staff. It is your customers and operators.

Any other advice, work routine, ideas, tips, or wisdom you would like to share for people who just started their career in the restaurant business?.

Stop-and-start advertising is close to a waste of money. To achieve regular and compounded growth requires consistent and steady advertising.

STEVE WIBORG

Marvin Alballi: I worked under Steve Wiborg's leadership when I led sixty-six Burger King restaurants in Western Canada (British Columbia and Alberta). At the time, Wiborg transformed the brand with many innovative ideas and initiatives, such as improving the ingredients and procedures for making our signature product: the Whopper.

Wiborg took the Whopper's taste and quality to another level and introduced a new type of high-quality french fries that our customers loved. Not to mention, new digital menu boards, new breakfast dishes, and new snacks and smoothies. It was an era of brand transformation.

Wiborg is currently an operating partner at Agman and has been affiliated with the firm since 2016. Before joining Agman, Wiborg served as chairman, executive vice president, and president of North America for Burger King Corporation, as part of the 3G Capital-sponsored acquisition. At BKC, Wiborg played an instrumental role in defining and implementing the tremendously successful turnaround strategy, including Restaurant Brands International Inc.'s public listing (NYSE: QSR).

Previously, Wiborg was president and chief executive officer of Heartland Food Corporation, at the time one of the larger franchise operators in the country. He held the position of chief operating officer from 2003 to 2006 and was named president and chief executive officer in December 2006. Prior to joining Heartland, Wiborg was an owner and operator of fifty-six Hardee's restaurants.

Wiborg is a former director of Carrols Restaurant Group Inc. (Nasdaq: TAST) and currently serves as executive chairman of Ampler Restaurant Group, which he cofounded with Agman in 2016.

What is your best business advice to restaurant owners and chain leaders?

Ensure you're communicating with the employees who interact with guests every day.

Often, as owners and chain leaders, we would communicate only to our top people and then allow them to communicate things down to the next level. When you are an owner or a chain leader, it is imperative that people hear your vision, reasoning, and excitement for change. Change is one of the hardest things for people to embrace or think about. I will give you an example: At Burger King, I decided to cut lettuce by hand instead of getting it precut and delivered already shredded. I knew the customer feedback scores were much higher using leaf lettuce, which would make for a better Whopper sandwich, but this was going to be a big change. We would bring in lettuce heads and properly wash, cut, and spin the excess water out. So much more work was involved for the teams: If I just said this was what we were doing, they would have seen it as a lot more work and not understood the why. It's the *why* that matters the most to them. So I recorded a video of *why* we were making this change: the benefits it would bring, the guest satisfaction increase, the increased potential sales, and making the Whopper sandwich the best in the industry. But, I said, I could not do it without their help and needed them to help me deliver to the guest what they wanted and something they could be proud to produce. If people know the *why* and how it benefits them, they have a real shot at success. This could mean more raises if sales go up or providing guests with better food so they return more often and have a great experience.

What are some of the common mistakes restaurant owners make?

The most common mistake I see restaurant owners make is lack of engagement in their business. When a restaurant owner starts out, they work very hard to make their one store successful and then get to two stores and more. They know every aspect of their business, they reply to every customer concern, and every dollar counts. As people grow their businesses, they have to rely on others to do the things they used to do each day. Remember, it's your business and nobody will care about it as much as you do or did. Success brings complacency, which is not good for your business, or chain, or brand. Reengage as if you have only one store and making the house payment next month depends on the next seven days of your business.

What are the most important elements for leading a successful restaurant or restaurant company?

Three of the most essential elements for leading a restaurant or company are the following:

- Having people's respect. People must buy into your plan or objectives for you to have any shot at success. You learn very fast in multiunit management that you can't do everything. In fact, as you move up the chain of command, you really don't do any tasks. You lead by your actions and words. One of the best examples of this that I used in training new managers was to have them run a shift one day normally and then the next day run that shift while holding a roll of quarters in each hand. They could not jump in and help or do anything. They had to use their voice and plan better to have a successful shift. They want to drop those quarters and do things themselves so many times, but you need them to understand that successful leaders will earn people's respect. Communicate prior to the task, coach them during the task, and give them feedback after. Holding the rolls of quarters during a shift teaches them to do just that.
- Don't ever underestimate what someone can do or is willing to do. You will be amazed what the right person can do or how much they can do. Too often, I see people afraid to ask or give others responsibility or tasks.
- Set lofty goals but with checkpoints and timelines. There is nothing wrong with setting what might be a lofty goal for your team to achieve as long as you set the right timeline and steps to accomplish it. It's not the goal that will set you back from achieving it—it's the steps along the way and the timelines.

Any other advice, daily work habit, business mantra, or wisdom you would like to share?

You will have many different types of bosses during your career. Many people get frustrated with the bad ones and quit or change jobs. I have learned as much, or more, from the bad bosses than the good ones. I believe that you have to start picturing and planning out how you would lead at the next level before you get to the next level. The bad bosses always seemed to help me do that better because I would hold myself accountable when I got the opportunity to make that decision and better envision how I would communicate a change or how I would motivate a team.

I have always believed that people don't wake up in the morning, jump out of bed, and say, "I am going to have a bad day and do a bad job at work today." Things usually happen throughout their day, and their busy lives, that make them have a bad day. So if you have hired the right person, then it is up to us as leaders to motivate, take away the obstacles, and make their job one of the best parts of their day.

CHEF AND RESTAURATEUR JASON ATHERTON

Jason Atherton[1] (born September 6, 1971) is an English chef and restaurateur. His restaurant, Pollen Street Social, gained a Michelin Star in 2011, its opening year. He was the executive chef at Gordon Ramsay's Michelin-starred Maze in London until April 30, 2010. In 2014, he cohosted the Sky Living TV series *My Kitchen Rules*.

Atherton's recipes and articles have appeared widely in magazines and newspapers, including *The Guardian*, *The Sunday Times*, *Observer Food Monthly*, *Waitrose Food Illustrated*, and *Caterer and Hotelkeeper*. Additionally, he demonstrates regularly on food shows in the UK and abroad. He is a regular guest on *Saturday Kitchen*, and in June 2008, Atherton won the third hugely popular series of BBC2's *Great British Menu*, cooking both the starter and main courses at the "Gherkin" building in London. In 2009 and 2010, Atherton returned to *Great British Menu* as a host. He has also won the Chef Award at the Catey Awards in 2012. Atheron operates several restaurants around the world.

What is the best business advice you can give to chefs?

The best business advice I can give chefs would be: don't rush into owning your own restaurant; take your time and make sure you have the right skills to make your place a success. You need to be many things to be a successful chef operator, like time management, financial awareness, confidence as a good leader, and overall determination.

1 Wikipedia, s.v. "Jason Atherton," last modified August 30, 2022, 19:24, https://en.wikipedia.org/wiki/Jason_Atherton. Used with permission from Jason Atherton.

What are the most important elements for leading a successful kitchen?

The most important elements for leading a kitchen would be: never ask anyone to do something you wouldn't do yourself, and also to listen to your team. You never stop learning; different cultures have different ideas and working practices, but also never let go of the DNA of what made you a success.

What are some of the common mistakes you see chefs or restaurant operators make?

Common mistakes that are made are: overexpansion without proper standards and leadership in place, and thinking you are great at everything. Be humble and always stay hungry.

Any other advice (wisdom, mantra, daily routine, time management, strategy advice) you would like to share?

Always have a master plan. It's important to have a long-term strategy, but as tastes change, you must change as well. Always focus on quality, and never try to master everything.

CHEF AND RESTAURATEUR PIERRE GAGNAIRE

Pierre Gagnaire[2] (born April 9, 1950 in Apinac, Loire) is a French chef and the head chef and owner of the eponymous Pierre Gagnaire restaurant at 6 rue Balzac in Paris (in the 8th arrondissement). Gagnaire is an iconoclastic chef at the forefront of the fusion cuisine movement. Beginning his career in St. Etienne, where he won three Michelin Stars, Gagnaire tore at the conventions of classic French cooking by introducing jarring juxtapositions of flavors, tastes, textures, and ingredients. On his website, Gagnaire gives his mission statement as the wish to run a restaurant which is "facing tomorrow but respectful of yesterday" ("tourné vers demain mais soucieux d'hier").

Gagnaire has made appearances on Fuji TV's *Iron Chef*. He represented France in the 1995 Iron Chef World Cup in Tokyo; the other chefs chosen were Italy's Gianfranco Vissani and Hong Kong's Xu Cheng as well as Iron Chef Rokusaburo Michiba representing Japan. Gagnaire also appeared in the France Battle Special at Château de Brissac, where he battled Iron Chef Hiroyuki Sakai. Gagnaire operates several restaurants around the world.

What is the best business advice you can give to chefs?

My best business advice to chefs is straightforward: to be authentic in their work, to work hard without seeking recognition, to believe in their dreams, and never to forget that our job is a business with a low profitability.

Do not expect to be Iron Chef; just be yourself.

2 Wikipedia, s.v. "Pierre Gagnaire," last modified March 11, 2022, 13:12, https://en.wikipedia.org/wiki/Pierre_Gagnaire. Used with permission from Pierre Gagnaire.

What are the most important elements for leading a successful kitchen?

To respect not only your clients but mostly the people who are in your team. Never to forget that a kitchen is based on teamwork, that they have to be respected, well paid, and have enough time to spend with their families. Through a chef's vision, the team has to be able to progress and to carry on enjoying themselves and dreaming. The kitchen's environment must be safe, and the utensils and equipment must be in good condition.

What are some common mistakes you see chefs or restaurant operators make?

They tend to follow trends too much, to copy others, and to try to be successful too quickly. Everything is highly based on concepts, which means that these projects are very short-term and won't last long. A lot of restaurants invest in decoration, and the culinary management aspects (equipment, lighting, and health and safety) are forgotten.

Any other advice (wisdom, mantra, daily routine, time management, strategy advice) that made you successful that you would like to share with others?

The most important thing is knowing that the road is long and that you need to lead a healthy life to keep the ship afloat. The chef is responsible for the well-being of his team; he is the leader and needs to have an exemplary life, both physically and mentally, like athletes.

ANDREW WALSH CHEF/FOUNDER CURE CONCEPTS

Hailing from the idyllic village of Breaffy, near County Mayo, Ireland, Andrew Walsh has established himself as a successful chef, restaurateur, and businessman since arriving in Singapore in 2011 to spearhead Jason Atherton's first Singapore outpost, Esquina, and modern British restaurant, The Study.

Andrew's ability to design and manage a portfolio of dynamic concepts that are so distinctly unique to him reflects his sense of astute business acumen and his unwavering commitment to his craft. Under Atherton's tutelage, Andrew learned not only the business and financial side of restaurant ownership but also the art of balancing inventive food within a creative space. These lessons proceed to stand him in good stead with his successful transition from chef to chef/owner with his first venture, Cure, which pioneered the "bistronomy" concept during its inaugural launch in 2015. Under the helm of the Irishman, Cure has since reinvented itself, revivifying the concept with what he holds dear—his Irish heritage.

"Nua" represents the evolution of Andrew's own brand of cuisine, where his Irish roots and the food of his childhood take centre stage, along with culinary techniques and global influences that have been refined over his career. His vision and efforts have proved successful with Cure clinching its first star at the Michelin Guide Singapore 2021 and continuing to retain it in 2022. The restaurant's success in garnering this award during a challenging time for the industry is a clear testament to the team's unwavering resilience, dedication, and passion for their craft.

In addition to Cure, the thirty-six-year-old has established four other distinctive dining concepts under the umbrella of Cure Concepts: Butcher Boy, an East-meets-West bar and grill inspired by his travels in Asia; Catfish, a contemporary fish grill and raw bar serving up seafood-centric fare highlighting the best of Asian ingredients; Ember Beach Club with One&Only in Desaru, Malaysia; as well as the latest addition of a progressive wine bar, Club Street Wine Room. Apart from his own ventures, Andrew also serves as a culinary collaborator at the Straits Clan members club, breathing life into their newly renamed Clubhouse Kitchen with his signature emphasis on quality ingredients and beautifully executed flavors from around the world.

What is the best business advice you can give to chefs?

The best business advice I can give to chefs is: don't always look at what's on the plate, but look at what goes in the bins and keep a close eye on the finance side of the restaurants.

What are the most important elements for leading a successful kitchen?

[The] most important elements to leading a successful kitchen [are] to lead from the front, be a good mentor, be a good listener, and know when someone is down or not at their best—look to bring them back up.

What are some common mistakes you see chefs or restaurant operators make?

[The] most common mistakes are chefs or restaurants getting way ahead of themselves with big egos. It's best to always stay grounded and also not to get too carried away or expand too fast and take your eyes off the business.

Any other advice (wisdom, mantra, daily routine, time management, strategy advice) that made you successful that you would like to share with others?

Time management is so important. It keeps everyone with a certain goal and time limit in sight, working as a team to achieve this. Also with goals, set team awards, like team days out or a nice treat. Always look at the bigger picture and stay humble to the core.

CHEF ANDREAS CAMINADA

Andreas Caminada, who was born in 1977 in Ilanz, Switzerland, is a Swiss chef and gastronomic entrepreneur. Since 2003, Caminada has been a leaseholder at Schloss Schauenstein in Fürstenau, Grison, which offers a fine-dining restaurant as well as nine guestrooms and suites. Caminada had been awarded three Michelin stars and 19 Gault Millau points by the age of thirty-four. His restaurant at Schloss Schauenstein has been on the list of the World's Best Restaurants since 2011 and on OAD's Top 100 since 2014.

What is the best business advice you can give to chefs?

Start humble, have a lot of patience, keep your costs under control, spend only the money that you have and on things that you really need, focus on the guests, try to build a strong repeating customer base, be kind and encouraging to your staff, and always lead by example. You need to be a good host and always give more than employees or guests expect.

What are the most important elements for leading a successful kitchen?

Be inspired and open but develop your own identity and stick to it. Your identity is very personal and you cannot delegate it.

What are some of the common mistakes you see chefs or restaurant operators make?

They are not patient enough for a long-term commitment. Beside everything, the economic factor is one of the most important elements to be successful. Make sure your restaurant makes money without someone else in the back having to feed your finances in order to avoid losses. Equally important, though, is the service culture and obviously good food. It takes at least seven years until you have established yourself and are known to a certain continuity.

Is there any other advice that made you successful that you would like to share with others?

It's nice to have Michelin stars, but at the end of the day, your restaurant must be full with happy guests.

CHEF RICHARD SANDOVAL

Chef Richard Sandoval is a global pioneer in contemporary Latin cuisine. His career as a chef, restaurateur, and entrepreneur also includes serving as a television personality, cookbook author, brand ambassador, and philanthropist. He is internationally acclaimed for his innovative approach in combining Latin ingredients with modern culinary techniques to create award-winning flavors that span sixty locations and four continents.

A graduate of the Culinary Institute of America, Sandoval has earned many accolades over the course of his career, including Mexico's National Toque d'Oro, *Bon Appétit*'s Restauranteur of the Year, Cordon d'Or's Restauranteur of the Year, and one of *Inc.* magazine's 10 Most Inspiring Business Leaders; he is a James Beard semi-finalist for Outstanding Restaurateur and received an honorary doctorate for culinary arts from Johnson & Wales University.

Chef Sandoval is commended for elevating Latin American dining in each market he has a presence with best-in-class concepts, with regular features in publications like the *New York Times* and *People*. Sandoval is also credited for introducing Latin cuisine to the UAE, Qatar, and Serbia.

What is the best business advice you can give to chefs?

Take time to understand the business side of restaurants. Being a successful chef and creating incredible cuisine that will be memorable for your guests is only half of the equation. Take time to review your P&Ls, communicate with your operations team, research restaurant trends, and fine-tune your budgets.

What are the most important elements for leading a successful kitchen?

Collaboration. All team members work together to create the experience that we are giving our guests in the restaurants. Listen to your dishwashers, your line cooks, your sous chef. Take their feedback and ideas and put it into motion. There's no "I" in team!

What are some of the common mistakes you see chefs or restaurant operators make?

Learn how to say no. In the years when you are building yourself and your company, it's important to stand back from the choices that are presented to you and take time to evaluate them before saying yes to everything. Like Richard Branson said: "Business opportunities are like buses; there's always another one coming."

Is there any other advice that made you successful that you would like to share with others?

One of the most important things to remember is to remain positive and surround yourself with people that will mirror that positivity and have the same high-reaching goals.

MICHAEL WHITEMAN

Michael Whiteman is president of Baum + Whiteman, the company that created two of the world's largest-grossing and most magical restaurants: the legendary Windows on the World and the Rainbow Room atop Rockefeller Center. Working with boldface names in architecture, design, and hospitality, his firm, based in Brooklyn, creates big ideas for diverse sections of the food industry—from supermarkets to museums, from public parks to drinking bars. His company has created high-profile dining destinations around the world, developed the world's first food courts, and masterminded restaurant concepts for Starwood, Taj, and Raffles hotels and rooftop extravaganzas in Singapore, New York, and Taiwan.

As founding editor of *Nation's Restaurant News*, Whiteman built the industry's first newspaper into its most powerful trade publication and lectures around the world as a futurist and food trends pundit. He is married to four-time James Beard award-winning chef and author Rozanne Gold (together they created CBE's soup kitchen during Hurricane Sandy, preparing 185,000 meals for those in need).

What consulting advice do you give to people who want to open a restaurant?

Here's the free advice we give to nonprofessionals who come to us with the notion of launching a restaurant. We urge them to: "Lie down until the urge passes." Or: "Take two shots of bourbon and sleep it off."

We explain that restaurants are all-demanding enterprises that can gobble up your psyche and your life, and the best way to survive in this business is to ensure sufficient freedom so you can have a life, which means developing a business plan that allows you not to become a slave. And if your business plan's economics force you to become chief cook and bottle washer, we suggest you do something else. For sure, we won't take you as a client.

Restaurants often are described as theater, but that's inaccurate. When staging a Broadway show, the entire team of actors and musicians is talented and eager, whereas a restaurant's talent roster often consists just of the owner, a chef, and a loyal sous chef. So, a restaurant is more like a high-stakes, high-wire circus act—requiring enormous balance and energy by its key people to keep it from plummeting without a safety net.

The joy in restaurants comes from getting this balancing act just right. Then you're in the zone and you can devote yourself gladly to what this business is about: creating memorable meals while providing memorable service. The most important word is "memorable"; what customers remember fondly is what brings them back.

What are your thoughts about developing menus today?

With ingredients readily available from everywhere in the world, restaurant cooking has become an unruly game—exciting but without much discipline. Chefs are playing mix-and-match by cross-breeding cuisines, and at the same time, bragging about the "authenticity" of their recipes when, in fact, there is no such thing. I have a feeling that in their quest to achieve exaggerated "flavor impact," many chefs are over-challenging their customers. We have our own mantra about restaurant food: Make "familiar" food interesting. And make "interesting" food feel familiar.

Why have restaurants become more difficult to run?

Restaurants today are whipsawed by conflicting objectives. We talk a good game about "personalization" and the "personal experience" of the customer. Yet the real world tells us something different: that minimizing human-to-human contact, reducing people to algorithms, clicking for automated reservation lines instead of talking to live people, repeated texting to confirm your reservation, settling your dinner bill on your smartphone, forcing the use of QR codes, drive-by pickup stations, and a dozen other such examples all are alienating the customer from the meaning of "service." So, we should recognize this split in our industry between what used to be called "restaurants" and what now are little more than petrol stations with as many self-service pumps as possible. And waiting in the wings, of course, will be the pleasure of watching your food being made by machines. And that leads me to the answer to your next question.

What is today's biggest challenge?

Juggling labor issues is our most significant problem, largely because we're not good at it. I believe there's no success unless restaurateurs figure out how to treat their employees with the same regard and concern as they treat their customers. It is not easy for an owner or manager to put himself in a customer's shoes *and* an employee's shoes simultaneously, but it has to be done—primarily because employees no longer accept being classified as "unskilled servants." And: We have to figure out how to pay living wages—which means getting customers to pay for the true cost of restaurant labor via higher prices. If that results in fewer restaurants, well, then, that's how economics is supposed to work. Even after Covid-induced shutdowns, we still have thousands of restaurants that are kept alive by government subsidies and welfare payments to supplement stingy wages. Stated another way, we have been transferring our labor cost to the government—which means transferring them to society in general, rather than directly to restaurant customers. There's an economic term for this; it's called "privatizing profits while socializing costs."

INNOVATION, STRATEGY, CULTURE AND FINAL WORD

A Note on Innovation and Staying Relevant

Eating habits change, new food trends emerge, new technology surfaces, and the list goes on. Change is constant.

Some businesspeople even go to the extreme and say "innovate or die." Staying relevant and fresh and practicing ongoing innovation are keys to your business survival and growth.

Just recently, we have seen that more people work from home now, so you need to ask yourself, how do you adapt and meet their wants and needs? Online ordering has grown significantly and so has delivery. How do you capitalize on that? Offer ordering from a website, delivery platforms, and through Instagram and Facebook.

Innovation and staying relevant can take place in several parts of the business. Let's start with culinary innovation that blends with current trends without moving away from your core menu. For example, can you add gluten-free or vegan options? Can you add at least one dessert that's Instagram-able, full of action, and somewhat eye-catching and theatrical?

Chefs' pop-up events and four hands dinners are growing in popularity. Many restaurants invite chefs from other restaurants and create a curated menu for a limited time period: typically one to three nights. Such initiatives keep your brand relevant and exciting.

For staying relevant in customer service, consider introducing technology to understand ordering habits, guest behavior, and speed of service.

Keep your interior and exterior modern and fresh, including new plateware, a new look for the staff uniform, and repainting.

All are examples of efforts restaurant owners should make to keep their restaurants relevant, exciting, and fresh. Watch trends, attend industry shows, and be open-minded and a risk taker. Do not just copy trends—create and lead them.

Strategy: Vision, Mission, Culture, and Values

One of the key elements for leading your team is to build a shared goal and strategy, which are generally represented through vision and mission statements, culture, core values, and behavior statements.

The mission, vision, and behaviors are core fundamentals of your business strategy. They represent the heart and soul of the business, the character, the positioning, and the end goals. They shouldn't only be part of the new hire's orientation or posters on walls.

I intentionally held team meetings in a hallway at one of our restaurants where four posters hung showing the mission, vision, culture principles/behaviors, and key hospitality standards of the business. I referred to the posters *every single day*. I made sure it was part of our team's lingo—from the dishwasher all the way to the operations managers. We held ourselves and others accountable to these statements. We built our culture around them. One of the key behaviors was "*Treat people the same way you like to be treated.*" We always referred to it when there was a conflict. It was one of our guiding principles. Another was simple: "*Take your job seriously but not yourself. Have fun!*" Our restaurant concept was casual; we wanted our team members to have fun.

These statements/posters create a vibe—an inspirational, emotional connection to your brand. Keep them alive! I still remember to this day, after twenty-three years, the mission and vision of one of the brands that I loved—powerful stuff.

Building a sound business strategy is monumental to any business. In simple words, strategy is a plan and set of goals. Building strategy is an in-depth exercise, including SWOT analysis, and requires a deep understanding of your business. In some cases, it's better to work with third-party specialists who are well-versed in building strategies.

This plan will incorporate several goals with one or two overarching objectives. Such goals include marketing, customer acquisition, positioning, pricing, expansion, growth, cost management, competitiveness, menu offerings, HR goals such as diversity and team satisfaction, and the list goes on.

There are different layers of strategy but they are all built and sync with each other: corporate level and unit/restaurant business level.

Some parts of the strategy could be confidential and only known at board members' level; other parts that manifest themselves through the mission, vision, and value are public.

The failure or success of such strategies is based on how much a frontline, even entry-level employee—a dishwasher, a cook, a chef—understands, believes, and supports such strategies and how attainable and realistic they are.

Whatever strategy you build, my advice would be to follow a bottom-up approach: listen to team members, ask for their opinion, engage them in building, and keep it alive and present in your day-to-day discussions. The pyramid that we shared can be a great foundation to any restaurant's tactical strategy. In fact, we used the word *strategy* more than thirty-six times in this book. It's that important.

Whatever strategy you build, my advice would be to follow a bottom-up approach.

Remember, the healthy work culture you build will bring strategy to life, or as many professionals say, culture eats strategy for breakfast! So make your culture and strategy go hand in hand.

Lastly, keep in mind that the business needs to have a soul, not only financial targets. It must motivate and inspire people.

Final Word

I hope that you found this book useful—I hope you got value out of it. Don't be afraid to try some of the tactics, strategies, and tips. There isn't a one-size-fits-all approach—some might work and some may not fit your brand, but never stop evolving, learning, and trying new things.

I wish you and your loved ones happiness, great health, and resounding success!

Get in touch;

- LinkedIn (linkedin.com/in/marvinalballi);
- Facebook (Marvin FoodandBev);
- Instagram (@marvin_alballi_fnb);
- E-mail fnbinsights@hotmail.com

Marvin

ABOUT THE AUTHOR

Marvin Alballi is an award-winning food and beverage executive with twenty-two years of international experience managing franchise chains, celebrity-chef restaurants, independent establishments, and global hotel F&B operations. Marvin spent several years apiece with the InterContinental Hotels Group, for which he oversaw 745 restaurants and bars for 212 hotels overseas, and the Fortune 500 company Brinker International (Chili's Grill & Bar), which named him Operator of the Year.

Marvin has also worked with the Burger King corporate office and led all of the western Canadian market. He has launched Caribou Coffee, Fuddruckers, Marble Slab Creamery, and Applebee's locations in international markets and worked for the award-winning Canadian chain White Spot. Marvin has consulted for several restaurant companies, including Boston Market, the Great Harvest Bread Co., Famoso Pizzeria, Cafe d'Arte, and many more top-tier brands. Additionally, Marvin delivers seminars and keynote speeches and offers consulting—both online and in person. Marvin, a Canadian citizen, currently lives with his wife and son in Dubai, UAE.

"Everything is possible when you are armed with knowledge, passion, and determination."

Marvin Alballi

www.ingramcontent.com/pod-product-compliance
Lightning Source LLC
LaVergne TN
LVHW020506100826
845148LV00003B/704